Analyzing Companies and Valuing Shares

How to Make the Right Investment Decision

D0543032

FT Prentice Hall
FINANCIAL TIMES

In an increasingly competitive world, we believe it's quality of thinking that will give you the edge – an idea that opens new doors, a technique that solves a problem, or an insight that simply makes sense of it all. The more you know, the smarter and faster you can go.

That's why we work with the best minds in business and finance to bring cutting-edge thinking and best learning practice to a global market.

Under a range of leading imprints, including *Financial Times Prentice Hall*, we create world-class print publications and electronic products bringing our readers knowledge, skills and understanding which can be applied whether studying or at work.

To find out more about our business publications, or tell us about the books you'd like to find, you can visit us at
www.pearsoned.co.uk

PEARSON
Education

Analyzing Companies and Valuing Shares

How to Make the Right Investment Decision

MICHAEL CAHILL

FT Prentice Hall
FINANCIAL TIMES

An imprint of **Pearson Education**

London • New York • Toronto • Sydney • Tokyo • Singapore
Hong Kong • Cape Town • Madrid • Paris • Amsterdam • Munich • Milan

PEARSON EDUCATION LIMITED

Edinburgh Gate
Harlow CM20 2JE
Tel: +44 (0)1279 623623
Fax: +44 (0)1279 431059
Website: www.pearsoned.co.uk

First published in Great Britain in 2003

© Mike Cahill 2003

The right of Michael Cahill to be identified as Author
of this Work has been asserted by him in accordance
with the Copyright, Designs and Patents Act 1988.

ISBN 0 273 66363 1

British Library Cataloguing in Publication Data
A CIP catalogue record for this book can be obtained from the British Library.

10 9 8 7 6 5

Typeset by Northern Phototypesetting Co. Ltd, Bolton
Printed and bound in Great Britain by Bell & Bain Ltd, Glasgow

The Publishers' policy is to use paper manufactured from sustainable forests.

This publication is designed to provide accurate and authoritative information in regard to the
subject matter covered. It is sold with the understanding that neither the author nor the publisher
is engaged in rendering legal, investing, or any other professional service. If legal advice or other
expert assistance is required, the service of a competent professional person should be sought.

The publisher and author make no representation, express or implied, with regard to the accuracy
of the information contained in this book and cannot accept any responsibility or liability for any
errors or omissions that it may contain.

To my Dad
Peter Joseph Cahill
1925–1984

Advance praise

"A welcome, well structured and common sense approach to the black art of equity analysis that will be extremely useful to anyone interested in how the City values companies in practice.

Successful investment is not rocket science, it's about thoughtful analysis and common sense. Michael Cahill's very readable book has both these qualities in ample measure. His approach clearly reflects the value of his real world experience in high quality investment research."

Derek Higgs, author of the report on *The Role and Effectiveness of Non-Executive Directors*

"Mike Cahill has written the definitive guide to deciding whether or not to buy a share. Thorough, well researched and clearly written – this is a long overdue return to common sense investing. Just what you would expect from a professional analyst who believes that in the long run a company's share price is determined by its fundamental value."

Tom Stevenson, Head of Research, Hemscott

"This book allows the reader to get behind the numbers and the City jargon to understand what *really* determines a company's share price performance. It de-mystifies investment analysis for those new to corporate communications, as well as providing a welcome point of reference for more seasoned professionals."

Tony Knox, Chairman of Financial Dynamics

"A comprehensive, detailed and clear guide to the fundamentals of equity investment."

Philip Coggan, Investment Editor, *Financial Times*

"Never has there been a better time to read a book like this. Valuation is at the heart of equity markets, and this book crystallizes the issues and is an invaluable companion for anyone looking to buy equities.

Remarkable for a book written by an ex-City professional, this book carries none of the waffle normally associated with the subject. It is punchy, highly readable and a very useful guide for investors of all levels."

Lawrence Gosling, Editor-in-chief, *Bloomberg Money*

"A practical and pragmatic approach to a complex subject. This book helps to de-mystify the concepts and techniques involved in company valuation for ivnestment purposes.

It sets out clearly the many judgmental factors that drive valuation and develops a sound framework and approach. The author has effectively combined anecdotal evidence and worked numerical examples to illustrate how valuations are achieved in practice.

The book is highly recommended as a sound grounding for a new practitioner or for someone who wants to gain an appreciation of just how difficult and subjective the topic of valuation is in reality."

Steve Webster, Group Finance Director, Wolseley

"Too many small investors rely on too little information to guide make-or-break decisions on their portfolios. Michael Cahill looks beyond the hype of City tipsters in this common-sense guide on how to determine a company's true worth. Thanks to his background as a City economic analyst, backed by a deft marshalling of evidence, Cahill shows why investors must look much more carefully at individual companies before buying shares. Along the way, he knocks back more than a few market myths, including the notion that blockbuster mergers create shareholder value. In a market environment where volatility has become the norm, Mike Cahill proves that knowledge is strength."

David Ellis, Editor, *Moneywise*

"*Analyzing Companies and Valuing Shares* is a modern-day bible for every investor, be they a recent entrant or a hardened professional in need of a top-up. Succinct, to-the-point and packed full of definitions of some of the most over-sued but least-understood phrases, Cahill provides a down-to-earth guide to investment.

Cahill's constant reminders that investors should look at the sector and the economy within which a company sits are vital; as no company is an island, entire of itself."

James Quinn, Small Companies Editor, *Shares*

"An invaluable jargon free guide to company valuation. A must for all active shareholders, whether novice or professional. There can be no shortcuts to making your investments grow and Mike Cahill sets out a clear and methodical approach to the research and valuation techniques necessary to become a successful investor."

Dr Jonathan Agbenyega, Head of Private Investment, ProShare

About the author

After graduating from Cambridge with an economics degree, Michael Cahill spent 16 years in the City as an analyst, working in both fund management and broking. Ten of those years were spent as part of a top-rated research team at investment bank Warburgs. This experience has provided an excellent background for getting to grips with the issues involved in analyzing and valuing companies.

Since leaving the City Michael has focused on writing about investment and developing his own business, Market Matters, which provides bespoke financial training.

Contents

Acknowledgments

This book has taken two years to develop and write and is based on 16 years of experience. Inevitably, over the years, in the development of my analytical skills a lot of people have provided valuable input and advice. Special mention must go to the building team, past and present, at Warburg's, where the high-quality environment helped me to learn a great deal about analysis. In particular thanks are due to Phil Raper for having faith in recruiting me and to Mark Stockdale from whom I learned a great deal. Andrew Rodgers has been extremely important in terms of his confidence in my ideas for both the training business and the book. Importantly, he also provided lots of excellent ideas (albeit not all of them used) and kept me up to date with market developments.

The content team at Infoshare were another great source of encouragement and ideas. Their input and patience greatly helped my approach to structure when writing about investment and the focus on a crisper writing style.

Mike Monkton provided excellent technical input with respect to the book. In particular, his faith in the idea, patience in going through early drafts and always useful suggestions are very much appreciated.

Special thanks are due to Martyn Ralph for his constant support and his constructive comments on major parts of the book. His thoughts on companies, sectors and valuation methodology have helped considerably in improving the finished product. His review of the glossary was also very welcome.

I am grateful to Keith Robinson for lending a fund management perspective and useful input on sectors and valuations. For road testing the final manuscript and some important observations thanks are due to Philip Hobday. Great assistance in dealing with those observations, along with much appreciated, high-quality advice, was provided by Sue Scott.

Clearly all of this input was vital in ensuring the quality and technical credibility of the book. Any errors or misinterpretations are very much my responsibility.

The excellent input of the editorial team at Pearson also deserves mention. In particular I am grateful to Richard Stagg for having faith at the outset and to Laurie Donaldson for his patience and support.

I very much appreciate the cooperation of Thomson Datastream in allowing me to use their charts. Extracts from *Warren Buffett Speaks* by Janet C. Lowe, copyright © 1997 Janet C. Lowe, used by permission of John Wiley & Sons, Inc.

On a personal note, big and sincere thanks are due to Cheryl Stroud for her considerable patience and wonderful practical support which made a crucial difference. And last but by no means least, to Patricia Bishop for her insight and help in dealing with the themes and issues that generate value in the long run.

Introduction

The message of this book is that doing your homework thoroughly can help you avoid potential investment pitfalls. This is a key consideration, especially given increasingly volatile stock markets worldwide. With share prices under such pressure, the focus has returned to the risk component of the risk–reward ratio. While investment is made on the basis of potential upside, understanding the key components of risk and your tolerance for risk is also crucial.

The considerable question marks that now exist over the independence of investment research have also put an increasing premium on understanding the valuation process and reaching your own conclusions.

This book is intended for those needing to understand more about how companies are analyzed and valued by the stock market, not only in theory but, perhaps more importantly, in practice. Hence it will have a wide appeal, from those looking for a user-friendly introduction to equity analysis to those with an academic grounding in the principles of accounting and investment who would like to have a better understanding of how the City really works. In addition, it will benefit active private investors aiming to improve the performance of their portfolios.

We here explore the investment-style debate, traditionally divided into 'value' and 'growth', in the context of the current market and how this might influence decisions. This is not to lay down a definitive guide, as these styles may not be mutually exclusive. However, knowledge of the issues behind the debate and how other investors may be looking at things will help you assess which approach may be most suitable for your circumstances.

The common sense of investing is often mystified through jargon. Throughout the book, the aim is to explain the importance of each concept and how it can directly affect your decision. A comprehensive glossary also explains simply the concepts behind financial terminology. An increased familiarity with the language you come across when reading investment reports or the financial press will help you feel more confident about your investment decisions.

Illustrative case studies are provided for two very contrasting stocks and sectors, with very different business drivers and valuation issues. These demonstrate how, from a starting point of little or no knowledge but using generally available information, a framework for establishing the key valuation drivers of a share and sector can be established.

A FRAMEWORK FOR YOUR INVESTMENT DECISIONS

The book's structured approach provides a practical framework for arriving at your investment decisions. It breaks down the process into four key stages:

- prospects for the sector
- prospects for the company
- valuation
- the investment decision.

These are all crucial steps in ultimately determining whether a share is attractively valued or expensive.

Assessing the sector's prospects

A sector's prospects are dependent upon the supply/demand, pricing and cost trends within the industry. If the industry economics are favourable, that provides an incentive to analyze a company's prospects in more detail. If a sector has been consistently unprofitable, volatile or has historically generated very poor returns, you may well save yourself a lot of time and money by looking elsewhere.

Challenging sector economics can be overcome, but it takes an exceptional company with special characteristics to achieve this. You may be attracted to such a situation – understanding the background will help you identify the qualities that are needed for success and make you more conscious of the risks you are taking.

Assessing a company's prospects

The analysis of the prospects for the company is based on four essential drivers of business performance:

- management and strategy

- performance and returns
- financial position
- outlook for earnings.

The combination of these factors determines the value put on a company's shares.

The management – is it working for or against you?

Strong emphasis is placed on assessing the quality of the management since, combined with the company's economic position, this is crucial to how the business will perform in the long term. As an investor, you are effectively backing a management team to deliver an adequate return to compensate you for the risks you are undertaking.

Wall Street's most successful investor, Warren Buffett, pinpoints management as a key concern when assessing risk. Three points identify the critical elements of management risk:

1. is the management running existing assets properly?
2. will it use cash flows properly?
3. is management working for shareholders or for itself?

The recent accounting and performance issues of companies on both sides of the Atlantic reinforce the importance of the quality and integrity of management. The more fraudulent activities have clearly been driven by management working for itself rather than for shareholders. This suggests that focusing on good corporate governance is another way of managing risk. This book will help you to concentrate on the main criteria, both quantitative and qualitative, that should be used to evaluate management.

Performance and returns – the wealth-creation triangle

Our attention then turns to the important numbers and ratios that indicate how the company is performing. These include sales, earnings before interest, tax depreciation and amortization (Ebitda), earnings, return on sales (operating margins), return on capital, and economic value added. We do not just show you how to calculate the ratios but also outline the business and investment implications of the answer, while explaining how this can affect valuation.

Some of these performance indicators have become controversial because there is considerable doubt as to whether they work in the interest of investors. The key area of concern, apart from the manipulation of the numbers, is whether the growth in these numbers is achieved while 'adding value' to the business. Given these issues, we will see that a blend of performance measures is required to highlight what is really going on within a company. A wealth-creating triangle of earnings growth (with close scrutiny of the quality as well as the quantity of earnings), cash generation and value added all need to be considered to assess performance.

Financial position – reading the tell-tale signs

The fear of credit downgrades has had a negative impact on many share prices. Understanding the financial position of a company can therefore save you a lot of money, so we examine the main ways of doing this. The simple calculation of interest cover can alert you really quickly to potential bankruptcy or major financial difficulties. Interest cover of 2x is normally a real source of concern – the financial risks are extremely high.

Outlook for earnings – futureproofing your investments

Given the importance of future profits and earnings in driving the share price, we then explore the difficulties and risks involved when assessing the trend in future profits. Understanding the impact of changing volumes and prices is crucial in understanding the key drivers of profits. Earnings downgrades can dramatically erode the value of an investment, so predicting when and why they are likely to happen is crucial.

Valuation – beauty is in the eye of the beholder

Having analyzed the numbers and the four factors driving valuation, we turn to how those numbers are valued. The traditional approaches of price/earnings ratio (P/E) and yields are examined and the strengths and weaknesses of these valuation methods are debated. In particular the dangers of being seduced by apparently 'cheap' valuations are clearly highlighted.

Thereafter, some of the more sophisticated valuation techniques are explored. Again the pros and cons of such methods are fully spelt out. Although some of these methods may not be easy to compute for a private investor, understanding the principles and the potential pitfalls will help you spot situations that are too complex or that exceed your appetite for risk. It is often the case that the more sophisticated the valuation technique used, the less compelling the investment argument.

Crunch time – the investment decision

Deciding whether to buy or sell a share rests on the interplay of the company's prospects and how those prospects are valued. The prospects for the company may be excellent, but you may not make any money if the shares are already very expensive. On the other hand, a company that faces a difficult future may be priced very cheaply and all the difficulties correctly reflected in the share price. Potentially this may be an attractive situation.

Opinions regarding appropriate valuations, even among investment professionals, are often sharply divided. Where does the disagreement lie? Is it in the prospects for the company or the valuation? The valuation matrix referred to earlier:

- management and strategy
- performance and returns
- financial position
- outlook for earnings

enables you to break down the valuation into manageable sections. Is it in the assessment of the management and strategy that people disagree or are there radically different views of the earnings outlook?

A low valuation may suggest that one, or all, of these factors is unfavourable. You need to understand the market's perception of these issues before arriving at your own conclusion. You can then take a view as to where you think the market is being too negative (or too positive). It also helps you identify what might need to change before the market reconsiders its valuation. This process will also make you focus on why you may be right and the market wrong – always an important discipline.

CAN YOU AFFORD NOT TO UNDERSTAND THE STOCK MARKET BETTER?

Demographics and public-sector finances mean that we are all going to have to be increasingly self-reliant when it comes to financing ourselves in retirement. With private and professional investors alike still feeling the pain of recent stock market excesses, one could be forgiven for thinking that the mattress is the best place to keep any nest egg. However, *in the long term*, investment in equities does yield higher returns than risk-free investments. The ultimate aim of this book is to equip the reader with all the skills required to understand the valuation process and make better-informed investment decisions. I wish you well.

Prospects for the sector

Why look at the sector first?

What drives sector profits?

General economic and stock market factors – how do they affect the sector?

Sector checklist

WHY LOOK AT THE SECTOR FIRST?

It is worth looking at the sector first as it gives you a quick sense of how difficult or otherwise it is for a company to make money. If the sector has historically found it difficult to make money and generate good returns, the reasons for this must be explored. This immediately may save you time as you can eliminate the sector as one where it is difficult to make money or importantly where the risks for you are too high.

What are the economic characteristics of the sector? What attributes does a company need to succeed in such an environment? Overcoming the difficult economics of an industry can be done, but it needs a special company with special characteristics to achieve this and it is quite rare. The sector may be prone to price wars, it may be cyclical or it may have a record of investing in huge amounts of capacity just as the economy turns down.

If you have found a stock that you find interesting in a sector that has historically failed to make money, you need to have a particularly good case for investing: what is different about the company that will enable it to succeed?

A number of sectors have historically failed to make money for shareholders over long periods. Steel, chemicals, paper and packaging, automotive and airlines spring to mind as areas that have been prone to losing investors' money on a long-term basis. This may reflect a combination of interrelated industry characteristics which profoundly affect the ability of a sector to create wealth.

- *Overcapacity.* This leads to poor pricing and severe competition for market share. In theory if it is making no return this capacity should be withdrawn. In reality it tends to be the case that there are 'barriers to exit'. It may be expensive to withdraw or there is a temptation to wait for things to get better. When demand does pick up, there is too much capacity (and/or too many competitors) chasing the higher volumes. This leads to pressure on prices and will prevent a profit recovery.

- *Highly capital intensive.* The high fixed costs that are a feature of highly capital-intensive industries mean that there is a tendency for the companies in the industry to go for volume. Again this leads to pressure on prices. The high amount of capital employed combined with weak pricing will lead to very poor returns on that capital.

- *Commodity products.* An inability to differentiate between products means that competition is likely to focus on price. It may also mean that there are few barriers to entry. Prices are likely to fluctuate a great deal, with management having relatively little influence.

- *No pricing power.* This will be a feature of market structure and will be influenced by the factors outlined above. It may also occur where the consumer shops around and can bargain on price. The internet has made prices increasingly transparent and makes shopping around much easier.

- *Internationally competitive markets.* Again this intensifies competition.

- *Cyclicality.* Demand patterns which fluctuate widely mean that an industry goes through a series of good and very bad years. It can be difficult to generate long-term wealth in such conditions.

These factors are not mutually exclusive. Indeed they tend to be interrelated. What is crucial is that they all tend to undermine prices. Poor pricing and shares underperforming is a key relationship which will feature throughout the book.

To illustrate some of these issues we will look briefly at two sectors where the historic performance has been poor, automotive and airlines. The points made are simple and general but describe some of the key factors accounting for the industries' inability to make money. We will also look at the characteristics of a company that has managed to make money in each sector.

Automotive sector – factors driving poor returns

Figures 1.1 and 1.2 for the US and European automotive manufacturers illustrate a history of long-term underperformance relative to their respective local manufactures. You would have lost a lot of money compared with just buying, say, an index fund that mirrored the overall market. The share price trend also shows great volatility, which suggests possible trading opportunities, although whether you have the skills to do that successfully is a different matter.

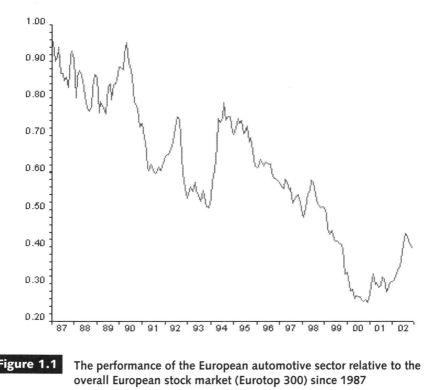

Figure 1.1 The performance of the European automotive sector relative to the overall European stock market (Eurotop 300) since 1987
Source: Thomson Datastream

The automotive industry is a classic example of an internationally competitive market. Developing countries have encouraged indigenous car industries often based on exports as an integral part of improving living standards. The industry has political importance in the developed world too – it is a large employer and the local company is often seen as a national symbol. State subsidies or loans have been important historically, helping to preserve capacity, as politically and economically it is expensive to close capacity in advanced economies while new capacity is being installed in developing countries. This new capacity will be more efficient than older facilities and labour costs are often substantially lower. It may be that the prospect for volume growth and perennial recovery hopes in the industry mean participants feel it is worthwhile to retain capacity. Closing capacity can also be an extremely expensive decision, which accounts for a reluctance to withdraw capacity.

High costs are involved in building production plants and developing new products (these are sometimes referred to as 'sunk' costs). A high pro-

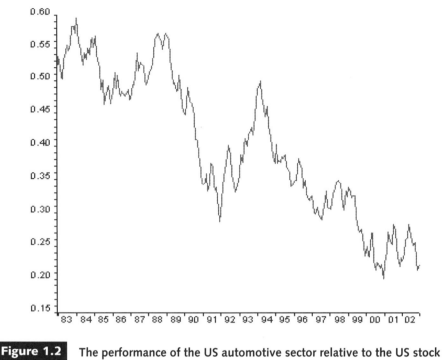

Figure 1.2 The performance of the US automotive sector relative to the US stock
market since 1983
Source: Thomson Datastream

portion of production costs are fixed. In addition, costs tend to rise as the
cars produced have more and more sophisticated features while the real
price of cars continues to fall.

These factors account for some of the difficulties. The industry tends
to have permanent overcapacity. This leads to significant competition,
domestic and international, which serves to depress prices and margins.
Volumes in the US automotive industry have been strong, but discounts
to consumers and interest-free loans have cut margins to very low levels.
Customers are increasingly shopping around and helped by the internet
are very aware of prices. This puts them in a position to negotiate keenly
on prices. The weak pricing leads to weak margins which in turn puts
pressure on cash flow – a major problem for an industry with lots of capital to maintain, high costs and new product developments to undertake.

Therefore the combination of a high cost structure and a very competitive
market makes for a difficult operating backdrop. This translates into poor
pricing, high costs, low margins and poor returns on capital employed.

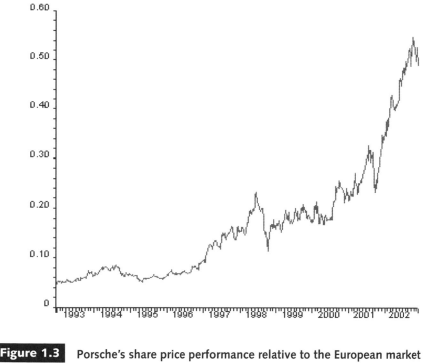

Figure 1.3 Porsche's share price performance relative to the European market
Source: Thomson Datastream

Given the issues surrounding the sector, Porsche's outperformance of the European equity market is quite exceptional (Figure 1.3). The trend in its return on capital is also impressive in the context of its industry (Figure 1.4). Its qualities and strengths contrast interestingly with the sector problems identified above. It has clearly defined itself as a luxury product and has not compromised this by going down market. This has preserved the value of the brand.

Having had difficulties in the mid 1980s the company radically restructured and reduced capacity. Rather than add capacity it has been happy to manufacture to order and has waiting lists for its output – this keeps capacity under control, keeps costs down and removes the risk of falling demand or producing so many cars that the exclusive cachet is lost.

Therefore, by keeping capacity well under control and operating in a distinct segment of the market where competitive pressures are much lower, the risk/reward ratio is much more in shareholders' favour.

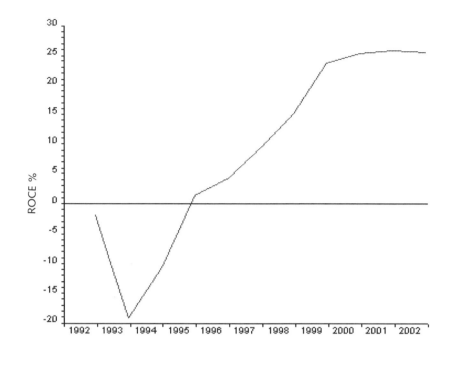

Figure 1.4   The trend in Porsche's return on capital employed since 1992
Source: Thomson Datastream

Maintaining exclusiveness of the brand is crucial in protecting sales and margins.

Airlines sector – factors driving performance

Figures 1.5 and 1.6 demonstrate that for both the world airline sector and the US sector there has been a clear, long-term relative underperformance against their relevant benchmarks. What is also a feature is the volatile pattern of these figures. Therefore the sector has lost money over time but has also been volatile. This may or may not suit your risk profile (an issue we will come back to frequently). If you feel that you have a thorough knowledge of the sector you may be able to trade it successfully. However, you need to be aware of the risks involved – you may want to have a short timescale or buy and sell on the basis of momentum (an investment style we will analyze later on page 218).

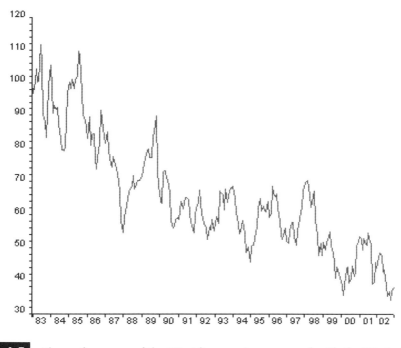

Figure 1.5 The performance of the US airlines sector compared with the US stock
market since 1983

Source: Thomson Datastream

The airline industry has also been affected by overcapacity issues. The
combination of politics and the fact that an airline is a symbol of national
pride makes for state subsidies and regulatory interference. As with the
automotive industry it tends to make it difficult for capacity to leave the
industry. Costs are fixed in the sense that for each plane trip the same costs
are incurred whether the aircraft is empty or full. Therefore small changes
in passenger numbers can cause dramatic changes in profitability. Payments for landing slots and other fees to airport operators may also be
unaffected by traffic. The cost of fuel oil is fixed and of course volatility in
oil prices can cause major changes to sector profits. This might account for
some of the sector's volatility. Capital employed is very high, although
sometimes the aircraft may be leased, not owned (if it is a finance lease
this will make no difference).

Demand tends to be cyclical – affected by economic activity but also by
global political stability. The cutbacks in company expenditure since 2000
have affected the travelling of high-margin business customers. Growth

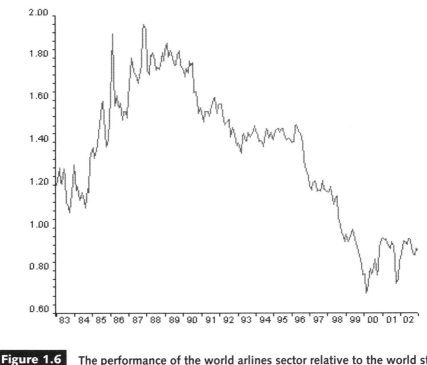

Figure 1.6   **The performance of the world arlines sector relative to the world stock market since 1983**

Source: Thomson Datastream

for low-cost operators has been strong, however. This highlights that barriers to entry have been circumvented by companies with a different business model. These operators and the transparency provided by the internet have put a downward pressure on prices and customers can make significant savings by shopping around.

Therefore, high capital intensity, high fixed costs, overcapacity and price pressure again combine to make the sector a poor home for long-term savings. These returns are disappointing given the risks involved.

In a sector known for its highly cyclical nature and wide swings in returns, Southwest Airlines has been profitable in every year since 1973 despite having the lowest fares in the industry. It demonstrates an impressive earnings growth record and consistently high returns on invested capital and equity. While Figure 1.6 demonstrates a sorry tale, Southwest Airlines has been a star performer relative to the overall US market, let alone a very poor sector. It has overcome all the industry difficulties cited above. Founded in 1971, it has provided the blueprint for other low-cost

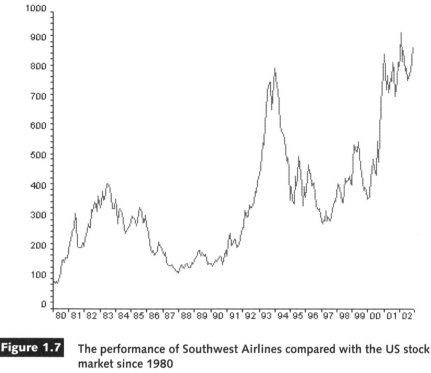

1000
900
800
700
600
500
400
300
200
100
0

'80 '81 '82 '83 '84 '85 '86 '87 '88 '89 '90 '91 '92 '93 '94 '95 '96 '97 '98 '99 '00 '01 '02

Figure 1.7   **The performance of Southwest Airlines compared with the US stock market since 1980**
Source: Thomson Datastream

airlines that have emerged since the 1990s. The focus on costs is demonstrated by the fact that it has the lowest cost per available seat mile of any of the US airlines. This is achieved through no-frill flights, only using 737s to economize on procurement and maintenance costs, avoiding the use of hub airports and maximizing the usage of the fleet.

The airline has also been driven to provide high levels of customer service and customer satisfaction. It has an excellent safety record. Clearly, as Figure 1.7 demonstrates, it has found a simple and effective formula that works for both customers and shareholders. Sales and earnings have grown strongly since the 1970s and the company has delivered excellent returns on equity. These returns historically have been between 18 per cent and 20 per cent before falling to 13.7 per cent in the year post September 11th.

The success of Southwest Airlines highlights what is wrong with many aspects of the industry. The focus on low costs and customer service has clearly created a significant amount of value for shareholders. The company has also been deliberate in choosing which segments of the market and which routes it believes will make money.

This process of examining the prospects and issues facing a sector is often referred to as a 'top-down' approach. Many investing styles will contest this on the grounds that we buy stocks, not sectors. But sector knowledge is a good starting point for providing a framework for understanding the key factors influencing the likely performance of a share. If, from the sector's historic performance and economic characteristics, it is clear that it has rarely made money, you can save money and time by focusing on sectors with more compelling money-making characteristics. Alternatively, if there are certain trends and themes in the sector that appear attractive you will want to focus on those stocks that offer effective ways of playing these trends. Critically you will be aware of the risks involved in investing in the sector. Porsche and Southwest Airlines clearly demonstrate that money *can* be made in sectors with a consistent tendency to lose money. However, the company must have special characteristics and a very different approach to the rest of the sector.

Once you understand what drives the sector you can then pursue a 'bottom-up' approach, focusing on the economics and strengths of a particular company. Chapter 2 deals with analyzing the individual company.

WHAT DRIVES SECTOR PROFITS?

Having established that it is worth getting to grips with the sector context before drilling down to look at an individual company, the next step is to examine what drives profits in the sector. You need to ask:

- What is the outlook for demand?
- What is the outlook for prices?
- What is the outlook for costs?

What is the outlook for demand?

When considering the outlook for an industry or sector you must of course take into account the overall economic outlook. This will include the prospects for interest rates, consumer and business confidence, all of which will give you an idea of where in the economic cycle we are at present. You should also consider any predicted significant population trends, for example a baby boom or an ageing population, and any other social trends that are likely to change spending habits. Any research company or survey which provides well thought-out predictions for the future will be widely reported in the financial press because it is exactly this sort of information all investors want in order to assess the prospects for one sector or company in comparison with another.

In assessing demand it is helpful to ask whether you are looking at a cyclical industry, a mature industry or a growth industry. This will immediately give you some information about the outlook for demand in your target company.

A *cyclical* industry is one that is known to have phases of doing well followed by lean periods; typically these follow the economic cycle or the interest rate cycle, which may be related. For example, the house-building industry tends to flourish during times of economic boom or low interest rates, but its investors and management expect it to do less well during a recession or when interest rates rise. This can mean that even if the economy is buoyant, if there is an expectation that interest rates will rise, housing shares may not perform as well as their business performance might warrant.

What drives demand?

If the sector is cyclical, it is important to isolate what drives the cycle. In essence this is trying to establish whether company, personal or government expenditure is what determines the overall level of demand.

The economic difficulties at the beginning of the 2000s are interesting in this context. The difficulties experienced by the corporate sector and its high level of indebtedness have seen companies cutting back severely on any discretionary expenditure. This has affected a whole range of sectors supplying the corporate sector, whether it be advertising or capital equipment. Conversely, the consumer has been surprisingly resilient. As a result consumer cyclical stocks have had a relatively encouraging demand backdrop.

Another factor that will determine how cyclical demand might be is whether the product is a 'high ticket' or 'low ticket' item. This means whether the item is costly or inexpensive. A major piece of capital expenditure would be 'high ticket' and likely to be deferred or cancelled in more difficult circumstances. For the consumer, a car or new kitchen might be deemed high ticket while going out for a pizza might be deemed low ticket. In difficult economic conditions one would expect high ticket areas to be especially vulnerable.

Where in the cycle are we?

If you are considering investing in a cyclical industry, you need to know at which point in the cycle the industry stands. This will give a good guide to the outlook for demand. How can you tell? If the sector's operating margins are very low and there have been several years of falling revenues, with prices depressed and poor demand, it is likely that the sector is close to the bottom of its cycle. Conversely, if margins are high and income (or revenue) is growing rapidly, it is likely that the industry is either at or approaching the top if its cycle.

Pinpointing the moment when the trend turns is by far the hardest part of the analysis for professional and small investors alike. Reading the cycle is not straightforward. In addition the sector may have 'structural' problems. These can include industry overcapacity, oversupply in the market, the impact of new entrants and problems among the customer base. All of these factors may mean that price, demand or profits do not recover when the economy or demand does and the share price continues to languish. The cyclical problems are prolonged.

A current example is the telecoms equipment sector where the high levels of debt among the customer base mean that demand is severely undermined.

A *mature* industry is one in which investors expect steady demand (for its products or services) at all phases of the economic cycle but where the capacity for strong growth in the overall market is unlikely. The industry is likely to grow in line with, or a little below, gross domestic product (GDP).

Examples of a mature industry in the UK would be food manufacturing or tobacco. Stable or gently growing profits over the whole of the economic cycle can be very useful, particularly during a recession. Mature industries are often good cash generators, which should mean a steady dividend. The strategic deployment of that cash flow will be a major issue at the stock-specific level.

A *growth* industry is one that is experiencing a significant increase in the demand for its products. The growth of the industry will considerably outstrip the growth of GDP. Often this is a young industry offering a new service or product, for example the mobile phone industry in the 1990s. It is also worth bearing in mind that in some instances growth sectors have turned out to be highly cyclical when the economy turns down. This has certainly been the recent experience of many technology stocks.

Growth industries are immediately attractive to the investor and will generate a lot of press and media comment. But a word of caution: high growth potential often attracts a lot of new companies which invest a lot of capital. This level of competition and high levels of capital investment make it difficult to generate the level of profits initially hoped for.

While the sectors have been broken down into cyclical, mature and growth components, a sector may have all these elements. The telecoms sector, for instance, tends to consist of mature fixed-line, conventional telephone operators as well as high-growth mobile operators.

What is the outlook for prices?

Prices are crucial to the investor. Falling prices are an effective method of destroying wealth. A price reduction comes straight off the 'bottom line', as revenues will fall sharply and so will profits as costs are relatively fixed (see operational gearing on page 135). Take a company making operating profits of £10m on turnover of £100m. If prices fall 10 per cent, revenues will fall to £90m – with costs unchanged, profit is eliminated. So the understanding of the key determinants of pricing in a sector is crucial.

We have already touched upon drivers of demand which are key elements in determining the outlook for prices. We now need to look at the other issues affecting the supply side and the competitive structure of the industry which influences price.

Nature of the product or service

Clearly a commodity product that cannot be differentiated will have less pricing power than a more sophisticated product (subject to the competitive conditions/market structure). Product differentiation should protect the company by building up brand loyalty and should provide a level of satisfaction that prevents consumers from switching to other suppliers.

Industry or market structure

This is a major determinant of price. If an industry is fragmented, i.e. there are many small players, there is typically a lot of competition and prices are kept low. As an industry matures it tends to go through a period of 'consolidation'. Companies merge with or buy each other, hoping to make it easier for them to keep prices higher and harder for new companies offering the same product or service to break into the market.

Consolidation does not always lead to higher prices. If the larger companies are determined to win an even larger share of the market, they may depress prices to win customers. The extreme example of this is a price war in which prices are cut now to enable a company to dominate the market in the future. *The Times* famously did this when it cut its cover price to 20 pence at the beginning of the 1990s. Waging a price war costs money and depresses prices across the sector. It is rarely good news for the investor, at least in the short term.

Market share aspirations

It is not just a consolidated market that is important – the participants need to be content with their market share as it is battles for market share that undermine prices. Therefore it depends on the aspirations and objectives of competitors. There may be a consolidated market, but if one of the competitors has a weak balance sheet and a need for cash, they may pursue a volume strategy to generate cash. This may or may not be sensible, but there is a danger it might happen.

Capacity position

Industries prone to large swings in demand are likely to see pressure on prices. The fluctuations in demand tend to be aggravated by the sector investing in new capacity at the peak of the market. The lags involved in bringing on stream new facilities invariably mean that demand has fallen by the time the new facility is ready. When demand does turn down, companies are keen to use this new capacity and tend to look for strong volume growth/market share. This inevitably depresses prices. It is perfectly understandable to look for volume – the new factories need to reach an efficient level of operation and this requires volume.

This capacity concern can be applied to a whole range of sectors. Chemicals, airlines, insurance and paper are just some sectors that historically have seen capacity coming on stream to undermine pricing and hence sector performance.

Barriers to entry

If the structure of an industry changes, so will the outlook for prices. Investors must consider how likely it is that new entrants will appear that could significantly change the picture. Clearly the easier it is, the more fragile the profits of the existing players. There may be a technological development that means that a new competitor can establish an efficient, low-cost alternative to the existing players. The development of the technology to build 'mini-mills' in the US steel industry changed the economics of steel production. New players needed relatively small capital sums to enter the industry, compared with the established players which had huge amounts of capital committed. Similarly, the arrival of the internet has reduced entry costs for many businesses that may have previously required a widespread distribution network to service the client base. Amazon's impact on book retailing is a case in point.

In general, barriers to entry will be determined by such factors as the following:

- *Economies of scale* – the greater the economies of scale, the more difficult it will be for a new entrant. They will need a very large amount of market share to make it worthwhile. Attempting to get this market share would lead to a price war, making the desired returns on investment difficult to achieve.

- *Amount of capital* – generally if vast sums of capital are required to enter an industry, new players will feel less inclined to take risks.

- *Experience and steep learning curve* – in some industries the skills and experience of the industry will deter new entrants. Customers may not want to buy a product or service from a new entrant if there is a lot of technical know-how involved. If the new player were to get it wrong, the customer would be massively inconvenienced.

- *Presence of patents or licences* – these make it extremely difficult for new entrants to copy the existing player(s).

- *Distribution issues* – the existing players may have such strong control over distribution channels that it would be very difficult to get a new product into the market.

- *Product differentiation* – genuine branding differences or performance characteristics will make it difficult for any new players to gain market share.

- *Efficiency/low cost base* – the more efficient and effective the industry is in serving its market, the less likely it will be that new entrants will feel there is an opportunity to take market share.

- *Customer service* – evidence suggests that when levels of customer satisfaction are very low, they are more likely to try a new supplier.

An interesting and important example of where barriers to entry have been circumvented is the emergence of low-cost airlines. They have made a big impact on the industry and taken a significant degree of market share. If they can lease the aircraft, then the capital limit to barrier to entry is avoided, that is, the company can rent the aircraft rather than having to find the substantial sums needed to purchase a very expensive piece of equipment. There may have been a feeling that the industry's cost structure was not sufficiently competitive, which meant there was scope to undercut the existing players. Similarly, the level of consumer satisfaction and the value for money equation provided by the existing players may have encouraged the low-cost airlines.

International competition

This is another important consideration. In general terms, barriers to foreign competition are coming down, encouraging new players into national markets, a process widely referred to as globalization. This obviously undermines the market structure and will create a struggle for market share. International companies may have a target market share of the domestic market to make their presence worthwhile and to build a base for a longer-term push.

Some markets are already fairly international, for example car manufacturing, while others are still dominated by national players, for example high street (retail) banking. If foreign competitors are on the horizon it is likely they will depress prices.

Bargaining power

Another useful question to consider is who has the bargaining power to determine prices in the industry. This will depend mainly on the relative sizes of the customer and the supplier. The food retail sector sees the power rest with the distribution end of the system. Much has been said and written about the ability of the supermarkets to control prices. Companies supplying the food retailers will, in general, have little influence on pricing.

Another important example is the automotive industry. The size of the multinational car manufacturers means they place extremely large contracts which are very important for the supplier to win. These orders may also be placed on an international basis so that the supplier must meet that requirement to be able to fulfil the contract.

The price competition for the end product (witness the prices and dealer discounts, including zero per cent finance offered in the USA), however, means that operating margins for the car manufacturers are very low. Accordingly, there is significant pressure on them to reduce costs which will be felt among all their suppliers. The danger for component suppliers is that while they may have to have the infrastructure to be able to supply their customer globally, and a commitment to research and development (R&D) to make the products attractive to the customer, the price received from the customer does not enable them to generate an appropriate return on the extensive assets required or compensate for the costs involved. Therefore it costs a lot to secure this contract but the pressure on prices may mean that the profitability is severely affected. This may not be an attractive situation for an investor.

Where distribution is more fragmented and customers are placing relatively small orders with a limited number of suppliers, the power may rest with the manufacturers.

Regulatory issues

For some sectors, such as utilities, there may not be any direct competition. To prevent monopoly profits the government may restrict pricing freedom by imposing a cap on price or restrictions on the returns the industry can generate. This is done by appointing a regulator who will determine the prices and returns that the industry can achieve in the absence of competitive pressures.

Summary

From the investor's point of view there are clear advantages to having 'pricing power'. This is arguably becoming even more important (and even rarer?) given the twin concerns of globalization and deflation.

What is the outlook for costs?

The costs an industry faces are often broken down into three categories.

The cost of raw materials is a *variable cost* because it will rise and fall depending on supply and demand in their own market. Where variable costs are a large proportion of the overall costs, the investor needs information about the outlook for prices of the raw material in question. For example, the plastic pipe industry will see its profits significantly affected by movements in PVC prices, so some research into the outlook for PVC production would be useful. Fuel costs are often a significant proportion of overall costs and may need watching. Rising fuel costs will also tend to adversely impact the airlines sector. A key issue is whether these cost increases can be passed on to customers, which will tend to depend on the factors discussed in the price section.

One of the most important factors an investor needs to understand is what proportion of an industry's costs are *fixed costs*. In a sector where fixed costs are a high proportion of overall costs, small movements in the volume of goods (or services) sold will have a relatively big effect on profits (see operational gearing). One aspect to watch here is a tendency for a management with high fixed costs to adopt a strategy of selling large quantities of goods (high volume) to spread the costs. To do this it may be tempted to drive down the price. However, competitors may retaliate to regain market share, leading to a price war in which only the consumer wins.

In some sectors such as the service sector, wage costs can be a key fixed cost. If there is a scarcity of the skills needed to perform this service, costs may rise sharply. An obvious example is the football sector, where shareholders have suffered as players have prospered.

The balance between fixed and variable costs is an important relationship. This determines what is called the 'operational gearing' of the sector and tells you the relationship between a change in revenues (price × volume) and the impact on profit. For high fixed-cost companies, say those involved in manufacturing, a small fall in revenue will have a significant impact on profit. A 5 per cent revenue fall might lead to anything up to a 40–50 per cent fall in profits. The impact is greater if the fall in revenues is driven by a reduction in price. There is a fuller discussion on operational gearing on page 135.

The third main element of costs is *sales costs*. These are important in assessing the cost structure of a sector to get a feel for what proportion of overall costs needs to be spent on advertising and marketing or research and development. These costs can be high where supporting an existing brand/consumer good is important, where new product launches are a regular feature or in a start-up situation. Many internet companies, which had relatively low fixed and variable costs, had a very high level of sales costs.

These costs are discretionary costs – they can be increased or decreased as the company sees fit. In a recessionary period a company may be able to cut back on sales and marketing without severely undermining its long-term competitive position. However, the company needs to be sure that it will not lose competitive advantage.

The net effect of demand, prices and costs is to determine the profits and returns of the sector – which is what you are investing for.

GENERAL ECONOMIC AND STOCK MARKET FACTORS – HOW DO THEY AFFECT THE SECTOR?

- Economic conditions
- Impact of interest rates
- Global sectors and currency

Economic conditions

Defensive v growth sectors

Knowing where we are in the economic cycle and the outlook for economic activity is an important factor in determining the attractiveness of a sector. A period of rapid and sustained economic growth, such as that which occurred during the mid to late 1990s, will tend to favour growth-oriented stocks. This was indeed a period in which growth stocks outper-formed value stocks, with the value stocks tending to occupy the more cyclical or low-growth areas of the economy.

This has been reversed since the market peak in 2000. The deteriorating economic environment, especially for companies supplying the corporate sector, combined with overinvestment in many growth areas and the related very low returns generated, has severely undermined the attrac-tions of growth. This has been an environment for more 'defensive' stocks. Defensive stocks are traditionally considered those that are not materially affected by the economic cycle. They should face a steady out-look for demand and prices. Often they are focused on the domestic econ-omy and not subject to pressures from exchange rates/imports.

Examples include food manufacturing and retailing, brewers, pharma-ceuticals, utilities (note: political/regulatory risk is important in these two areas) and tobacco (where political/litigation risk is a major concern). These areas have on the whole been very good for investment since 2000, with tobacco a notable winner, although utilities and pharmaceuticals have had problems specific to their own sectors.

The difficulty for these areas is that demand tends not to grow as the economy/people's incomes grow – they become a lower proportion of household expenditure and the economy. It is difficult to see long-term growth for these businesses. Nonetheless, in difficult economic circum-stances their attractions are clear. The low growth is outweighed by stabil-ity. In addition, the financial attractions of being in a defensive or mature area of the economy can work to shareholders' advantage. Strong balance sheets and cash flow can either be used to invest in new areas of growth or be returned to shareholders through dividends or share buy-backs.

There may also be specific difficulties for these sectors that undermine their defensive characteristics. These include the purchasing power of the big food retail customers for food manufacturers, which has caused mar-gin pressure.

'Defensive growth' plays, which is where the growth is not dependent on the performance of the economy, such as pharmaceuticals, may also look interesting in such an environment. Demand is underwritten by demographics, the fact that using drugs is a much more cost-effective solution than hospitalization and the need to alleviate illness and disease. Risks tend to focus on the failure of drugs to gain regulatory approval and the need for governments to control health care costs, which may lead to pricing pressure.

Impact of interest rates

Falling interest rates will affect sectors in different ways. House builders, for example, tend to have a strong correlation with interest rate trends. For other sectors the link may be more complex.

The performance of cyclical stocks depends on the trend in the cycle and the trend in interest rates. While cuts in interest rates should benefit a cyclical stock, it may be that demand does not revive or industry over-capacity threatens pricing – the structural difficulties we referred to earlier.

However, there is a 'Catch 22' situation for cyclicals with respect to falling interest rates. A cut in interest rates is good for cyclicals for the following reasons:

1. Profits are very sensitive to GDP and falling rates should stimulate economic growth in time.
2. Often these companies are highly geared financially so their interest burden is likely to be reduced.

Be aware though that the reason interest rates are coming down may also be important. If interest rates are cut because the economy is slowing rapidly and inflation is under control, this may well see volumes and pricing come under pressure. At the time of writing the concerns over the impact of deflation are relevant here. Deflation has been a particular concern to the manufactured sector for some time. Globalization and the transparency created by the internet have been deflationary forces for many internationally traded goods.

This concern is particularly acute in the current environment – a downturn characterized by falling company expenditure, excess supply, inflation well under control and prices for many products on a downward trend.

Growth

Falling interest rates are positive for growth stocks as they reduce the rate at which future earnings are discounted. Historically, growth stocks (and especially 'cyclical growth' stocks such as software) have performed well coming out of a bear market. This might suggest that good-quality, lower-risk growth stocks with some GDP sensitivity would be an excellent way of playing the current market recovery. This is, of course, subject to the caveat that this economic cycle is very different and overcapacity exists in many cyclical growth areas that may weaken the earnings recovery this time round.

The investment style guide (page 211) provides more on the pros and cons of defensive and growth stocks/sectors.

Global sectors

Increasingly, due to globalization and the consolidation of many sectors, it is becoming less and less appropriate to think about sectors on a national basis. Sectors are being driven by events and developments all over the world. The technology, medicine and telecoms (TMT), pharmaceuticals, automotive and chemicals sectors, to name but a few, are all increasingly international. This has profound implications when examining trends and valuing these sectors (which we will turn to later). As a matter of interest the investing institutions have adapted to this environment by increasingly looking at sectors on a global basis (or at the very least a pan-European basis). Many of the larger US investing institutions are already structured along these lines.

On this perspective, looking at/comparing GlaxoSmithKline and AstraZeneca in the UK context may not be appropriate when there may be more attractive, better-value opportunities in the US or European pharmaceuticals sector. This may be important if it is a sector with overseas exposure. Different constituents will have differing exposures to the various regions. This may well be relevant to your decision in that you may feel that prospects are better in, say, Europe than in the USA. It will also be important in terms of the impact of currency movements.

The impact of currency

When assessing the impact of currency it needs to be established how currency movements affect the company or the sector. There are two key ways in which profits are affected by currency movements, normally referred to as the translation and transaction effects.

The translation effect
This is straightforward as it is simply the impact of a rising or falling domestic currency and how it affects the recording of the profits of an overseas subsidiary. Let us take a company reporting its profits in sterling

with a substantial part of its earnings from European subsidiaries. If the euro is very weak, profits will be lower when translated into sterling. Conversely, if the euro were to strengthen, profits might rise.

These movements may be mitigated by a company's hedging policies. It may be that the company has a lot of euro-denominated debt. Then t he servicing cost of that debt would fall, which would reduce the impact of the currency depreciation. The company might also enter into contracts in the currency markets by buying or selling the currency in the futures market.

The impact of translation on a share's value should be relatively short-lived as the movement may be a one-off boost (or reduction) to the company's profits. In that sense the improvement is a low-quality source of earnings (see earnings quality on page 86). If you choose to gain overseas exposure to a particular country or region you should do it on the basis that the prospects for volumes and prices in those regions are attractive.

The transaction effect

The transaction effect is far more complex and can have a profound impact on the value of the business. This is because it affects the competitive position of the company. It affects those sectors which deal in internationally traded goods and sectors. Manufacturing sectors such as engineering and automotive are the most obviously affected.

If the domestic currency strengthens, imports are more competitive and exports less competitive. This leads to a decision for the domestic producer – whether to lower prices and protect market share or to try to maintain prices and margins. This is a difficult decision and will depend on a number of factors, such as how big a threat import competition is going to be and whether importers, distributors or consumers will be attracted to these products. It may be that increased promotional spending will highlight the benefit of the domestic product or will try to get customers to focus on non-price areas of competitiveness. This marketing will reduce margins at least in the short term, but with the obvious intention of protecting longer-term market share and seeing off the import threat.

If prices are cut, the impact on operating margins and profits will be severe (see price/operational gearing). If volumes fall, profits will also fall but perhaps by not as much as allowing prices to fall. However, as ever, it is not as easy as that. Once market share is allowed to slip, there is the danger that importers will use this base to take even more market share.

Many of these issues are of a long term-nature and will be more costly if there is a prolonged strengthening (weakening) of the domestic currency. In a worst case scenario this could see the progressive erosion of market share for the domestic companies.

As the transaction effect can have such a profound impact on the sales, long-term market share, operating profits and operating margins of a sector, it clearly can have an enormous effect on its valuation.

Summary

At this point you have completed the first step – you have assessed the prospects for your chosen industry or sector. Taken together, demand, prices and costs determine profits. Understanding the outlook for each of these elements in your chosen industry will give you a strong background against which to begin analysis of your target company.

▮ SECTOR CHECKLIST

Demand

1. Is it a growth, mature or cyclical sector?
2. How do movements in interest rates and GDP affect it?
3. If cyclical, is it the business (capital expenditure) or consumer cycle that drives demand/profits?
4. How discretionary is this expenditure?
5. Is it 'high ticket' or 'low ticket'?

Pricing

1. How consolidated is the sector?
2. What are the barriers to entry and how high are they?
3. How powerful are its customers?
4. Is there overcapacity and/or fierce struggles for market share?
5. Is there significant international competition in the sector?

Costs

1. How operationally geared is the sector?

2. Are trends in raw material costs likely to make a big hole in sector profits?

3. Are employment costs a key component and are the skills scarce?

General economy and stock market influences

1. Is it defensive or growth sector . . . how will it perform in difficult economic environments?

2. How is it affected by interest rates?

3. Is it dominated by a few stocks?

4. Is it a global sector?

5. How do currency movements affect the sector?

6. Does this impact on the translation of overseas profit or on the competitiveness of the sector (transaction effect)?

7. Is political and/or regulatory risk a feature?

2

Prospects for the company

When you have fully assessed the outlook for the sector it is time to look at the prospects for the company you are considering. Armed with the sector knowledge you will know what the company does. You now want to establish how well it does it.

You need to ask yourself:

- What is the company's market position and strategy?
- What is the quality of management?
- Strategy – mergers and acquisitions: do they add value?
- Key performance numbers and ratios: how is the company doing and how well managed is the company?
- What is its financial strength?
- Outlook and prospects: what are profits and earnings going to do?

These factors all are key influences on valuation. When we come to discuss valuation we will explore it in the context of four fundamental drivers of value. These are based on the factors above and have been simplified to:

- management and strategy
- performance and returns
- financial position
- outlook and prospects.

WHAT IS THE COMPANY'S MARKET POSITION AND STRATEGY?

Having looked at the factors influencing the sector, the company's market position is another key consideration when debating how well a company is likely to do in the future. The company's current market and competitive position needs to be evaluated before assessing its plans. Investors should expect every company to have a believable strategy for growth as a means of increasing shareholder value. However, such plans should not be taken at face value. It is worth considering the following:

- What is the company's market position?
- Is it gaining or losing market share?
- What is the profile of the company?
- What is its strategy?

Having assessed the company's competitive position the other critical issue is to determine:

- the quality of the management.

It is crucial to assess both the position and quality of the business and the management. The quality and integrity of the management and its focus on delivering value for shareholders are crucial elements in the investment and valuation decision. There are debates over whether the issue is to buy a good company or good management. When investing in shares you are getting both and both are crucial. Moreover, a good management team will struggle against poor industry conditions or a poor market position.

Some of the issues to be considered when looking at the company and its market position include:

- Is it a market leader?
- How consolidated or fragmented is the market?
- Is it a low-cost producer?
- Is it gaining or losing market share?
- Is there a customer that dominates sales?
- What are the barriers to entry? How might they be broken down?
- What is the record for innovation and introducing new products?
- Does it have the ability to move into new markets?

Is your target company one of the top three in the industry? If so it should be able to influence industry trends and prices. An ability to influence prices is a huge advantage and should secure both higher profits and a greater degree of stability. The issues surrounding pricing power/profitability were discussed in the section on sector characteristics (page 15). It is worth stressing that barriers to entry and a high degree of product differentiation (branding) are likely to establish a strong economic franchise that should face little threat. The sustainability of this franchise is critical to the long-term performance of the shares and how we value them.

Conversely, where there is little product differentiation (a commodity product), price wars or struggles for market share may well be a feature. This tends to be avoided only if the market is highly consolidated (very few players) and the market shares have reached a level where the agents believe they have a natural market share. The competitive position of the company and its ability to translate this into high margins will very much depend on the market structure.

As discussed when examining the prospects for the sector, margins are likely to be threatened if there is a customer that accounts for a large proportion of sales or that is such a significant purchaser that they can bargain down prices aggressively.

Smaller companies may face some disadvantages in terms of pricing power but alternatively may be more nimble at exploiting industry trends. You should also consider whether the company has a track record as an industry innovator. Particularly if it is a large organization, you will want to know whether it can still move quickly to meet changing market circumstances. A track record of introducing new products/ services and responding to developments in the marketplace is a crucial indicator of the company's ability to look outwards to the needs of the market. (You may want to see whether you can establish what proportion of sales comes from products that were not part of the portfolio say five years ago.)

Being a low-cost player is also a key element of a company's market position. Again this is one of the issues identified by Warren Buffett when he cites that management should 'exert tight cost control at all times' (see management culture page 41). Again this can be crucial not only for competitiveness but also for deterring new entrants. If potential competitors can see that a major player has an inefficient cost structure it may well encourage them to think they can serve the market in a more cost-competitive way and establish a strong market position relatively quickly.

Winning market share

- Can market share be increased?
- Consequences . . . price war?
- New product development
- Product mix changes
- Growing segments of market

Winning market share can be a very obvious way of growing the business (assuming that the company does not have a monopoly position). This is particularly true of smaller or medium-sized companies. The danger is of course that competitors react aggressively and a price war ensues (the newspaper market in the UK has gone through various price wars). This can be costly for an industry and ruinous for investors.

There can be a lot of sense in building market share on a long-term basis. To do this the company needs to be a low-cost producer and financially strong enough to take a long-term view. The US computer equipment company Dell has had a clear policy of building market share by being a low-cost producer. Being a dominant player when the market has matured can be a very attractive position.

Market share can also be developed by focusing on segments of the market that offer higher growth potential. Again the culture of the company is important here. It needs to be very market aware and focused, enabling it to exploit new trends and developments in the market, a move which is far less likely to cause a price war. If the segments of the market are performing well and have slightly different requirements, addressing these needs may even command higher prices and margins. So a combination of new product development and changing product mix can be an effective way of both gaining share and enhancing margins.

Growth from the gaining of market share and new product introductions is sometimes referred to as 'organic growth'. Similarly, when people refer to 'like for like' expansion they are also referring to organic growth. Essentially this means growth from the existing operations and is used to differentiate it from growth achieved via acquisition.

The risks attached to growth by acquisition tend to be much higher than organic growth, so the market tends to value organic growth more highly than acquisition-led growth. The risks and issues surrounding acquisitions are detailed on page 58.

What is the company's profile?

A good way of quickly getting to grips with the company is to get a feel for its overall profile. By this I mean a balance of operational and financial characteristics that will determine whether it is likely to make money. Some of these factors will be determined by the characteristics of the sector.

The following is a brief list of factors you may want to consider.

- Is it a one-product company?
- Is it focused or diversified?
- What is the geographic profile of earnings and is one of those regions about to run into trouble?
- Does the business generate cash?
- What is the balance of cash-generating and cash-absorbing businesses?
- Is there a significant need for capital expenditure (capex) in the business?
- What is the relationship between growth and replacement capex?
- Is the company growing organically or through acquisition?

If the company is reliant on one product, this can be both an advantage and a disadvantage. It depends on the strength of that product and its economic characteristics, such as the degree of market dominance, quality of the brand, low-cost production and barriers to entry. Focus has been increasingly seen as an advantage over the past decade or so as companies increasingly stick to what they know. The downside is if the product becomes out of date due to technological change, becomes unfashionable or is subject to a competitive threat from another product or service. Profits are likely to come under severe pressure in this situation, what the famous industrialist Lord Weinstock referred to as a 'niche becoming a tomb'. Again this stresses the need to know the economic and market position of the company.

Analyzing the divisional breakdown of profits (normally Note 1 to the accounts) is important. This will help establish how focused or diversified the company is. It is worth getting a sense of whether the activities are related to each other and if so how. If the skills required for the divisions vary enormously, does the management have the requisite skill set to manage this portfolio effectively? The divisional mix of profits will also point out some strategic issues. If a division is a small percentage of profit and the division has been owned for some years, what is the case for keeping it? Similarly, you will want to check the returns of each division. If the returns are low, again one must question why it is part of the company. (We will examine measuring returns on page 107.)

The geographic profile of earnings may be important as the prospects may vary between different countries. Is the company overdependent on one country and does this country offer reasonable prospects? If the business is cyclical this can be crucial. The building company RMC had a strong position in the German building industry, the largest in Europe. This was a major advantage in the late 1980s early 1990s as the UK market was suffering from weak volumes and prices and Germany was enjoying a reunification boom. However, from the mid 1990s German construction activity entered a downturn from which it has yet to recover. With pressure on prices as well as volumes, the business is scarcely profitable.

In the first of these periods the shares were a reasonably good investment, but they became a very poor investment in the second period. RMC allocated a lot of capital to these German operations when things were going well. Arguably it should have been diversifying into other regions. This is not trying to be wise after the event but illustrates that the geographic profile of earnings and how those markets are performing will directly affect the performance of your investment. It is worth stressing that the cyclicality of the business, its operational gearing and the sensitivity to price falls are all economic characteristics that need to be taken into account.

A good spread of regional/country operations may be an effective way of diversifying risk as you are not dependent on the fortunes of any one market. Increasingly in internationally competitive markets a position overseas may be relevant to ensure a lower cost base. In the case of a company with a number of overseas subsidiaries, it is important to check what its market position is in each market.

Presence in emerging markets can provide good long-term growth potential, but earnings can also be affected severely if the country runs into trouble. It can take a long time to build up an effective position in these markets and results can be disappointing for a number of years. In the initial stages the company may generate very low returns. With respect to its geographic profile you will need to consider the influence of currency, as discussed on page 24.

As well as examining the geographic profile, you may want to consider the balance of cash-generating and absorbing businesses. This is trying to get a feel for whether there are businesses that have a good market position with good margins which consequently generate a lot of cash (sometimes referred to as 'cash cows'). While attractive, these businesses may not offer any growth. Therefore, if there are other products or areas that offer good growth potential, the cash can be allocated to these areas to improve the growth outlook. As ever, with any investment it is not just the growth but the return it generates that is important.

The need for capital expenditure within the business also needs to be determined as it influences many other elements, such as the dividend, that affect you as a shareholder. This might be detected by looking at the relationship between capex and depreciation. If capex has been systematically and significantly below the depreciation charge, this may suggest the company has been underinvesting in assets, which may well catch the company out at some stage. It may become less and less competitive as it uses equipment that is progressively less efficient. The risk then is that a massive catch-up investment programme is needed and that all the available cash and management time will go into this project. Yet regaining the lost market share can be a difficult process.

The capex/depreciation ratio can also be a useful way of determining the growth of the company. If the capex number is significantly higher than the depreciation ratio, this can be an indicator of potential growth. Again it needs to be considered in the context of what the company is investing in and what the returns are likely to be.

The other aspect of the company's growth profile to monitor is the extent to which growth is achieved by acquisition rather than organic growth. The reliance on acquisitions for growth can be an issue of potential concern. The record of acquisitions adding value is on the whole poor. This is explored on page 58. Ideally one would like to see high organic growth rates supplemented by low-risk, in-fill acquisitions that improve the company's market position and range of capabilities.

Strategy and growth

- Key to longer-term value
- Effective strategy effectively delivered
- Implementation is key
- Does the management have the skills required?
- Management – the scarce resource?

Top management teams make strategic decisions. They decide on the allocation of resources – capital and personnel – that will deliver shareholders the best returns. This involves deciding which divisions should be kept, which will prosper and which are best disposed of. Getting this right is crucial in making money for shareholders.

Supporting the right divisions with appropriate capital expenditure and investing in product support and R&D should generate returns on investment that reward shareholders for taking on the risks involved. The returns generated from these decisions will influence share prices and consequently return on investment.

Key to longer-term value

The allocation of capital to add value for shareholders will drive the share price in the long term. There is of course an assumption that the current portfolio is performing effectively and is run properly.

If a discounted cash flow valuation is used to appraise capital investment, 50–60 per cent of the value is normally generated after the first five years, highlighting the longer-term importance of strategy. Share prices are often depressed because a company is perceived to be ex growth and to have no strategy. Alternatively, there may be a perception that the management has no credible strategy or does not have the resources (financial or managerial) to execute a winning strategy.

Effective implementation is crucial

Once the strategy is decided, there remains the key issue of implementation. The board will need good people to run the key divisions and carry out the board's instructions and objectives. Indeed, the whole workforce needs to be motivated to see effective implementation of strategy.

This combination of strategic and implementation skills is critical for setting the company on the right long-term course for adding value. The management's track record (see page 75 for an evaluation of performance) will provide an immediate check on what management has been delivering. The best plans in the world are likely to fail if the management is poor or inexperienced and cannot deliver. Conversely, simple and/or conservative strategies executed by competent managers may do well for investors.

Different skills required

Different businesses may need very different managerial approaches to be successful. A highly regulated utility, for example, requires a very different approach from a highly cyclical commodity business, which in turn requires very different skills from a fast-growing technology business. Similarly, companies at different stages of development (start-up, high growth, mature, declining or recovery) may require very different skill sets. This can often be seen in recovery situations where the skills and approach needed to cut costs and reorganize the portfolio may not be those needed to start developing a growth strategy.

The blend of skills on the board should also be consistent with, and complementary to, the strategy. The financial implications, risks and impact on returns from any given strategy will require a detailed and thorough examination by the finance director (FD). The FD should be an effective check on the chief executive (CEO) to ensure the financial aspects of the strategy make sense. He will need to address issues such as:

- Can the strategy be funded?
- What returns will it generate?
- What is the cash flow profile of the move?
- How will it affect the share price?

What can happen is that the finance director is very good on matters of financial control and reporting but not so good at appraising the strategic aspects of what the company is undertaking. The debate on strategy then becomes less effective.

The ability to delegate and empower people is critical if the strategy is to be implemented effectively. So there needs to be strong divisional and operational management that can drive the strategy through and ensure the required results are delivered.

Do the skills match strategy?

This raises the issue of whether the skills of the board match the strategy the company has. Reading the biographical notes in the Report & Accounts (R&A) may help with this. Do the board members have a lot of experience in what the company actually does? Marconi expanded and focused on its telecoms operations when both its CEO and FD had little experience of this market. This was not the only problem that Marconi ran into and maybe not the major one. But the relationship between skills and strategy is an important issue here and needs to be taken into account. It should also be noted that there was a fashion for both focus and the telecoms sector at this time and the moves were initially well regarded, as evidenced by a soaring stock price. Again sensible business strategies and doing what is right for a business may be divorced, short term, from stock market trends. The dangers of acquisitive companies will be discussed in detail on pages 73–4.

Management – the scarce resource?

The shortage of high-quality management is a major constraint on corporate performance and the implementation of strategy. This has been highlighted dramatically by the high-profile corporate failures of recent years. It is also very much an issue with the failure of mergers and acquisitions to add value. While earnings dilution is always the number people focus on when deals are done, 'management dilution' is often a much greater determinant of whether the deal is successful in creating value for shareholders and the impact on share price performance. (This is discussed in more detail in the mergers and acquisitions on page 58.)

The availability of high-quality management will have a crucial impact on the longer-term performance of the company and its shares.

THE QUALITY OF MANAGEMENT

This is critical for the success of your decision. To get a sense of the quality of management and the extent to which it is working for you, it is worth examining:

- management culture

■ corporate governance

■ management change.

The other critical issue in assessing the quality of management are the results and returns it delivers. This will be covered in detail on page 101.

Management culture

While difficult to define, it is nonetheless interesting to have a sense of what the culture of the management/company is. This can be decisive in whether it is successful at what it does. Warren Buffett has neatly encapsulated the key elements of a successful corporate culture. This is a management that:

● behaves like owners

● exerts tight cost control at all times

● does ordinary things extraordinarily well.

This sounds and indeed is wonderfully straightforward. However, it is rarely found. Management often loses sight of these key guiding principles. It may be that as companies get larger they lose the ability to think and act like 'owners'. The important thing is that a management that is working on this basis firmly has its interests aligned with the shareholders'. This is a key requirement for avoiding many of the management scandals that have dominated the headlines in recent years. For investors it is crucial to ensure that the management culture is driven by adding value for shareholders.

The need for tight cost control at all times is interesting in the context of companies that have periodic major restructurings to deal with an uncompetitive cost base. This clearly implies that they allow costs to get out of hand until they decide that a massive attack is needed. This inevitably tends to mean big write-offs, exceptional charges and a related cash outflow on redundancies. All of these things impair the net assets or cash position of the company to the detriment of shareholders. They are often an integral part of recovery stories, but caution should be exercised (see problems with recovery stocks on page 215).

Long-term business perspective

Taking decisions in the long-term interests of the business is an important factor in delivering returns to shareholders in the long run. As we will discuss when we come to look at earnings (page 79), decisions to hit short-term earnings targets may, in an immediate sense, please the market. However, if it is being achieved by reducing discretionary expenditures on marketing and R&D, or underspending on critical investment that the business needs, then the long-term position of the business is likely to be undermined.

If management is driven by short-term financial goals, this may jeopardize the value of the investment in the longer term. So if hitting an earnings target is important to management, the decisions it takes to do this may not be in your interests. There may not even be a short-term benefit as, if the market sees that earnings have benefited from the reduction in marketing or research and development, the shares are likely to be marked down.

What do they target and why?

This leads us to examine what the management targets for performance and why. There is a legitimate question as to whether targets should be set in the first place. As mentioned above, the danger is that targets are hit by decisions that harm the business. Even worse is fraud. The accounting scandals of 2001/2002 invariably revolved around numbers being manipulated to hit sales or earnings growth targets. (The other principal reason for accounting trickery was to conceal the extent of the company's debt levels.)

It is interesting to note how management is remunerated, which will normally be detailed in the R&A. If performance bonuses are linked to growth in earnings per share (EPS) or even worse earnings before interest, depreciation and amortization (Ebitda), this immediately suggests a potential conflict of interest between management and shareholders. This will be explored in more detail later, but essentially actions that deliver growth do not necessarily create added value (i.e. returns compensate shareholders for the risks they are undertaking by exceeding the cost of capital). Mergers and acquisitions (M&A) may well deliver growth in EPS (and are guaranteed to increase Ebitda), but M&A has a poor record of delivering shareholder value. The other great danger is that if debt is taken on to fund the deal and deliver an increase in EPS/Ebitda, the risks will increase considerably. This is on top of the risks of the deal itself (overpaying, buying a poor business, buying at the wrong point in the cycle, etc.).

These actions benefit management as they help reach performance targets, thus triggering bonuses and the higher remuneration that goes with running an ever larger business.

Another danger of targets is the impact when they are missed or no longer relevant. This can cause disappointment in the market. Targets that are absolute are also likely to cause problems. For example, setting an earnings target of 15 per cent when inflation is 6 per cent becomes a totally different proposition when inflation is 2 per cent.

So targets can be dangerous in a number of ways. They may encourage accounting gimmickry, which must be avoided. Again this is putting a gloss on the company's performance and position which distorts the reality of its real performance and position, which is what drives value. They may also encourage management to take decisions which destroy shareholder value but help hit targets – and of course trigger their bonuses.

Bullish v conservative

If possible it is worth getting to know whether management normally takes a cautious view of developments and likely profits or whether it tends to be optimistic and upbeat about prospects (bullish). This enables you to form a sense of how realistic the company's announcements and assessments of the outlook are likely to be. Reading R&A and results announcements and seeing what the chairman's statement indicates will give you a clue, as will reading the financial press. If the management is perennially bullish you may want to 'aim off' its indications of future results. It may also be the case that a company that is conservative by nature will also be conservative in how it presents its numbers and not engage in attempts to distort the numbers through flexible accounting policies. Companies that are bullish by nature may be tempted to flex the numbers to reach their bullish targets (though this is certainly not always the case).

Growth culture – organic v acquisition

If the company has a growth culture and relies heavily on acquisitions to achieve this, the risks may be much higher than in a company with a culture of expanding its core operations organically. Again it is worth stressing that many of the companies that have crashed following the bubble years were highly acquisitive by nature. Often this was to disguise difficulties in their core operations and to provide growth and the accounting flexibility that often goes with integrating acquisitions. The destruction in value that acquisitions often deliver will be discussed on page 58.

Growing a business organically tends to be lower risk and more likely to deliver higher value. Accordingly it will be valued more highly by the market.

Production or technology driven, cost or market driven?

It is always worth trying to establish whether there is a particular bias in the company towards production or marketing. In effect you are trying to establish how inward or outward looking the company is. Many companies have developed a new product or production process but have not had a sufficiently strong marketing culture or distribution network to exploit the product. Many technology companies have historically been guilty of this. This can be particularly important if there is a relatively short product cycle as the company may not capitalize on the product and before it realizes it another product has taken its place.

Importantly many companies make the mistake of emphasizing technology or production skills when actually it is a focus on costs and/ or marketing that is the most critical requirement to ensure competitiveness. The majority of consumers buy a product on the attractiveness of its features, how it performs, and not the technology. It is also easier to understand what the market is likely to be for a product than for the technology.

Monopoly culture

Another potential problem exists in companies that have historically enjoyed a dominant or monopoly position in a market. This can breed inefficiency and a culture of not having to try too hard. Arrogance towards the market can alienate the customer base. If an alternative competitive product or provider emerges, customers are more likely to switch allegiance. Market share can then fall sharply as the management has never had to deal with this encroachment on to its territory.

The attitude and performance of many newly privatized companies in the UK has been interesting in this regard. Arguably BT had a large bureaucratic structure with a lack of commercial awareness that is not surprising in a company that had been in the public sector for so long.

Accordingly it has missed potential market developments or in some instances not made the most of its position.

Culture of privatized companies

Partly related to this monopolistic culture is the culture often found in recently privatized companies. Having been previously government or local authority owned, utilities are often bureaucratic and not commercially oriented. Interestingly, when they find that the regulator is looking to control and regulate their core business, their natural reaction appears to be to buy overseas utilities or to diversify domestically. This has tended to lead to them overpaying for acquisitions, not running them effectively when they have them and then finally selling them at a loss.

Culture determines whether management will make money for you

It can often be difficult to assess something as intangible as 'culture'. Nonetheless, it is well worth thinking about it when looking at a company as it can be critical in whether you make money. In this sense the most important aspect is that the management is clearly and emphatically working for shareholders. A focus on doing what is right for the long-term benefit of the business – in Buffett's terms acting as owners – is going to deliver returns to you in the long run. An openness and directness in its dealings with you is also an indicator of a culture that is conducive to treating owners properly.

Corporate governance

The spate of scandals over accounting fraud and management receiving massive salaries while companies perform poorly and share prices slump has put the issue of corporate governance firmly on the agenda. How and why this is allowed to happen and why the checks and balances to protect the interests of shareholders (who happen to own the company) have so often failed are the crucial issues that corporate governance must seek to address.

Buffett's rationale for managers to behave like owners becomes abundantly clear in this context. While one can legislate for 'best practice' in corporate governance matters, there is no substitute for a management that is fundamentally committed to acting in the interest of shareholders.

The principal-agent problem and conflicts of interest

The issue of why shareholders' interests are sometimes poorly served reflects the twin issues of the 'agency' problem and related 'conflict of interests'. The agency problem refers to the fact that there is an effective separation of owners (shareholders) and those who are employed to manage the company on their behalf. Will they really, as agents of the owners, manage in the interests of shareholders? Conversely, the owners may be disinterested or feel they have little impact on influencing the management team. As a result there are few constraints on management.

The decisions taken by the board may well be taken in its interests rather than to benefit shareholders. That it is in a position to decide things immediately raises the 'conflict of interests' element of the equation. If it appoints non-executive directors, there is immediately a conflict of interests. Does the loyalty of the non-executive lie with the chief executive who appointed him or with the shareholders he should be representing? If these non-executives are on audit committees this conflict arises again. It might be compounded by the fact that the board may hire remuneration consultants to deliver evidence to the remuneration committee. Again the consultants' interests lie with the executives who hire them.

Conflicts and bonuses: what triggers the bonus?

The other area where major conflicts arise is that of pay, the award of stock options and bonuses. Bonuses in particular have been and remain a key concern. Remuneration packages are often triggered by hitting earnings or Ebitda targets, an acquisition being completed successfully or the company's shares outperforming the market. The problem is of course that these targets may have nothing to do with good management and may not be consistent with shareholders' interests. In particular acquisitions can help you hit Ebitda or earnings targets while subtracting a lot of value for shareholders (i.e. the returns from these deals are massively below the cost of capital).

In certain sectors there may be a boom in volumes and prices that has nothing to do with good management performance and adding value. In effect in a bull market anyone would be able to hit targets set in absolute terms. So you need to think about how demanding the targets are. Let's say bonuses are triggered by earnings growth of 7 per cent. In a company with high operational gearing these payments could be generated by relatively small trading improvements. If there is a 3 per cent uplift in profit for each 1 per cent increase in revenue, a 3 per cent revenue uplift could trigger a 9 per cent uplift in earnings. For some industries this could be easily achieved if volumes and prices are on a rising trend. Alternatively a company facing poor volumes and weak pricing, or where there are high variable and low fixed costs (i.e. low operational gearing), might find it incredibly challenging to have a 7 per cent earnings trigger.

Best practice is to use a combination of internal targets which are difficult to achieve and targets set against the performance of competitors (if you happen to be in a growth sector it might be easy to beat the market or FTSE; you are certainly not comparing like with like).

Therefore these targets will encourage strategies and policies that are likely to hurt shareholders in the long term. In the meantime the remuneration package for the board can rise dramatically. An acquisition being completed should not be a source of extra pay; generating a return and making the deal work is where management should distinguish itself. Similarly, linking rewards to the shares performance against the market overall may not be appropriate. In many respects the shares may perform by default against the market – a defensive share may perform brilliantly in difficult economic environments but that may owe little to the performance of the management.

Good examples of these policies include Vodafone where remuneration has been triggered by Ebitda targets and where the CEO did receive payment for successfully completing the Mannesmann acquisition in 2000. Similarly GlaxoSmithKline ran into controversy during 2000 over an attempt to reward its CEO more generously. This has revolved around earnings targets being 9 per cent over inflation over a three-year period, the shares performance relative to the FTSE and being in the top third of a group of chosen drug company peers. The issue is whether these targets are relevant and how challenging they are. Similarly, might an acquisition be undertaken to help with these targets? It is far from clear whether previous acquisitions have added value. Indeed, the poor performance of the company's drug pipeline might argue that a further acquisition would make this problem even worse. In effect it may be that there are diseconomies of scale in the company's R&D division – a key driver of long-term value.

Therefore the issues of agency and conflicts of interest lie at the heart not just of the corporate governance issue but of profitable investing in shares. While this is increasingly a feature of the regulatory environment, it works far more effectively if the culture of the company is deeply committed to adding value for shareholders, i.e. it is part of the company's culture.

Governance and strategy

With the need to create shareholder value increasingly being recognized, one of the key aspects of corporate performance is strategy. This is an area where shareholders are increasingly trying to influence company boards.

This tends to revolve around the company's portfolio and the pressure either to sell underperforming divisions or to ensure that value-destroying acquisitions are prevented. An interesting case in point is the fund manager Hermes and its public involvement in influencing Six Continents (formerly Bass). In January 2002 Hermes wrote to the management of Six Continents urging it to avoid value-destructive acquisitions and return cash to shareholders. There was institutional pressure to demerge the pubs and hotels side of the company. In February 2003 the possibility of a break-up bid emerged before the demerger was implemented. Clearly this pressure implicitly suggests that there is little confidence in management's ability to allocate that cash in value-added ways. The track record generally on acquisitions adding value is poor and if a particular company has consistently subtracted value, it is likely to come under pressure.

Ensuring good governance

Focusing on corporate governance is crucial to ensure that management is acting in your interests. In effect it is another way of reducing risk. There may be one or two instances of founder owners breaking the codes on good governance which do not harm the returns to shareholders – the managers are owners to a significant extent. The founder may hold such a large share of the equity that his interests are aligned with those of the shareholders. More generally, however, it is crucial to ensure that 'best practice' is being followed.

The best practice checklist should cover such matters as:

- quality and integrity of management
- separation of chairman and CEO roles
- ratio of non-executive to executive directors
- independence of non-executives
- contract length
- remuneration policies
- what triggers performance-related bonuses
- open and timely communications to shareholders.

This list is to ensure a proper board structure, with a split between the roles of chairman and CEO and high-quality, independent non-executive members of the board. The splitting of the roles of chairman and CEO is important in order to avoid an overly powerful and influential figure who proceeds to make decisions without sufficient scrutiny from and debate with the board.

Similarly, independent non-executives are important to represent the interests of shareholders on the board and to challenge the executive members to justify their decisions. It is normal to have three independent non-executives on the board, although some commentators are now advocating having a higher number of non-executive to executive directors.

The independence aspect is clearly crucial – non-executives should not be dependent on work coming from the business or have commercial relationships with the CEO or chairman. Otherwise they will not provide an independent check to boardroom discussions. This is why there is so much concern about the number of directors who sit on each other's boards. If you have a non-executive director (NED) on the board where you are CEO and you are a non-executive on their board, there is an obvious conflict of interests and lack of independence (I do not challenge you, you do not challenge me).

The importance of a board having high-quality and independent non-executive directors was the focus of the review by Derek Higgs on 'The role and effectiveness of non-executive directors', published in January 2003. This addition to the combined code and suggestions for improvement to best practice was instigated by government in February 2002 in response to the fallout from Enron and other financial scandals. At the same time Sir Robert Smith was asked to look into the role of the audit committee.

While there has not been anything on the scale of Enron in the UK there have been many instances of companies pursuing strategies which have destroyed value on a grand scale. On this basis improving the quality and independence of the debate over strategy and whether the allocation of capital will create value has to be beneficial for shareholders.

In terms of improving the functioning of the board and the decision-making process, the review focuses on avoiding concentration of power on the board. Here the independence of NEDs is crucial. To this end the proposals revolve around having a higher proportion of independent and well-informed NEDs on the board with their role defined more clearly. To achieve this, the review suggests that the selection and appointment process needs to be broadened and made more rigorous. There also needs to be a step change in the provision of training and development of NEDs to maximize their contribution to the decision-making process.

An important aspect of the Higgs proposals is the appointment of a senior NED whose responsibilities would include chairing meetings of non-executives where the chairman is not present and significantly to act as a link with shareholders. They may sit in on regular meetings with shareholders and also act as a point of contact for shareholders if they feel grievances are not being dealt with effectively by the chairman or CEO.

The proposals in the Higgs review are an updating of best practice and are incorporated into the combined code. A critical part of the approach is rather than focus on legislative requirements the onus will be on best practice, with the board having to 'comply or explain'. There may be good reasons why a company cannot comply with best practice but these must be explained to shareholders. If you as an investor feel that management is not operating in your interests by complying with best practice, you need to think through the implications.

Some of the key features of the Higgs Review are as follows.

- The division of roles of chair and CEO should be clearly defined, written down and agreed by the board.
- The CEO of a company should not become chairman of that company.
- NEDs must be independent – that is, the individual should not be receiving fees from the company or have a business relationship with it, should have no family connections, should not represent a major shareholder or have been on the board for more than ten years.

- Half of the board, excluding the chairman, should be NEDs.
- NEDs should lead audit, nomination and remuneration committees.
- A senior non-executive director should be identified.
- If shareholder concerns are not addressed effectively by normal channels and fail to be resolved, the senior NED should be used.
- NEDs, and in particular chairs of committees, should attend the annual general meeting and answer relevant questions.
- A full-time executive board member should not have more than one NED role.
- No individual should chair more than one board of a major company.

Concerns and objections to the review have centred on potential conflicts between the senior non-executive and the chairman. Some critics argue that in some instances the senior NED might emerge as an alternative power base and this would disrupt the 'unitary board' that characterizes the UK's approach to corporate stewardship. It is also feared that confusion will arise if the message from the senior NED to shareholders differs from that of the chairman/board. While this may occur in some instances the potential upside of the proposals, if managed properly, far outweighs any downside.

One of the features of the accounting scandals in the USA has been complicity or negligence by the auditors. In some cases this has been because of auditors earning non-audit consulting fees, which makes the rocking-the-boat option a costly one. In such a case the auditors' independence is severely compromised. The auditors should be representing shareholders, not executive management.

Reflecting these concerns the Smith proposals revolve around the audit committee being made up of the non-executives, ensuring the independence of auditors and the enforcement of accounting standards. As with the Higgs Review, a 'comply or explain' approach is adopted.

Some of the key features of the Smith proposals are as follows.

- The audit committee should comprise at least three members, all independent non-executive directors.
- At least one member should have significant, recent and relevant financial experience.
- The role of the audit committee is clarified to include monitoring the integrity of the financial statements, reviewing financial reporting

judgments and reviewing the company's internal audit function and financial controls.

- The audit committee is also responsible for making recommendations to the board concerning the appointment of the external auditor and for monitoring the external auditor's independence, objectivity and effectiveness.

- The audit committee should develop and implement policy on the engagement of the external auditor to supply non-audit services.

The length of employment contract for key executives is another area of concern. If they are on a long-term contract (say three years), it can be expensive to get rid of a poorly performing board member. Not only have they destroyed value, they receive a payoff for leaving the company. Accordingly, the code advocates that contracts should be of 12 months' duration and no longer.

The use of share options and bonuses that are triggered by certain targets should also be monitored carefully. This can lead to massive payouts but, as discussed earlier, this may be for achieving objectives that do not assist shareholders, and indeed may be positively harmful to their interests. Again there is a temptation to use sharp accounting practices to help hit these targets. Clean accounting should be a fundamental part of the quality and integrity of the management team.

An open communication policy is not necessarily part of any strict governance code but it is an important part of how your company is run. Critically, it tells you a lot about the culture of the management – that it is interested in doing the job properly for all those who employ it: the shareholders. The company being open with all its shareholders at the same time is a legal requirement.

Many companies do in fact talk to analysts and brokers to guide expectations one way or another. You can see this from the way share price movements in stock market reports in the papers are described. Again this is not best practice. A trading statement at the end of the half-year and full-year trading periods is a more effective way of communicating fairly to all shareholders.

Upside of good corporate governance

The benefits to you as a shareholder/potential investor of good corporate governance are considerable. At the very basic level, the quality and integrity of the management will be a crucial determinant in the success or otherwise of your company. Knowing the company is being run in your interests is critical. Increasingly, good governance is being taken seriously and large shareholders in particular are keen to ensure that boards are more aware of their views on these key issues. Evidence is also starting to show that valuations are benefiting from good governance practices.

Management change – responding to underperformance

Management teams and chief executives are judged on how well they use the money shareholders have invested and what subsequently happens to the share price. If management has consistently failed to deliver and change is needed, what issues must be addressed if you are to continue to hold the shares or consider buying them?

News of management changes

When returns have continually disappointed and this has been reflected in a sharp fall in the share price with little prospect for a recovery, things need to change. A new management focused on generating higher returns is very much needed. This may be a buy signal if the new management has a realistic chance of turning the company around.

How does poor performance show up in the figures?

The return on sales and capital employed are likely to have fallen to low levels in absolute terms and will certainly be a lot lower relative to others in the same sector or industry. The return on capital may be so low that it is not covering the company's cost of capital and it would be better putting money in the bank. This may have occurred over a long period. The share price is also likely to have underperformed both the sector in which the company operates and the broader market. (We will discuss the returns issue in a lot more detail on page 101.) A collapsing share price will inevitably lead to close scrutiny of management and its failings.

Are the key problems endemic to the industry/business itself or to management failings?

Poor corporate performance, or even failure, is often ascribed to deficiencies in the trading environment rather than to a poor management team or performance. It needs to be considered, therefore, whether the market conditions are genuinely difficult, with both prices and volumes under significant pressure.

It might be the case that returns are low due to significant overcapacity and weak pricing across the industry. In this instance it may not be a demand problem and may well require action across the industry before returns register any improvement. However, it might be that blaming a poor trading environment is a diversion from more long-standing and deep-seated problems within the company. We have continually stressed the need to take long-term decisions to protect and enhance the company's competitive position. If the management has consistently failed to do this, ultimately the company will lose market share and see returns on sales and capital come under pressure.

Careful analysis is needed to determine whether this is due to any of the following scenarios.

- Has the company lost touch with what is going on in its markets and what its customers want?
- Has an acquisition gone badly wrong (a strategic error)?
- Is a particular division seriously underperforming its peer group?
- Is the cash flow seriously deteriorating?
- Have the returns on a large investment programme disappointed?

Who decides management should change?

This is a complex question and realistically represents a variety of factors/issues coming to a head. If the performance has been poor for a significant period, then shareholder pressure combined with media coverage should galvanize the non-executives to initiate change. This presupposes that large shareholders are ready to wield their influence. Alternatively, the threat of being taken over may either lead to action to improve performance or to the management deficiencies being remedied by a takeover.

What management needs to do and can it do it?

In essence, the key options to raise returns, and hence the share price, open to management are to:

- improve revenues (prices and volumes)

- reduce costs
- reduce the amount of capital that is used in the business.

Improving the revenue side of the equation requires either extra volumes or higher prices to be achieved. This may be problematic because the market is too difficult and/or the response of competitors prevents extra volume or higher prices being obtained. This may be especially true if one of the players in the market is driven by gaining long-term market share. Problems will also arise if there is a lot of competition from imports. If the company has seen a long-term erosion of market share, generating higher revenues may be far more difficult to achieve. Significant investment in the product and marketing will be required to regain market share. This will take time and success is not guaranteed.

Costs are the one variable within management's control and so tend to feature prominently in recovery stories. The cutting of overheads, closing of factories and discontinuance of loss-making or poorly performing product lines/divisions are the first port of call for any restructuring programme. This arguably represents the easy first stage of the recovery. If prices or volumes continue to fall, however, this may not be sufficient for a profits recovery. So buying shares for a profit recovery in these circumstances may well fail to make you money. In addition, it is worth stressing that these restructuring charges and asset write-offs will have a negative impact on shareholders' funds/net assets and cash flow (to pay for the redundancies, etc.).

If massive restructuring charges are taken, it may well be future earnings that benefit from this action. One needs to be careful in these circumstances to determine how much of the uplift is a benefit of accounting matters rather than the underlying performance of the business. The danger is, of course, that shareholders' funds are written off to benefit earnings growth so that shareholders are in effect paying for the earnings growth.

Strategic issues – disposals and acquisitions

As well as trying to rectify a poor trading performance, the management may need to address the company's strategic position. This may involve selling off poorly performing or non-core activities. However, as recent evidence has amply demonstrated, this is far from straightforward. Selling companies at a sensible price in a bear market when companies are highly indebted and have little access to new funds is very difficult.

Assuming disposals can be achieved, this should allow management time to be focused on the core and raising its performance (as well as improving the financial position of the company). As indicated earlier this may be a long-term process. Improving its operating performance may then allow growth opportunities to be considered. Acquisitions may improve the product coverage and growth profile (subject to the caveats about acquisitions made in the M&A section on page 58).

Culture

One of the great difficulties in turnaround situations is gauging how far the culture of the organization needs to be changed and how long this will take. This can be especially true when once great companies have under-performed for years but still believe themselves to be great. A bureaucrat-ic structure may have evolved during the years of success. This invariably prevents the radical change that is needed. This can also be the case when a company had monopolistic control over a market and has come under pressure. BT has been a classic case of this. The important thing to bear in mind here is that any investment on a recovery basis will take time to come through.

How long will it take? How long should they be given?

This is impossible to answer as each situation will be different and the complexity of issues will vary enormously. Is it just a cost problem or are there fundamental problems with the company and/or the market place? Critically, both the external environment and the extent of the internal problems will have a big bearing on the success of the turnaround – and the time needed to do it. A turnaround in a stable market where revenues are not under pressure may be much quicker and easier to effect than in a cyclical commodity business with huge overcapacity, high import pene-tration and price weakness. Where the culture has become bureaucratic and unresponsive to developments in the market and the needs of cus-tomers (leading to a significant loss of market share), combined with pressure on volumes and prices, there is a much stiffer challenge – a turn-around will not be achieved quickly.

Is it an internal or external appointment and is this significant?

Some chief executives have good reputations as agents of change. It may be that a fresh approach is just what a company needs. Track record is important here. The new members of the top management team, if brought in from outside, will have no loyalty to past decisions or to any particular division where they cut their teeth, nor will they have been affected by a possibly inefficient or lazy corporate culture. This will hopefully counteract any inertia blocking the implementation of change.

What skills does the new CEO bring?

Is the new CEO a cost cutter, a product/marketing expert, or does he have skills in restructuring portfolios? What does the company need? If he has a proven record in cost cutting, what happens when the company needs to grow? Similarly, if his track record is in running dynamic growth businesses, what happens when the company matures? In most recovery situations a blend of these skills will be needed to transform the company's fortunes.

Again it is worth stressing Warren Buffett's dictum on management, which is particularly relevant in situations where there are management changes in companies that are struggling:

> ... with few exceptions, when management with a reputation for brilliance tackles a business with a reputation for poor fundamental economics, it is the reputation of the business that remains intact. (in Janet C. Lowe, *Warren Buffett Speaks*, Wiley, New York, 1997)

Waiting for a takeover?

It can be tempting when holding the shares of a severe underperformer to wait for a bid approach (indeed you may consider that the shares are attractive on the basis of a likely bid and be a potential buyer). The danger is, of course, that the company's market position and performance have deteriorated to such an extent that the company is no longer as attractive as it was. It no longer enjoys the market share that may have made it a genuinely attractive bid candidate. Indeed, the competition may have been so successful in gaining market share from this weakened competitor that they, correctly, feel they can gain even more market share by undercutting the company (the customers are also those most likely to have noticed poorer performance). Furthermore, there is no desire to take on the difficulties of an ailing company.

This is not to argue that potential takeover situations cannot be a potentially profitable investment area. However, it is important to be aware of the risks involved and that a bid may take a long time to materialize (if ever). In the meantime you may be invested in a company that is going through a difficult time and as a result you may lose a lot of money while waiting. So if you are thinking of buying shares in a company on the basis of a potential takeover, try to ensure that its underlying performance is reasonable, that it genuinely has features (high market share, good technology, brands, distribution network) that make it still attractive to potential suitors and that the takeover hopes are not the only reason you are holding the shares. A takeover should be the icing on the cake.

Management change and recovery stories – will you make money?

All in all it is quite complex to assess whether new management coming into a company will reverse its fortunes. A key issue is the extent to which the company's market position and returns have deteriorated – the steeper the descent, the more difficult the turnaround. Another key issue is the stability of the markets in which the company operates. The more volatile the pricing and volume environment, the more difficult it will be to improve returns. In an environment where prices are falling rapidly, any cost-cutting initiatives will be needed just to stand still.

Doing your homework to assess the company's market position and performance is crucial as there are significant risks involved. The changes are likely to take a long time to implement and correspondingly it may be a long haul for the shares.

MAKING SENSE AND CREATING VALUE OUT OF MERGERS AND ACQUISITIONS

A merger is when two companies of roughly the same size join forces. An acquisition is when one company takes over another. Mergers and acquisitions remain an important part of the financial landscape even though much of the academic and empirical evidence casts serious doubts on whether they fulfil the promises made at the time of the deals, and more than half destroy, rather than enhance, shareholder value.

In the light of this evidence it is worth exploring:

■ why companies are keen to do deals

■ what to consider when evaluating deals

■ why deals do not add value for shareholders.

Why deals are done

The principal drivers of acquisitions tend to involve attempts to improve earnings and returns on investment by:

● controlling costs

● influencing prices

● growth from new product or geographic areas.

In theory, deals done for these reasons should benefit shareholders. A stronger business with a better earnings outlook and long-term growth potential should deliver a higher share price. Considering these objectives, the most common reasons advanced to justify deals include to:

● improve the growth outlook for the company

● enable costs to be cut

● improve pricing power

● increase market share

● take out excess capacity

● gain access to a new product area

● gain access to a new geographical area

● gain access to a key technology

● gain control of key raw materials or inputs

● gain a stronger control of the way the product/service is sold.

It could be argued that the risk/reward profiles differ with the various reasons for doing a deal. A move that is made because it enables costs to be cut and gives the combined entity greater market share (and better pricing power) is arguably lower risk. It should be easier to implement the required actions as the management is working in an industry it knows. It might be that these benefits are one-off and improve the earnings growth for a couple of years. This may limit the longer-term rewards but then the risks are also lower.

The more growth-oriented deals may involve more risk. Moving into a new product or geographic area will inevitably pose the management with more unknowns and potentially therefore be higher risk. For example, moves into new geographic regions often prove to be disappointing, or at the very least take a lot longer to deliver value than originally anticipated. This can be the case especially when the deal leads to a very small market position being established.

Types of deal being done

The probability of a deal 'adding value' may well depend on the type of deal being undertaken. As mentioned earlier, the risks increase dramatically as more unknowns are taken on. It may also be the case that the larger the deal, the more risks are likely to be present, certainly in terms of the management resource needed and the size of the 'bet'.

The type of deal can vary enormously and might include the following.

- *Strategic* – this might be a very large acquisition to take the company into a new regional market in a business it is already in. For example, a company entering the US market for the first time might make a 'strategic' acquisition to gain access to that market. Alternatively, it might take a company into a related product area where the technology is different and the technological know-how is as important as the product.

- *Vertical integration* – this is when a company acquires a supplier (sometimes referred to as 'upstream') or a customer ('downstream'). Reasons for doing this might be to gain control of a critical raw material to ensure a regular supply or to gain market share through a distributor to ensure an outlet for the product instead of that being given to a competitor.

- *Horizontal integration* – this is when a company acquires a competitor in the same market or industry and might be referred to as 'industry consolidation', as discussed earlier. This should be lower risk, although the competition authorities may express an interest.

- *In-fill acquisition* – this is normally a low-risk way of expanding. A company buys a small competitor that operates in an area of the market to which it does not have exposure. This may be a region or a certain segment of the product market. By their nature these deals should be lower risk and fit into the existing business very easily.

● *Agreed/hostile deals* – whether a deal is agreed between the two boards or whether it is hostile may make a difference to the outcome. A premium paid to secure agreement may depress returns, but if it means that key personnel do not leave and the integration process is conducted efficiently and effectively, the premium might be worth paying. Alternatively a hostile deal might avoid the need for a premium and allow the aggressor the freedom to do exactly what they want as quickly as they want.

Evaluating the deal: what to look for

While management may make all sorts of claims when looking to do deals, investors should focus on the:

● impact on earnings
● economic return from the deal.

One of the most commonly used phrases in statements accompanying deals is that the 'deal will not dilute earnings in the first year' or the 'deal will enhance earnings in the first full year'. This reflects the focus that is placed on earnings per share by the management and the market.

Earnings are one of the key numbers monitored by investors and the growth in earnings is a key driver of valuation and hence share prices. Therefore, when a company is doing a deal, attention inevitably focuses on the impact it has on the company's earnings outlook. Whether this is the correct number to focus on is highly debatable. In the wake of the degree of value destruction that followed the deals of the boom years, attention has correctly turned to the returns on investment and the value added of the transaction.

The return on capital that a deal is expected to generate is crucial for shareholders. If the company is going to be allocating capital to a deal, it is important that it generates an appropriate return to compensate shareholders for the risks involved. Again there is a clear correlation between the return on capital a company generates and its valuation/performance relative to the market.

So how does the impact on earnings and returns flow through? This very much depends on:

- the price paid
- how the deal is financed
- the benefits of putting the two businesses together
- how effectively these benefits are realized.

The price paid

Clearly, paying an appropriate price is the critical cornerstone of any successful deal. Even if the deal makes all the commercial sense in the world, if it reduces earnings and generates a very poor economic return, shareholders will lose out heavily.

Debt finance

If the deal is paid for out of debt, the earnings effect is simply

> The profit from the new business, plus the cost-saving benefits from combining the businesses, plus the pricing/revenue benefits from the combination, minus the cost of paying the interest on the debt.

There may be a complication in the form of whether the deal influences the tax charge – earnings being struck after tax. (Indeed, sometimes deals may be done because of the tax advantages that a target brings, but on the whole doing deals simply for the tax benefits may not be beneficial in the long run.)

Equity finance

When shares are used, the calculation becomes a question of adding the overall profit impact from the deal (as detailed above) and dividing by the enlarged number of shares (adjusting for any tax impact). If the deal is done part way through a year, the profits for that part of the year are included and a weighted average of the number of shares is used.

Cost of capital

This is important for assessing the economic impact of any investment project or deal. A company must generate a return that exceeds its cost of capital to make the deal worth doing when set against the risks involved. This is referred to as 'adding value'.

The cost of debt is relatively straightforward and is effectively the rate of interest at which the company can borrow. This will normally be at a premium to long-term government bonds, which is regarded as the risk-free rate.

This risk-free rate is also important in determining the cost of equity. The 'opportunity cost' of investing in the shares is that you are forgoing the risk-free rate of return. Put simply, if you can get 5 per cent returns from simply putting your money into a deposit account and your feet up, then you need considerably more than this to compensate for all the risks and effort involved in investing in a business. To reflect this, the cost of equity is normally calculated along the following lines:

Risk-free rate + (equity risk premium × beta).

The equity risk premium is the premium over and above the risk-free rate of return that is demanded by equity investors in (risky) equity investments. Its level is subjective but is usually thought of as being somewhere in a range of 2–5 per cent. Let us assume it is 3.5 per cent for our example.

This equity risk premium is a catch-all figure and needs to be adapted to the individual circumstances of the shares in question. This is usually done by measuring how volatile the stock is against the movement of the underlying equity market. This is referred to as the stock's beta. It is calculated by measuring discrete stock and market movements over a period of time (monthly intervals over five years are typical). A stock that tends to overshoot the market will have a beta greater than one; a share that moves less emphatically than the market – up or down – will have a beta less than one. It can be seen then that the beta is an additional measure of risk and has to be priced accordingly. The higher the beta, the more expensive it is to issue equity. In our example let us assume the beta is 1.2×.

So if the risk-free rate (the yield on long-term government bonds) were 5.5 per cent, the cost of equity would be:

$$5.5 + (1.2 \times 3.5) = 9.7 \text{ per cent.}$$

The cost of capital therefore reflects the make-up of a company's balance sheet between debt and equity. Debt may 'cost', say, 7.0 per cent. But the interest payments are tax deductible (they are debited before we get to pre-tax profit). Correspondingly the cost of debt, post tax, would be 70 per cent of this figure, i.e. 7 × 0.7 is 4.9 per cent.

As we have seen it is more complicated with equities but it is likely to be around 10–13 per cent. A more comprehensive assessment of the issues involved in the cost of capital can be found on pages 172–9.

Therefore an investment or acquisition that is funded by shares needs to generate a much higher return to exceed the cost of capital, i.e. generate a positive economic return.

The weighted average cost of capital simply reflects the extent to which the company is funded by equity or debt. If the ratio is 70 per cent equity and 30 per cent debt and the cost of equity is 10 per cent and post-tax cost of debt is 4.9 per cent, the WACC is (10 × 0.7) + (4.9 × 0.3) = 8.47.

To show the impact of debt on reducing the cost of capital, if we say the company is funded 50 per cent equity and 50 per cent debt, the WACC is reduced to (10 × 0.5) + (4.9 × 0.5) = 7.45. Therefore a company that is more heavily funded with debt will have a lower cost of capital.

The problem is of course that the risks go up the more heavily indebted the company is. In this case the beta would rise and this would increase the cost of equity to reflect the greater risk (see the factors influencing beta on pages 175–6).

Debt v equity finance – the impact on earnings and returns

To consider the impact of the various methods of financing an acquisition, let's consider a takeover by company A of company B. The total consideration (or enterprise value, EV) is detailed in Table 2.1. You need to ask yourself the following:

- What is the impact on earnings per share?
- Will the deal add value?
- What will be the financial position of the company after the deal has gone through?

The equity value on takeover takes into account the premium needed to secure the control of the target company. The provisions reflect liabilities that would be inherited when the acquisition is completed. It may relate to environmental responsibilities the company has or the need to fund pension payments to current and former employees. The costs of the transaction will relate to such things as the documentation needed, legal advice and fees for getting the share issue underwritten.

Table 2.1   The cost of buying B (£m) with 70% funded by equity and 30% by debt

Pre-bid value	600	
Equity value on takeover	780	
Debt	100	
Provisions	40	
Costs of transaction	20	
EV	940	
70/30 equity/debt		
Shares	£658m	
Debt	£282m	at 8 per cent

Share price of A = 650p, market cap = £1.95bn
Share rights issue at a 20 per cent discount to share price, i.e. 520p
Therefore the number of shares that need to be issued = £658m/520p = 126.5m

Table 2.2   A takeover by Company A of Company B

	Company A	Company B	Merger effect	70/30 equity/ debt	All shares	All debt
Operating profit	150	65	25	240	240	240
Interest	10	10	22	32	10	85.2
Pre-tax	140	55		208	230	154.8
Tax	−42			−62.4	−69	−46.4
Post-tax earnings	98			145.6	161	108.4
Earnings						
No of shares	300		126.5	426.5	481	300
EPS	32.7			34.1	33.5	36.1
P/E	20×					

Buying company B would bring operating profit of £65m. It is assumed that the benefits of putting the two businesses together, the merger effect, is an incremental operating profit of £25m. These benefits may come from a range of cost-cutting measures: removing head office costs, purchasing economies, and economies of scale of putting extra volume through the operations. These benefits are often referred to as the 'synergies' of the deal. Clearly at this stage they are hypothetical and management has to deliver these benefits.

The central case assumes that the deal is financed by the issue of shares for 70 per cent of the cost of the deal and 30 per cent by extra debt. The shares are issued in a rights issue at a 20 per cent discount to the prevailing market price. At a share price of 520p the company needs to issue 126.5m shares to meet 70 per cent of the acquisition consideration. The debt component of £282m is financed by debt with an interest cost of 8 per cent.

Table 2.2 demonstrates the impact of financing the deal entirely with debt and entirely through the issue of shares, where the assumption is that the shares are issued at 520p. This is perhaps unrealistic given how many shares are being issued, which might suggest a bigger discount than the 20 per cent. If it was, say, 30 per cent, 207m shares would need to be issued and not the 181m shares in the example. This would reduce earnings to 31.7p, representing dilution of a relatively modest 3 per cent. Table 2.2 demonstrates that the deal improves EPS (enhancement) in all the proposed financing methods.

The advantages of 'gearing up', i.e. using debt, are clearly illustrated in the all-debt option. Earnings rise by 10.4 per cent when the all-debt option is pursued. The tax efficiency of the debt option is evident as the tax charge increases by only 10 per cent despite a 60 per cent uplift in operating profit. With no extra shares in issue, the EPS benefits significantly.

The danger of the all-debt option is of course the financial position of the enlarged company post the deal. In this instance we can see quickly that interest cover falls to $2.8 \times$ (240/85.2). Whether this is comfortable is very much dependent on the type of business it is (i.e. how cyclical or stable the revenues are), the need for capital expenditure and the cash generation expected of the enlarged business. (See financial position, interest cover on pages 127–30 for a fuller discussion.)

If the business was cyclical with a high level of fixed costs, where volumes and prices are subject to significant swings, this level of interest cover would be a source of some concern. A relatively small fall in revenues could reduce interest cover to dangerous levels. The risks to shareholders in such a scenario rise dramatically. However, if the business was very stable with strong pricing and good visibility of revenues, one might feel more relaxed about the all-debt option.

As the impact on earnings is positive for all three options, management could argue that as growth is enhanced by the deal it represents a sensible move for shareholders. However, we need to see whether the deal actually 'adds value'. We also need to bear in mind that there are considerable risks that the deal will not deliver the hoped-for results.

Looking at the value added we need to assess the cost of capital and see whether the returns exceed this. The returns are relatively straightforward. We are buying £90m of operating profits (£65m of operating profit plus the £25m of merger benefits) for a total outlay of £940m. This gives a pre-tax return of 9.6 per cent. With tax at 30 per cent the return falls to 6.7 per cent.

The cost of debt we know to be 8 per cent in this instance. However, as discussed above there are tax advantages of debt – the interest payments are deductible before arriving at the pre-tax number. Accordingly the cost of debt is 5.6 per cent.

The cost of equity is more complicated and the process is illustrated on page 173. In this case we are assuming it is 12 per cent.

For the central proforma case we take the 'weighted average cost of capital'. Here we simply take into account that we are funding 70 per cent of the deal at 12 per cent and 30 per cent at 5.6 per cent. This gives an overall cost of 10 per cent.

Table 2.3   Value added

	Pre-tax	Post-tax
Returns (90/940)	9.6%	6.7%
Cost of debt	8%	5.6%
Cost of equity	12%	12%
WACC (70/30)	10%	10%

Table 2.3 demonstrates that economic value is added only when the deal is funded by debt. This is because debt is cheaper than equity and crucially the tax deductability of interest payments reduces the post-tax cost of debt considerably. As discussed earlier, the issue here is what happens to the risk profile given the higher financial gearing associated with this option. As an investor you would have to feel confident with the higher risks being undertaken.

The other two options clearly destroy value. The only way they might add value is if the 'synergy' benefits are much higher than the planned-for £25m. Obviously the higher the assumption, the greater the risk of not realizing the benefits. In this case it would take a further £45m of synergy benefits to ensure the deal did not destroy value (£130m/£940m is 14.4 per cent. Taxed at 30 per cent gives a post-tax return of 10.1 per cent). In the context of a company making £65m, a further £65m would be a very tall order.

The other way of trying to make the deal more beneficial in terms of economic added value is to reduce the extent of the premium that has been paid. In this case it is 30 per cent, which is a fairly standard premium to secure a takeover. Trying to secure the company with a 15 per cent premium would save £90m. Whether the management and shareholders agree to this is a moot point. It does illustrate that the problem with acquisitions is that they are good for the shareholders of the company being taken over but not so good for the shareholders in the acquiring company.

Earnings growth or returns?

Therefore, when evaluating the success or otherwise of the deal, you need to be clear about what is being delivered and what you feel is an appropriate way of assessing the deal. Conventionally there has been a tendency to focus on the impact on earnings. However, following the raft of poor deals in the past few years and a disillusionment with management and their far from shareholder-friendly policies and actions, there is much greater focus on deals delivering value. With balance sheets constrained and the appetite for risk having fallen significantly, this again argues for an approach based on value being created for shareholders.

The issue of growth is also perhaps even better understood if one considers the aggressive acquisition policies of companies in the 1980s and early 1990s. The 'trick' here was to use 'highly rated paper' (i.e. shares standing on a very high P/E) to acquire lower rated companies. This would both deliver the growth needed to justify the high rating and ensure a re-rating of the earnings acquired. The higher the rating, the less paper you need to issue.

By way of example look at the previous case and assume the stock was rated at $30 \times$ earnings rather than $20 \times$. Let's consider the all-share option in this case (Table 2.4). On $30 \times$ earnings the share price would be 981p (32.7 $\times$ 30). If we are issuing shares at a 20 per cent discount we need to issue only 120m shares (120 $\times$ 784p generates the required £940m) rather than the 180m for the all-share option with the share price on 20 $\times$ earnings.

Here we can see that the earnings enhancement is dramatically better – 38.3p of earnings represents an uplift of 17 per cent compared with the 2.4 per cent increase in the first example. This obviously drives a great earn-

Table 2.4	The all-share option (using highly-rated paper)

	All shares
Operating profit	240
Interest	10
Pre-tax	230
Post-tax earnings	−69
Earnings	161
No of shares	420m
EPS	38.3p

ings growth story. Critically, however, there is absolutely no difference to the value added of the deal. The returns on the price paid are exactly the same – £90m on an outlay of £940m. The cost of capital is 12 per cent because of the all-equity nature of the deal.

This provides an even more dramatic conflict between the two ways of evaluating the deal. Earnings are boosted dramatically but the economic result of the deal is precisely the same.

Benefits of the deal

How much profit is to be added when performing this calculation? This figure depends crucially on the 'integration benefits' of adding the new business. This will depend on the scope for cost cutting and/or generating extra revenues from combining the two businesses.

Costs

If there is significant overcapacity in an industry and this has led to weak pricing (with the target company especially aggressive in looking for market share), then taking over a competitor *may* make a lot of sense. If fixed costs are high and the number of factories can be reduced, then costs will benefit from a) the closure of uneconomically performing factories and b) greater efficiency at the factories that are now producing greater volume at lower costs. In addition, there may be cost savings as a result of bigger discounts when buying greater quantities of raw materials/supplies ('procurement economies'). These procurement economies can be an important saving for retail or distribution-related businesses as they will give them a much more effective hand when dealing with suppliers.

The issue with costs is whether the benefits are just a one-off and do little to improve the longer-term growth outlook for the business. As a result earnings growth over a (say) two-year period will be valued relatively low by the market. An interesting example here is the merger trend in the pharmaceuticals sector. There can be many savings in R&D and marketing in such situations. However, if investors have been investing for growth through new product introductions they may fear that the cost-cutting initiatives (and indeed the merger itself) are being implemented to conceal the poor performance of the drug portfolio. Therefore the cost cutting will be valued differently compared with the earnings growth that may be generated from 'top line', i.e. revenue growth.

Another important issue to bear in mind with cost cutting is whether the benefits are offset by price or volume weakness post the deal. In our earlier example of taking capacity out of an industry the danger is whether the deal does enough to lead to price stability. If the industry remains fragmented, with a number of players committed to gaining market share and import competition a key threat, the prices are likely to remain weak. In this case weak pricing will offset the cost reduction programme.

Price benefits

Revenues will obviously benefit from the contribution of the acquired company. However, the removal of an aggressive competitor will hopefully lead to a less competitive market place. This will help pricing stability. This process is often referred to as consolidation: the industry sees fewer players with greater market shares. In theory this is beneficial to pricing, although there can be exceptions as mentioned above (a powerful competitor may still be driven by market share considerations and/or cash flow to service a high level of debt or need for income, in a family-run business for example or more simply when there is an economic downturn).

Therefore the removal of a disruptive competitor and the subsequent improvement in industry pricing could see quite a significant benefit to the company and its shareholders. It is worth bearing in mind that the benefits of higher pricing have a 'geared' impact on the bottom line – a few percentage points increase in prices can dramatically improve profits. This would reinforce the cost savings benefits described above.

These cost and revenue benefits are why a company is prepared to pay a premium to acquire the business in the first place. If it is the case that the pricing environment has improved, this makes a crucial difference. Post the deal the management has a greater influence on the market and this helps to improve the 'quality of earnings', that is to say the earnings stream is more stable and management has greater influence on matters that affect its profits. (Quality of earnings is discussed in more detail on page 86.) Deals which help improve the pricing and revenue potential tend to be the most successful.

Volume benefits

The benefits from extra volume can also have an important impact on both revenues and the bottom line (again the impact of operational gearing). The extra volume also equates to an enhanced market share which will improve the quality of earnings. Volumes may benefit from access to a bigger and better distribution network or to different distribution channels.

Revenue benefits

These volume and pricing benefits of acquisition combine to generate an overall revenue impact. The ability to grow revenues, the 'top line', and not just enable one-off cost reductions to be made, will make a crucial difference as to whether the deal adds value. These revenue benefits will be valued much more highly by the market as they will improve the quantity and quality of earnings.

Timing of benefits

Some deals will inevitably be more complex than others. Therefore it may take time for the full benefits of a deal to come through. The company may well make it clear that the deal will take time to yield the maximum benefit and that it will incur short-term earnings dilution. This sort of deal is often referred to as being 'strategic'. If the company has a good track record in delivering returns and living up to its promises (as well as having a clearly articulated long-term strategy), the investment community will support the deal. Alternatively, if the management has a poor record and a reputation for subtracting 'value' when doing deals, it will be hard pressed to convince investors.

When deals work

Given the high risks attached to acquisitions and their poor record in adding value, it is worth having a sense of when they have a good chance of working. Clearly, management track record is crucial here – a history of not overpaying and then making sure the acquisition is effectively integrated is essential. While it sounds easy, the number of deals that do add value suggest very few do it well.

A checklist of factors that give the deal a chance of succeeding would include the following (although this list is not necessarily comprehensive):

- a sensible price is paid which enables the weighted average cost of capital (WACC) to be exceeded
- acquisition made at right point in cycle
- consistent with stated strategy
- acquisition is part of an overall strategy . . . the strategy is not to acquire
- core business is performing well with few problems
- management not trying to avoid difficulties within core
- management fully understands the business/market – the acquisition is part of core business
- known target company well for some time
- management has the resources to ensure integration is done effectively without the core being adversely affected
- pricing in the industry is improved
- revenue growth is delivered
- genuine cost benefits/economies of scale
- improves quality of earnings
- improves growth profile of business
- adds a key capability, a new product, new region or technological skill
- balance sheet not too stretched post the deal
- bolt-on deals more likely to add value than strategic deals.

As the list demonstrates, management discipline and focus are essential. The demise of many of the high-fliers in the TMT boom was interesting in that many were highly acquisitive. They often used highly rated paper which would immediately have boosted earnings but not necessarily added value (as discussed in the example on page 68). A number of acquisitions occurred at the peak of the cycle at valuations that could never possibly have added value.

Therefore companies that are continually acquisitive may well be trying to hide a far from flattering performance of their core operations. It is also likely that they will engage in accounting practices that put them in the best possible light. Accordingly, if you are invested in such a company you are running a much higher degree of risk than you may appreciate and your chances of making money are much more restricted.

Why deals do not create value

The academic evidence suggests that few deals add value or work to the benefit of shareholders in the acquiring company and it is worth examining why the above theory does not appear to work in practice.

The most common dangers tend to be:

- the price paid is too high, making it impossible to generate an appropriate return
- the company is bought at the wrong point in the cycle – earnings from it immediately drop dramatically
- the strategy is ill-conceived
- management takes on too many unknowns, e.g. a business it doesn't know in a region/country it doesn't know
- management is overstretched at the acquiring company – 'management dilution'
- the business is not integrated as effectively as planned – does not deliver promised benefits
- diseconomies of scale – the enlarged company is too big to run effectively
- target is in a weaker position than envisaged
- loss of more revenue than anticipated
- loss of top people in acquired company.

The price paid and the point of the cycle at which the company is bought are the key drivers of a successful deal. Having bought the company, however, it has to be managed and integrated to deliver the appropriate returns. Good-quality management is a scarce resource and while the strategy may be well conceived much can go wrong in the integration process. While we have discussed the importance (or otherwise) of earnings dilution, many deals fail due to 'management dilution'. This dilution is likely to be more exposed if the company has gone into product areas or regions that it has no knowledge of – the risks are much greater. Management is spread far too thinly across the enlarged company, resulting in problems in the entire business in a worse case scenario. This can be especially true if the acquisition is in a much poorer position than was envisaged originally. It may have a weaker market position than thought and be in need of a lot of catch-up capital expenditure. These weaknesses may well be why the company was very happy to sell out, of course. It is always worth trying to find out why the acquired company was selling.

As well as these problems, it often appears that among some management there is a size for size's sake approach and an attraction to the glamour and excitement of doing deals. Running the number one business in an industry confers status – returns to shareholders may be a less important item on the agenda.

More cynical reasons for deals being done include:

- size for size's sake
- to protect jobs of top management/boost their salary
- fear of being taken over
- to cover up problems in the core business
- it is easier/more exciting to do a deal than run the existing business.

The market's reaction to the deal?

Given the potential benefits and drawbacks of doing deals, how will the stock market react to a deal being announced by a company in which you are interested? This will depend on the interplay of the factors determining why deals work and why they conspicuously fail.

A good test is to ask yourself how far you trust the management. If it announced a deal would you immediately think it deserves the benefit of the doubt or would you be concerned? This view will be formed by its track record in doing deals that add value, the performance of the existing operations and the financial position.

The market's reaction will also be very much determined by the financing of the deal – how much is financed by the issue of new shares and how much by debt? Again a useful checklist would cover such factors as:

- Is the deal consistent with stated strategy?

- Is there compelling commercial logic . . . does it fit?
- Management track record – is it trusted, will it deliver?
- What is the size of the deal (in-fill v strategic)?
- What is the price paid? What is the valuation of the target?
- How is the deal financed?
- What is the post-deal financial position . . . gearing and interest cover?
- What will be the financial impact – effect on earnings and returns v cost of capital?
- What will be the impact on longer-term growth potential?
- What will be the impact on quality of earnings?
- Are the main benefits due to cost savings, pricing power or extra volumes?
- What is the quality of the target?

KEY PERFORMANCE NUMBERS AND RATIOS: HOW EFFICIENT AND WELL MANAGED IS THE COMPANY?

Five-year trading record

The five-year trend in sales, profits and earnings relative to the sector will tell you a great deal about the characteristics of the company and its performance. Has the company demonstrated consistent growth in sales, profits and earnings? Have there been wide swings in sales and profits? Have sales grown rapidly while profit growth has been slow, implying progressive deterioration in operating margins?

There will be a five-year record in the R&A which will detail the trend in the key numbers and ratios. This is a useful and quick way of getting to grips with recent trends. Hopefully this five-year record will reveal the performance of all the company's divisions. This will enable you to see the contribution of those various divisions and whether they have been a spur to, or drag on, performance.

This will immediately tell you whether the company is a growth or highly cyclical company. Alternatively, if sales and profits have been on a steady downward path this might reveal a company in long-term decline. A rapid growth in sales but falling margins may reveal a company looking to grow market share at all costs.

The company's performance relative to its sector will demonstrate whether the company has been performing better or worse than its peer group. You will need to ask:

- What has been the trend in sales, profit or earnings?
- Has it been losing market share?
- Has it witnessed an erosion of margins due to costs increasing more than its peers?

This track record is a good starting point for quickly getting a sense of what has been going on and how the company has been performing. For a more thorough view, looking at its key ratios will reveal a great deal.

SALES

Sales are a good indicator of how the company is performing. In sectors such as retailing, 'like for like' sales growth is monitored closely. This is the performance of existing outlets and strips out the impact of acquisitions. The level of sales will indicate the health or otherwise of the market – or whether the company is taking market share (i.e. the company's sales exceed those of the market overall). This performance relative to the industry peer group is obviously a key indicator of both the company's competitive position and management's ability to deliver.

The performance of sales does need to be put in context, however. The profitability of those sales is crucial. If sales are growing but at the risk of causing a price war, this is potentially very dangerous. Similarly, if the sales are growing rapidly while margins are falling sharply, the value of those sales is clearly deteriorating. If there is a long-term strategy of taking market share, this may make sense, especially if the company has a very low cost base and a strong financial position. These characteristics make the longer-term strategy far more credible.

To get a clearer perspective on the performance of sales you need to ask yourself what the key drivers of sales have been, in particular:

- To what extent is sales growth organic and what has been the impact of acquisitions?
- To what extent has the revenue figure been influenced by volume or price?
- Has the company been chasing volumes and market share?
- Is the sales pattern stable? Are sales sustainable and easy to predict?
- What is the divisional breakdown and performance?
- Are there any noticeable leaders and laggards?
- What is happening to the mix of sales and the margins generated?

As a general point it is best to be careful when company statements start with proudly announcing record sales. This often tends to mean that the profits and earnings generated by those sales are disappointing. The company may have pursued volumes at the expense of margin.

Accounting for sales

Historically it has been felt that the sales figure was one of the few numbers not subject to widespread accounting manipulation. However, recent accounting scandals, especially on Wall Street, have tended to revolve around sales manipulation. Indeed, in 2000, 70 per cent of Securities and Exchange Commission (SEC) accounting and audit enforcement cases were problems of revenue recognition – either recognizing future revenues too early or recording revenues that did not exist at all (*Financial Times*, 6 June 2002).

Therefore you should try to understand the company's policy on sales recognition. It is a particular concern where there are long-term contracts involved such as building or software contracts. The photocopier company Xerox was forced in June 2002 to restate its sales and profits to a significant extent. The SEC alleged that it had inflated revenues by more than $3bn and earnings by $1.5bn over a four-year period. Revenues were being booked well before sales actually took place.

The manipulation of sales was also a feature of the technology and telecommunications sector, with 'hollow swaps', where telecoms companies sold capacity to each other and booked it as revenues even if no money changed hands. Related party transactions, selling to companies in which you had a significant stake, were also undertaken to boost the sales figure. These devices gave the appearance of high growth and reflected the fact that sales were featuring increasingly as a valuation driver.

This manipulation of sales tends to boost profits as there is a 'mismatch' – the costs related to those sales are invariably not recognized until they are incurred at a much later date.

Profits

As with sales, assessing the trend in profits over a five-year period (and longer if possible, especially in highly cyclical businesses, to establish what a complete cycle might look like) enables you to quickly get a sense of the characteristics, quality and performance of the business. Used in conjunction with sales, profits provide a major performance measure (operating margins) which we will explore in detail on page 101.

The same issues as with sales need to be explored:

- To what extent is profit growth organic and what has been the impact of acquisitions?
- To what extent has profit been influenced by volume or price?
- To what extent has profit benefited from cost reductions?
- Is the profit pattern stable? Are profits sustainable and easy to predict?
- Are there any one-off boosts to profits?
- Are profits depressed by investing in marketing or R&D to foster long-term growth?
- What is the divisional breakdown of profits?
- Are there any noticeable leaders and laggards?
- What is happening to the mix of profits and the margins generated?

It is important to have a sense of the divisional contribution to overall profits. The value attaching to the different divisions will vary depending on their economic characteristics, returns, growth and quality of earnings. Therefore a company can hit profit expectations, but that is not the end of the story. How did it do it? If it is achieved through the help of a one-off contribution such as a property disposal or selling an asset or a volatile, low-quality business doing extremely well while a better-quality one disappoints, the share price will suffer.

The benefit from disposals and the impact of exceptionals are important issues. They influence the quality of earnings. We will discuss these factors in detail when exploring the trend and influences on earnings. Earnings are an important measure of performance and influence on valuation.

Profits can be made to grow through acquisition while earnings per share can fall correspondingly (as more shares are issued). Accordingly we will concentrate the discussion on earnings rather than on profits. The issues and concepts are applicable to both.

EARNINGS

The trend in earnings per share, defined as earnings attributable to ordinary shareholders divided by the number of shares in issue, is often regarded as a key measure of a company's performance. Much of the stock market's attention is focused on the projected earnings of a company. Analysis of corporate results invariably revolves around an assessment of what earnings have been reported compared with what had been expected. Whether this focus is correct is perhaps debatable and we will explore other important measures of performance later. Nonetheless, the growth in EPS is a critical guide to how well a company is doing. This will normally drive the share price. Poor earnings results or downgrades will put pressure on the share price. The growth in EPS, especially when compared with the market overall, is often a key component of management bonus and option arrangements.

Given the crucial importance of this figure it is worth being aware of:

- the various definitions of earnings per share that can be used
- how companies may distort the numbers to hit targets.

Earnings definition

The calculation of earnings per share is in principle very straightforward. You take the profit left after tax that belongs to ordinary shareholders. This is sometimes referred to as 'attributable profit' as it is profit that is available to ordinary shareholders. The earnings per share figure is then derived by dividing the attributable profit by the number of ordinary shares in issue.

Example

A fictional brake-unit manufacturer, Full Stop, had operating profits of £7.5m in 2001. Let us assume that interest costs were £2.5m, so deducting that from the operating profits gives a pre-tax profit of £5m. If the standard tax rate of 30 per cent is applied, post-tax profits, called earnings, are £3.5m.

If there are 30.5 million shares in issue, the earnings per share number is 3.5m/30.5m, or 11.5p per share.

It should always be remembered that the numerator (earnings or attributable profit) must be that which belongs to ordinary shareholders. Therefore, if there are any preference dividends due to preference shareholders, these must be deducted before arriving at the earnings figure. Similarly, if there are any minority charges these must also be deducted. Minority charges relate to outside shareholders' claim on the profits of the company – again they are not attributable to the ordinary shareholders in the company. So if an outside company has a 25 per cent investment in the company (or a subsidiary), it is entitled to 25 per cent of the earnings of the company. In this situation ordinary shareholders do not own and therefore are not entitled to 100 per cent of the earnings generated by the company.

The denominator

The number of shares can be found in the notes to the earnings number in the accounts. There will normally be the weighted average number of shares used for the period in question. To calculate the year-end position you may need to check the called-up share capital note to the accounts. This will detail any changes in the number of allotted shares in the year.

As well as considering any distortions to earnings from exceptional or amortization charges, you will need to ensure there are no distortions arising from the number of shares in issue. In particular, there might be convertible shares that need to be taken into account or outstanding share options.

If there is a convertible issue, you need to work out what the conversion terms are. This is normally stated in the accounts. For example, each £1 of convertible may convert to four ordinary shares. Then this is multiplied by the outstanding amount of convertibles. This gives you the number of shares on conversion. To get to the earnings number, you need to add back the interest on the bond or the cost of the preference dividends to the earnings amount (as the bonds or preference shares are 'converted' to ordinary shares there would be no need for these payments). The new earnings per share will normally be lower than the original one. This is called dilution and you will usually find that the 'fully diluted earnings' calculation is done in the R&A.

What earnings are we using?

There is often an abundance of earnings numbers (and hence P/Es, the share price divided by the earnings per share, which we will come to in the valuation section) and potential misunderstanding as different methods of computing and using earnings are employed. To avoid confusion, it is important to be clear about the two ways of looking at earnings. It is crucial to define carefully:

1. the time period to which the earnings relate
2. the accounting definitions used.

Prospective v historic

Investment is a forward-looking business. Therefore, wherever possible it is important to look at what the future earnings of a company are likely to be. There is clearly risk in doing this (the forecast may prove to be far from accurate), but again this is an integral component of investment – the confidence you have in the forecast is also an important element in your decision.

When looking at P/Es it is extremely important to differentiate between forward-looking multiples – often called prospective P/Es – and historic (earnings for the last fiscal year) or trailing P/Es (i.e. based on the past twelve months or the last four reported quarters). While many information sources such as newspapers quote historic/trailing P/Es, this is far less useful than a forward-looking measure – investment is about the future. The prospective P/E takes into account how well a company is expected to do in the current and subsequent financial years. So wherever possible try to use the prospective multiple.

These forecasts are available on some financial websites, normally in the form of the 'consensus earnings'. The consensus earnings is the average of the numbers expected from stockbroking analysts covering the company. They will be reached using their forecast for the companies' key markets and in consultation with the companies. In addition, when a company has reported results the financial press will often carry a guide to what profits are going to be in the current year or for the next full year.

The forecast is useful when looking at the growth rate in earnings delivered by the company and how that compares with both the company's sector and the overall stock market. The valuation of the share will depend on the company's earnings growth rate compared with the market average (see P/Es, page 146).

Calendarized earnings

This refers to the earnings of a company when adjusted to a calendar year basis. This is done to ensure comparability of companies with different year ends. For example, to arrive at this number for a company with a March year end you would take a quarter of the last financial year's earnings and three-quarters of the current year's earnings to establish the earnings in the calendar year. This would be done on the same basis for future years so it is crucial for using prospective earnings. The numbers are then broadly comparable to companies with a December year end.

Pre-exceptional pre-amortization earnings v stated earnings

When looking at P/E multiples it is critical to compare like with like. What can sometimes confuse investors is where analysts or commentators use different methods to compute the earnings. The simplest and easiest way to compare earnings on a standardized basis is to use pre-exceptional, pre-amortization numbers. The rationale for using this definition is that exceptional charges, by definition, are one-off by nature and should not be allowed to distort the earnings series of the underlying business.

Exceptional items

Exceptionals can come from a variety of sources. It could be the costs associated with closing a factory or division, or the writing down in value of assets. These items would appear as a negative in the profit and loss (P&L) account. Exceptional credits might derive from the disposal of investments or a piece of property. These charges/credits will not be related to the underlying performance of the business. Also, a really large credit will lead to an abnormally low P/E, while a significant charge will lead to a very high P/E which is not representative.

As well as comparing across companies, using pre-exceptional earnings makes for a fairer and more effective assessment of a company's earnings progress. Again it is important to be aware of the earnings number being used. For example, if a company has a large exceptional credit in one year, if you do not strip this out of the earnings number it might appear that the next year's earnings are going to fall. This could lead to a wrong conclusion about how the company is doing.

What should be deemed exceptional?

There is a danger, however. Companies may be tempted to include (usually large) items that are in fact normal costs of doing business. So you need to ask yourself, is the exceptional charge really exceptional and what does it relate to? A danger sign is if these charges occur year in year out – so that they are hardly an exceptional occurrence. In addition, if the costs relate to the core business, some commentators would tend to ignore them on the basis that they are not exceptional.

The Institute for Investment Management and Research (IIMR) has its own definition of earnings. The broad rule is that if the items relate to 'capital' items they are legitimate exceptionals, whereas if they relate to operating events within the core business they are not exceptional items. The capital item may refer to profit or loss on a disposal of an asset such as an investment, a subsidiary or a property. It may also reflect a change to the value of that asset.

You will often see in the R&A in the note relating to earnings an explanation as to how they have been calculated (a note always worth looking at, especially if there are exceptional items). This will normally include an IIMR definition also sometimes referred to as 'headline' earnings. The IIMR definition will normally be lower and stricter if there are exceptional charges than the definition used by the company. This will essentially reflect the exclusion of exceptional charges that relate to the core business, such as large restructuring or redundancy charges.

An interesting example is the UK food retailer Sainsbury's. The company had an exceptional debit of £20m in the 2002 R&A debited from the UK stores' performance. This figure was down from £37m in 2001. The reason for this charge was cited as being due to:

The costs in Sainsbury's supermarkets relate to the business transformation programme which involves upgrading its IT systems, supply chain and store portfolio. These costs are exceptional due to the scale, scope and pace of the transformation programme. These costs primarily relate to the closure of depots and stores and associated reorganization costs. (page 24 of the 2002 accounts)

Are these charges really exceptional? On a strict IIMR definition they would not be as they relate to the core business. In addition, it is worth looking at this in terms of the position of the underlying business. The reason these costs are exceptional relates to the scale of the charges and action needed to upgrade the IT systems, supply chain and store portfolio. However, as discussed when looking at the company's economic and market position, spending to maintain the competitive position of the company is crucial. One interpretation of the scale of this needed upgrade is that the company failed to invest properly on a consistent basis, hence the need for 'catch-up' spending. The company had fallen behind its main rival Tesco, partly attributable perhaps to this lack of investment in its 'IT systems, supply chain and store portfolio'. On this basis, it seems inappropriate to treat this item as exceptional.

Exceptionals and earnings comparisons

Exceptional items can distort performance comparisons. A competitor that consistently invested in these crucial areas for a food retail company would have incurred these costs. This would have depressed its operating margin compared with a company such as Sainsbury's that did not invest regularly. Similarly, by taking the charge as an exceptional means that the operating margin does not suffer if you use a pre-exceptional number to calculate it.

Performance comparisons can also be distorted if a company makes a major restructuring provision, which might be deemed exceptional due to its sheer scale. This then will flatter future performance as the use of provisions means costs are lower than would otherwise be the case. A company that has consistently kept costs low and incurred redundancy costs as a regular feature would not have the advantage of this provision to help its future performance. But its continuing focus on low costs at all times is a much more effective management approach (as identified by Buffett, see page 41). The subsequent figures are much cleaner.

So what has started out as a simple issue of earnings per share has become complicated by the issue of exceptionals. The message is that care needs to be taken and just because a company calls it an exceptional item does not mean you have to agree with it. Indeed, a company's frequent use of exceptionals may be worth investigating in detail to make sure it does not reflect a historically overinflated cost base that is finally being treated or a systematic underinvestment in the business. This approach may not be one that will make you money in the longer run.

Amortization

This refers to the writing off of goodwill that a company is obliged to do when it acquires another company at a premium to assets. The premium to book value is called the goodwill and reflects the value of the group's brand names, market shares, etc. Some businesses, most notably service-related businesses, have little by way of assets, so goodwill on acquisition can be quite considerable.

This goodwill is then 'written off' over the course of its 'economic life'. This may be ten years. So if a business with £20m of assets is purchased for £100m, the goodwill is £80m. If this is written down over ten years it generates an £8m per annum charge to the P&L. It should be stressed that this charge to the P&L does not involve an outflow of cash (referred to as a non-cash item).

Therefore when comparing a company that has made an acquisition with one that has not, the acquiring company is penalized if you use a post-amortization charge. Similarly, a company may have made a series of acquisitions prior to the accounting policy of writing off goodwill to the P&L was introduced. This company will have higher earnings growth as the goodwill was written off to the balance sheet.

Using a pre-amortization definition irons out these difficulties and means that you can compare like with like. Therefore, whenever looking at quoted P/Es try to be clear as to whether they refer to the past or the future and whether they are before or after various exceptional charges. You should also question the legitimacy of charges deemed exceptional.

The earnings calculation

In Table 2.5 (page 90), Company A demonstrates a more complex example of earnings and earnings per share. Here one can see that there are effectively three earnings per share that I have used. The a, b and c references are to both the pre-tax profit number and the corresponding earnings per share figure.

a) Stated earnings – these are earnings post all charges for whatever reason. So this number is struck after amortization and exceptional charges. It is also struck after the appropriate deduction for minority charges and preference dividends, but this is done for all earnings measures.

b) Pre-exceptional profit – here the exceptional debit of £15m is reinstated. In this case I have assumed it will be taxed at 30 per cent when calculating the earnings number. (Often this can be quite complicated as there may be different tax treatments of the exceptional charge.)

c) This is the pre-exceptional pre-amortization profit – as well as adding back the exceptional charges, we add back the amortization charge.

The question as to which earnings number you should use is dependent on the issues discussed above. Normally to get at the underlying performance of the business one would use the pre-exceptional and pre-amortization definition. However, it does depend on the nature of the exceptional charge. If it is for an ongoing restructuring of the core business, one would be sceptical about treating it as an exceptional – it is an ongoing charge against the core business. This would be reinforced by the fact that the same charge occurs in consecutive years. One should be wary if large exceptional charges are a recurring feature. If, however, the debit relates to a loss on disposal, then this would be very clear cut and one would use the pre-exceptional pre-amortization level.

We will come back to discuss the earnings profile of Company A when we examine the quality of earnings.

Quality of earnings

While all the focus on whether earnings are hitting targets and what the growth rate is tends to grab the headlines, it is crucial to identify the quality as well as the quantity of earnings. The quality of earnings is a vital component in the valuing of any company. While there is no one definition of earnings quality, the following factors need to be considered:

1. The use of very straight and conservative accounting policies by the company which ensures that the earnings number is a true reflection of what is really going on with the business – how it is really performing.

2. The sustainability and visibility of earnings in terms of the trading out-look which in turn derives from the volume, pricing and cost outlook. In this sense it is much easier to predict the earnings of the company.
3. The profits are being generated by the core and not any one-off dis-posals or other benefits.
4. What management has control over and can influence.
5. The earnings coming through into cash flow cleanly/efficiently.

The first two are clearly related. The more a company engages in account-ing manipulation to 'hit' earnings targets, the poorer the quality of its earnings is in the first sense. Critically, however, to the extent that earn-ings are benefiting from manipulation, its performance is less sustainable – at some stage it will run out of room for manoeuvre and the reality of the trading environment will catch up with it. A company that has, for exam-ple, been using provisions to hit earnings targets (by reducing the actual costs of doing business) may run into difficulties once all the provisions have been used up. The real costs of doing business will then reassert themselves. This was a feature of many of the acquisitive growth stocks of the 1990s.

This is especially true with the onset of a recession or more difficult sec-tor trading conditions. The economic slowdown since 2000, combined with overinvestment in many areas, has cruelly exposed the lack of earn-ings quality in many growth stocks. With growth stocks the management may hope that the high rate of growth or benefits from new acquisitions will prevent the problems ever coming to light – either continued growth or a recovery will bail them out.

The IBM example (page 95) regarding disposals and the pension fund dramatically highlights the issue of earnings quality. Critically, achieving earnings targets or expectations through one-off benefits, while the per-formance of the underlying business disappoints, will ultimately come to light and the share price will suffer. As these 'benefits' to earnings drop out of the equation, earnings growth will be dependent purely on the per-formance of the business. If, for example, revenues have disappointed and the company has been losing market share, this will drive the valuation. Investors should always be wary when scrutinizing the results of compa-nies that have a record of using dubious accounting policies to hit earn-ings targets. The valuation will reflect these concerns.

The other important aspect for earnings quality is what management can influence. In commodity-based businesses, for example, earnings will, by their nature, be volatile. A timber trading company will be subject to the vagaries of price movements and the impact of currency movements in determining its profits. Both of these may be difficult to predict and lie outside management's control. This is not to say the management is not extremely good at what it is doing. But earnings are clearly going to be volatile. If the business benefits from sharp price rises, how much of the improved performance is attributable to good management and its control of the business? As well as lying beyond management control, the sustainability of these higher prices needs to be questioned.

In our case study comparison of the engineering company Tin Can and pharmaceutical stock Pink Tablet (page 154) one can immediately identify that there are many things beyond the control of Tin Can's management that can seriously affect the company's earnings. These include the potential for higher raw material prices, falling selling prices due to industry overcapacity (and the threat from foreign competition) or a major customer taking away a contract. Pink Tablet, with patent protection, a diversified range of products and stable to rising demand, enjoys better-quality earnings.

Earnings and cash flow relationship

The ability to generate cash is crucial to a company's health and wealth. It is also the ultimate driver of value, which we will discuss in more detail later. Therefore it is important that earnings growth translates into cash generation.

There are a number of ways that the earnings growth can be registered (on top of accounting duplicity) without cash flowing into the company. One of the most important is where earnings growth may be achieved through the performance of what is called an associate or related company. This is where the company has an investment of over 20 per cent but below 50 per cent. In this situation the company 'equity accounts' its investment, i.e. it books its share of that company's profits. If the investment is growing rapidly, the company's P&L will show this. If it accounts for all the growth being achieved, one needs to consider what is going on within the core business.

Critically, the impact on cash flow is very different. The cash received from this investment will only be the dividends paid out – something the management of the company may not be able to influence. If the investment is growing rapidly there may be no dividend at all – the cash will be invested in the business.

Therefore strong earnings growth is not generating any cash. The quality of earnings is further reduced as the management has no control over the investment/source of the profit. The sustainability of the performance of this investment must also be questioned.

As well as related companies, there can be situations where management has a subsidiary of which it does not own 100 per cent and hence does not exert full control over the cash flows. This can occur with an investment in an overseas market where the culture and approach may be different from the domestic market.

Another key area to watch is the use of provisions and cash flow. If earnings growth is being achieved through aggressive write-offs so that the cost base is reduced, there may be a lot of cash going out on redundancy payments or other costs associated with the provisions. This can be particularly true for highly acquisitive companies and very much needs to be monitored.

Problems with earnings quality and cash may occur where profits are generated in overseas markets where inflation and currency issues may complicate the picture. In addition, repatriation may be a problem from countries with exchange controls or where weak currencies make it uneconomic to bring funds back to the home market. The volatility of earnings from emerging markets, albeit that there may well be a good long-term growth story, raises question marks over earnings quality.

Analyzing earnings quality

To illustrate the issues that are relevant when assessing the company's earnings, let's take two companies with similar pre-tax profits and explore the differences in their quality of earnings. We can also see how the EPS number is calculated.

Companies A and B are identical in size in terms of turnover, pre-tax profit and the number of shares in issue: 545m. However, the business and earnings profiles differ in certain key respects. Company B is focused on one core business in which it has strong market positions in the key developed countries. Company A has a spread of businesses in both advanced and emerging markets, many of which are not wholly owned. The exceptionals for company A relate to costs of the ongoing downsizing and restructuring of the company's core operations. This reflects the fact that the company has invested less in its facilities and has seen its cost base grow more rapidly than its rivals.

Both companies have an amortization charge of £5m.

The P&L schedules detailed in Tables 2.5 and 2.6 reveal the financial differences. The results for 2001 have been declared and are referred to as actual (abbreviated to A) while the numbers for 2002 are forecasts and are therefore 'expected' (abbreviated to E).

Table 2.5   Company A's P&L schedule

£m	2001A	2002E
Turnover	1500	1600
Depreciation	15	17
Amortization	5	5
Operating profit	135	155
Associates	30	35
Investment income	15	10
Interest cost	−12	−13
Redundancies	−10	−10
Exceptionals	−15	−15
Pre-tax(a)	143	162
PX-PTP(b)	158	177
PXPA PTP(c)	163	182
Tax	−42.9	−48.6
Tax rate (%)	30	30
Minorities	−20	−25
Preference dividend	−8	−8
Attributable	72.1	80.4
No of shares	545	545
Stated EPS(a)	13.2	14.8
PX EPS(b)	15.2	16.7
PXPA EPS(c)	15.8	17.3

Looking at the two businesses, some of the key differences are as follows.

- *Where the profits come from.* When considering how the pre-tax figure is arrived at, the principal trading difference is that Company B is generating a greater contribution from its core business, and its operating margins at 10.7 per cent compare favourably with the 9 per cent achieved by Company A. For Company A, 17.5 per cent of trading profit (i.e. income including associates and investment income) derives from associates, while a further 9 per cent derives from investment income. Furthermore, the exceptional debit of £15m makes for a less

Table 2.6	Company B's P&L schedule	
£m	2001A	2002E
Turnover	1500	1600
Depreciation	20	22
Amortization	5	5
Operating profit	160	180
Associates	5	5
Interest cost	−12	−13
Redundancies	−10	−10
Exceptionals	0	0
Pre-tax	143	162
PX-PTP	143	162
PXPA-PTP	148	167
Tax	−42.9	−48.6
Tax rate (%)	30	30
Attributable	100.1	113.4
No of shares	545	545
EPS	18.4	20.8
PX EPS	18.4	20.8
PXPA EPS	19.0	21.4

'clean' contribution. Importantly, these debits may be helping the subsequent year's operating performance.

- *Earnings calculation.* When calculating the earnings per share apart from the exceptionals, the difference in earnings per share is accounted for by the debit of the minority and preference charges. These need to be deducted to arrive at the amount of earnings available for ordinary shareholders.

- *Exceptional charges.* The fact that the restructuring charges occur in successive years immediately raises suspicions as to how 'exceptional' they are. In addition they clearly relate to the core business and so while more work is needed to reach a firm conclusion, they certainly need to be challenged. An IIMR eps measure would exclude them as they relate to the core business. It might be that these charges reflect a cost base that has slipped out of control and is belatedly being brought back into shape.

- *Earnings quality.* Crucially, the earnings quality varies significantly between the two companies. The profile of the businesses immediately raises issues over earnings quality. Company B is clearly focused on its core operations with strong market shares which, in theory, should produce some influence on price/price stability in its markets. The higher return on sales highlights these strengths. The emerging market exposure of Company A may make earnings less easy to forecast (i.e. lower quality) given issues over exchange rates (possible translation and transaction risks), inflation and the higher risks that often attach to emerging markets (though offering good growth potential in the longer term). The exceptional charges may also be benefiting the numbers by reducing costs in subsequent years.

- *Sustainability of profits*. The proportion of earnings coming from in-vestment income and the difficulty of assessing its sustainability also raises issues over earnings quality. If the investment income is partly made up of disposals, this may not be repeatable. The same may be true of the associate income where there is also a cash flow issue (see below). Effectively earnings are being influenced by a number of things beyond the control of management (value of investments, currency, performance of associates, etc.).

- *Cash flow*. There are major differences in how the earnings convert into cash. Company A will only receive a dividend from its associate contribution. It may also have cash costs related to the exceptional charges. There may be repatriation issues from some of the emerging markets to which it has exposure – exchange controls or unattractive exchange rates may make it impossible or uneconomical to bring back the cash to the company's HQ. In addition, the cost of servicing its preference dividends and also its minority holders make its cash flow profile less attractive than that of Company B. The higher operating margins will also enable better cash generation.

Comparing these two companies it can be seen that Company B has a much better-quality earnings stream and the earnings and cash flow pro-file are much 'cleaner'. On a fundamental basis, therefore, Company B would be far more attractive.

Not all earnings growth is created equal

Thus, when looking at earnings it is important to look at the quantity and quality of those earnings. The source of earnings growth is crucial to the quality and hence valuation of those earnings.

Earnings growth achieved by a one-off gain due to a one-off contract, currency movements or an asset disposal (if not deemed exceptional) will be valued very low. This is because it does not represent a repeatable source of earnings. The example of IBM meeting expectations through the disposal of a business saw the share price fall and question marks raised over its quality of earnings. (Those results had seen sales come in below expectations which pointed to difficult trading conditions and perhaps a loss of market share.)

The same reservations might apply to reduction in costs, though of course these are critical to the efficiency and competitiveness of the company. The problem is that they may be responsible for providing a one-off boost to earnings and not for sustainable long-term growth. (It is not quite as straightforward, as the lower cost base enables extra market share to be won.) Market comment on US retailer Home Depot's third quarter 2002 figures indicated that, while the company's earnings met market expectations, the shares fell 13 per cent as this was achieved entirely through cost-cutting initiatives. It can be seen that the market is very aware of where earnings growth has come from and will adjust its valuation accordingly.

In both the IBM and Home Depot examples the market's disappointment revolved around the performance of the business. Despite the fact that numbers were in line with expectations, the 'top line' or revenue performance suggested that things were not quite as encouraging as one would hope. This obviously raises the issue that it is wrong to focus just on earnings – it also depends on the underlying performance of the business.

Growth achieved through volume and price growth, if sustainable, is indicative of a company performing well. However, in a commodity business large, unsustainable hikes in price may increase earnings but would not be valued highly by the market. Again the concern here is that the uplift is a one-off or unsustainable – prices will fall back to previous levels in due course.

Another sensitive area is growth in earnings following provisions. This might occur if there has been an acquisition or a major exceptional charge. In the case of a large exceptional charge, shareholders will see shareholders' funds written down. In addition, there is likely to be a cash outflow to pay for this earnings growth. It is always worth checking post a large exceptional charge whether the subsequent earnings growth has been offset by a decline in net assets per share. In the case of acquisition-related provisions there may well be problems when the provisions run out. This may lead to the company pursuing another acquisition to maintain momentum.

Earnings from acquisition growth will tend to be valued far lower than those generated organically. As discussed in the M&A section, earnings growth can be achieved easily via acquisition while failing to add value – doing deals that are against shareholder interests. The risks attaching to growth through this route are also much higher. So it is important to ensure that growth is not being achieved at the expense of economic returns or through an increase in the risk profile.

Therefore while people correctly monitor earnings and how they may measure up to expectations, it is important that the issues of what has been driving the earnings are fully taken into account and understood. Critically the make-up of earnings will be a key influence on how the shares are valued.

How earnings might be distorted – the accounting

When considering the accounting methods used to arrive at the earnings number, it pays to be sceptical. Management's credibility and rewards are intimately connected with delivery of earnings targets. This scepticism may be especially warranted if any change in accounting policy or one-off items of a dubious nature allow a company to hit market expectations.

Below is a list of areas in which a flexible approach might be adopted to flatter the earnings number. It is by no means comprehensive but covers some of the key areas of concern.

Things to watch for include the following.

- *Profit smoothing* – this may not be a bad thing necessarily. The stock market/investors prefer to see a smooth earnings trend rather than experiencing huge volatility. This at least gives the impression of earnings quality even if the reality is rather different. This may lead to profits being stored away in good years and released in lean years. This may involve provisioning or recognizing costs earlier in a very good year. This then reduces the current year's profits, which means that the benchmark for the following year is set at a lower, more 'realistic' level. If trading conditions in the next year are more difficult, then due to the provisioning and transferring of costs into the previous year the company can meet its profit expectations.

- *Sales recognition* – an aggressive policy on sales recognition can bring forward future profits (while not recognizing the costs) and boost earnings (as discussed on page 77). This is a major issue when long-term contracts are involved.

- *Asset disposals* – while this should be clearly stated separately, it may not be immediately apparent that the company has disposed of an asset or business. It may be netted off cost of goods sold. This was done in IBM's fourth quarter 2001 profits when a business was sold to JDS Uniphase which generated a profit of $280m, which added 10c a share to earnings. Importantly in this example revenues were below expectations, suggesting that the focus should be the underlying performance of the business – not just the earnings target.

- *Pension benefits* – again this may be legitimate but if there is a change of policy it should be clearly stated. Again, a reduction in the cost of goods sold can obscure this, with the pension credit being buried deep in the notes to the results/accounts. CAP Gemini Sogetti did this in the summer of 2000.

  Optimistic assumptions about returns from the pension fund may flatter earnings as pension contributions are lower than they would be on the basis of more realistic assumptions. IBM under its previous chief executive assumed future returns of 10 per cent. A downgrading of this assumption to 9.5 per cent in March 2000 was likely to increase costs (and hence reduce earnings) by $350m in 2002. With many commentators expecting returns to be much lower than this, there is likely to be pressure on the 9.5 per cent assumption in the future.

- *Option costs* – this has been a big area for debate, with Warren Buffett stressing that as far as he is concerned, the granting of options is an employment cost. Interestingly, IBM (along with many other tech companies) would see its earnings reduced by 15 per cent if the granting of options was taken into account. Some have suggested that the technology sector would see a reduction in earnings of up to 50 per cent if option costs were expensed.

- *Provisions* – a fairly common way of boosting earnings is to make big provisions in one year which then effectively allows costs to be lower in subsequent years. This may involve provisions for cost reductions or the write-down of asset values. If earnings are deemed more important than assets, asset write-offs may be used to help reach earnings numbers. (To make sure a company is really creating wealth it may be worth checking that the net asset value grows as well as earnings.)

- *Acquisition accounting* – when a company acquires another company its accounting policies may be less conservative than those of the target company and this will benefit earnings. In addition, big provisions may be set up to fund the integration of the two businesses. Stocks may be written down and then sold at a higher level, with a benefit to profits.

- *Capitalization of interest* – instead of charging interest costs associated with a large investment project to the P&L as a cost, they might be capitalized as part of the cost of the whole project. This would then be depreciated in the normal way.

- *Depreciation policy* – this might be lengthened (suggesting that the useful life of the asset would be longer than anticipated) to reduce the depreciation charge. This would lower costs and hence boost earnings (it makes no difference to cash flow).

- *Deferring marketing/advertising or capital projects* – this gives a short-term gain as costs are reduced but inevitably leads to potential market share issues. Some investors may feel that a more long-term approach is required to investing in the product and supporting market share. Ironically, companies may do this because they do not want to disappoint investors' short-term earnings expectations.

- *Currency* – this can have a big impact on earnings for companies with sizeable overseas activities. The translating of these overseas profits into the reporting currency can cause earnings to be a lot better or worse than expected. Cynically a company with a policy of using a year-end rate may change to an average rate if the drop in the overseas currency occurs in the second half of the year. This will result in a higher earnings number being recorded. This may indeed be a fairer reflection of the performance of the subsidiary during the course of the year – it is the change in policy that generates the questions.

- *Tax charges/policy* – the tax charge is another variable that impacts upon the earnings per share number. Therefore it is always worth monitoring whether there has been any change in the underlying tax rate. This may reflect, for example, a changing geographic profile of earnings (different countries have different rates and allowances) or a change in the tax rules in any of the areas of operation. Changing policy may cover such areas as deferred tax and again it is worth noting if the policy changes. Sudden rises in tax charges can have an impact on share prices as they lead to downwards revisions in earnings growth.

- *Low tax charges* – a very low tax charge can be an indicator that the earnings are being considerably overstated and not just due to the low tax charge. The tax authorities' view of (taxable) profits may be that they are considerably lower than the company is reporting. This immediately raises question marks as to the company's accounting policies and its approach to profit recognition. The other danger is that the tax charge at some point rises towards the standard level, which reduces the earnings growth quite dramatically.

Ebitda

Ebitda stands for earnings before interest, tax, depreciation and amortization (see Table 2.7).

Table 2.7   Calculating Ebitda

	Year 1
Pre-tax profit	£20m
Interest	£2.5m
Forecast operating profit (Ebit)	£22.5m
Depreciation	£20m
Amortization	£2m
Ebitda calculation (in millions)	22.5 + 20 + 2
Ebitda	£44.5m

Many of the issues explored under the quality and quantity of earnings apply equally to Ebitda; the issues over accounting policies are especially relevant.

Why it's used

Ebitda developed as a performance number partly because it strips out the effect of different depreciation and amortization policies that companies may have. In particular, with the growth of investment on a pan-European or global basis, it became important to avoid the distortions of different countries' accounting policies. For example, some countries had tax regimes which encouraged the accelerated depreciation of assets. This would lead to a very high depreciation charge because it was tax efficient but would correspondingly depress earnings. Therefore comparing across countries was rendered invalid at the earnings level. It should also be borne in mind that companies in the same country and indeed the same sector might have different policies with respect to depreciation, hence making comparisons very difficult. Similarly, amortization of goodwill and the treatment of goodwill varies across countries.

Ebitda is also struck before exceptional items, thus avoiding another potential accounting distortion to comparisons (see page 82 for analysis of exceptionals).

The other (contentious) reason for using it is that it serves as an approximation for cash flow and it is often referred to as a cash flow-based measure of performance/valuation. This is because depreciation and amortization are non-cash costs, i.e. while they are deducted before arriving at a profits number there is no actual payment that goes out of the company. Accordingly it gives an indication of gross cash flow. Cash flow, as we will discuss in more detail on page 124, is regarded as the key driver of value.

The other advantage of using Ebitda when comparing companies is that it takes into account the different capital structures the companies may have. As we have seen there are advantages to using debt over equity, so a company that has used a lot of debt in its capital structure can be compared with one that has used very little debt.

Ebitda is also used and indeed promoted as a performance measure by companies that have no earnings. This may reflect a company with cyclical earnings being at the bottom of the cycle. The other situation of course is where a company is at an early stage of development and has yet to generate a profit. If it can generate a positive Ebitda, it will hopefully reassure investors. It might be that a major programme of capital expenditure has been completed to get the business under way. These assets will be depreciated so the business is generating cash though not earnings.

What is driving Ebitda?

As with the section on earnings it is crucial to assess what is driving Ebitda. Investing in the business can certainly help Ebitda grow. The investment will hopefully improve revenues and lower costs and of course will attract additional depreciation charges as the asset base expands. However, in the first few years it may be that the depreciation charge increases but profits (earnings) do not. So Ebitda grows but profits do not. The real issue is that earnings need to increase.

However, the Ebitda measure of performance excludes the financing costs of this extra investment – the interest charge. If the interest component is rising rapidly, the investment is not actually improving the earnings available to shareholders. It may be that both the depreciation charge and operating charge do in fact rise, but that rising interest costs prevent this coming through to profit or EPS. Many companies using Ebitda are at an early stage of development and are in precisely this sort of situation. This is not to say that they are bad investments but that care is needed to ensure that the investments will generate appropriate returns. This brings us back to a central concern when looking at performance – that growth is not driven at the expense of returns on investment or value added (i.e. the returns on the investment exceed the cost of capital).

Another key concern is where the focus on growth in Ebitda leads to an aggressive acquisition policy, i.e. the growth is achieved through buying other businesses rather than through the underlying performance of the company. (We have already discussed the issues accounting for why acquisitions rarely add value.) Such acquisitions have been very destructive of shareholder value. Bought at the top of the cycle, at very high valuations, these businesses failed to deliver. While the growth failed to materialize, the funding, whether debt or equity, needed to be serviced. The (often severe) deterioration in companies' financial position then left them in much weakened positions and dramatically increased their risk profile.

While the fashion in the mid to late 1990s was that debt was good (it reduced the cost of capital and helped improve earnings growth), deteriorating economic conditions and weak financial markets have made overstretched balance sheets a major concern. This is especially true for those companies suffering from poor volumes and price. Debt servicing has become increasingly difficult and has led to a serious downgrading of credit ratings and higher debt servicing costs as a result. Inevitably this undermines the company's competitive position and makes investing for growth impossible.

Aggressive accounting policies have also been a factor. As discussed under corporate governance, Ebitda has been the trigger for remuneration packages. On the basis that if it is targeted it can be manipulated, care needs to be taken. The evidence is clear that accounting policies have been extremely aggressive (if not in some instances fraudulent) to ensure that performance targets were hit.

Not a true measure of cash flow?

Another of the major disadvantages of Ebitda is that depreciation is a very real cost of doing business in many industries and should be taken into account. It is crucial for the company to protect its competitive position and maintenance capital expenditure is critical in this regard. This, combined with the need for working capital and movements in provisions to be taken into account, prevents Ebitda from being a useful proxy for cash flow.

A performance measure in disrepute?

As a result of all these factors Ebitda has fallen into disrepute in the post-bubble years. Many of the companies, especially in the USA, that championed it as a performance metric have either run into serious financial trouble or have been very poor investments. The demise of many of these companies has raised serious issues over its use as a performance measure.

Given the importance accorded to Ebitda, its complexity and the publicity it has generated, it is worth summarizing the pros and cons of this performance measure.

The advantages of Ebitda are:

- it takes the whole funding structure into account (unlike P/Es)
- it allows comparisons between companies with different accounting policies towards depreciation and amortization
- it ignores exceptional charges, again allowing comparison
- it is a cash flow-based measure.

The disadvantages of Ebitda as a performance number raise various issues.

- Is it being used when all other measures are disappointing?
- Maintenance capex is a key cost and working capital also requires cash, so is it a true measure of cash flow?
- What does it measure – neither cash nor profitability?
- Earnings can still be manipulated.
- Earnings before interesting things . . . are we missing the story?
- Investment can grow Ebitda (Ebit, depreciation and amortization), but what is the rate of return on that investment v the cost of capital?
- What is happening to interest costs?

- What is the impact on gearing and risk?
- It is used in capital-intensive high-growth industries where no profits/EPS are generated . . . but overinvestment and low returns?

KEY PERFORMANCE RATIOS:
PROFITABILITY AND RETURNS

Checking the performance of a company against others in the sector is a useful way of assessing how well the company is positioned, how efficient it is and how well the management is performing. There are three key ratios you should concentrate on:

- operating profit margins
- return on capital employed
- economic value added.

Operating profit margins

The company's operating profit margins will be available from its P&L. Some companies spell this out while for others you will have to divide the operating profit by the turnover. Operating margins are the proportion of revenue that is pure profit.

Operating margins are essentially the outcome of changes in volume, prices and costs and therefore these crucial drivers of margins should always be considered. They convey a wealth of information about how well positioned, how efficient and how well managed a company is. They can also raise issues of strategic importance – is the company ex growth or are there likely to be new entrants attracted to the industry? Prices are a key influence on margins, as discussed in the sector section, page 15, and the company position, page 32.

In terms of the message and information that may be deduced from operating margins it is important to consider the following.

How does the profit margin compare with that of similar companies?
Comparing margins with the peer group provides an excellent way of judging the performance of a management team. However, care needs to

be taken to ensure that 'like for like' comparisons are being made. For example, one company may include an overseas subsidiary in a division that distorts comparisons with a company operating solely in the domestic market. One business may be 'vertically integrated' (performing many functions between its suppliers and its customers rather than outsourcing them) while the other concentrates on one element of the process. Company reporting does not always facilitate easy comparisons.

If margins of one business are consistently higher than those of another very similar company in the same sector, then clearly as a business and as a management they have found a winning formula. The investment issue is then whether to go for the winner or whether there is a 'catch-up' story in the weaker margin business. If it is a strong winning formula, the scope for catching up might be far more limited than it may appear. This is especially true if the higher-margin business has built up a dominant market position, an effective way of generating higher margins and a culture that enables it to continue to do well. Conversely, the weaker-margin business may have a weaker product offering and market position and a less attractive formula and a management culture that is not as effective at generating value. Overcoming these weaknesses is far from easy and so buying the company on hopes of restoring margins to those of the competitor can be a risky policy.

What has been the trend in margins?

Have margins been improving, static or declining over the past five years? What is the longer-term trend? Steadily rising margins are usually a good sign that the business is performing well, while declining margins are a cause for concern. As ever, care needs to be taken before reaching firm conclusions. A higher-quality, and higher-priced, product and/or progressively lower costs should see margins going higher to the advantage of shareholders. However, a company with a good-quality product and tight costs may consciously and perfectly sensibly decide to be very price competitive as it looks to increase its market share. This will see short-term margins decline but overall sales and profit increasing. This strategy will benefit the longer-term position of the company as it develops its market share position.

Conversely, a company may cut back on product development and marketing expenditure and boost short-term margins. However, this may progressively erode its long-term product offering and market position. The business and shareholders are likely to suffer.

If margins have been moving about widely (say from very low to high and back again), volatility is clearly a feature of the business. This suggests that the quality of earnings is very low. If you invest when margins are at the top of their historic range, there is a serious possibility that margins and earnings are about to fall. Accordingly the shares are likely to fall in value.

What has been driving margins?

It is important to have an understanding of what forces have been driving margins. This will affect the sustainability of those margins and the potential risks. If, for example, margins have risen following a rise in prices due to a shortage of the product or a temporary price hike in a volatile commodity, the higher margins will prove to be temporary – they will reverse as prices decline. Importantly, as discussed in the section on quality of earnings (page 86), in these cases management or the actions of the company are not the driving force behind the higher margins.

Similarly, temporary boosts to margins from lower raw material costs are likely to unwind relatively quickly and owe nothing to management action. However, a concerted effort by management to improve its purchasing policies and source more cost-effective/higher-quality components is likely to offer sustained benefits.

If margins are being boosted by solid volume growth, firm pricing, new product developments and improved product quality, this augurs well. Not only will margins expand but the company's position and profile in the market will be enhanced.

If margins are low, can they be improved? Is this a recovery stock or just mismanaged?

Low margins relative to the peer group may provide potential upside. However, they may reflect years of underinvestment in both plant and machinery and product range/development. This will inevitably lead to a worse cost structure and an inferior product offering than the competition and a continuous erosion of market share. Restoring margins and market share in this scenario is likely to be extremely difficult and take a long time (if ever) to achieve. Buying margin recovery stories is fraught with difficulties. Often the weak market position of the company or the degree of mismanagement are underestimated by outsiders – the company is in a much weaker position than anticipated.

One of the classic difficulties is a situation where costs are cut dramatically to restore margins. However, rapidly falling prices offset the improvement in the cost base. If you are going to invest in a margin recovery story, ensuring a stable revenue background is an important part of the equation. Alternatively, if it is a more simple case of an inflated cost base that can be addressed easily, then a margin recovery story is possible (though typically this will require a different management approach to the one that presided over the initial inflation of the cost base).

If margins are low due to start-up costs, investing in new product development or sales and marketing, this will reverse in due course. This may be a buying opportunity if these initiatives are part of a sensible long-term strategy.

If margins are low, is there a risk of going into loss?

If margins are low this can be a significant source of risk as there is little scope for anything to go wrong. If margins are low because things are already going wrong, it may not take a lot to see profits swing into loss. A contractor with operating margins of 1 per cent, for example, may run into problems with a large contract and quickly run into loss.

The risks are higher if the business is highly volatile and subject to wide swings in volume and price (high operational gearing).

Industry structure a big influence on pricing and margins

The degree of consolidation in an industry is a big influence on margins. At the obvious extreme a monopolist will enjoy very high margins, though this should not necessarily be construed as the result of good management. A high degree of industry consolidation – i.e. a few players accounting for the vast majority of the market – should lead to a better pricing environment than a fragmented industry where a large number of small players are jockeying for position.

There can be exceptions. In some industries with high fixed costs, for example steel, chemicals and cars, profits may be very sensitive to volume. Accordingly some players may decide to ensure they protect/increase market share by increasing volumes/cutting prices, which will inevitably hurt margins. Similarly, a company that takes the view that, in the long term, it will be better off by increasing market share may achieve its objectives by cutting prices aggressively in the short term. It may want to be seen as the most competitively priced player in the sector at all times. This again may cause margins to fall for all the industry as others try to compete.

Changes in industry structure which allow pricing, and hence margins, to improve can be a buy signal. Therefore watching industries where the market is fragmented (shared by a high number of players) for signs of consolidation may alert you to some potentially interesting possibilities.

If margins are a lot higher than competitors', can the figures be believed? Is the accounting prudent?

On the basis that 'if something looks too good to be true, it probably is', margins that are significantly greater than the competition should be closely scrutinized. They may genuinely represent the superior efforts of management – better products produced at much lower cost generating a much higher price. However, they may reflect a less prudent approach to accounting – low depreciation charges, valuation of stock, recognizing profit earlier than is sensible or capitalizing costs that other companies expense. Therefore it is well worth being aware of any accounting issues that are flattering operating margins. The policies adopted may be entirely within accounting guidelines, but they might be stretching the rules to the limit and far from conservative.

Similarly, if a company is generating high margins for producing a basic commodity, care needs to be taken.

If margins are low, does it indicate pricing power lies elsewhere?

Companies that supply big, powerful customers, for example the automotive industry or food retailers, will inevitably find that prices and margins come under pressure. The car manufacturers themselves tend to earn low margins and are almost permanently engaged in driving down component prices.

To counteract this trend, companies need to be able to display a tight control over costs and/or improve product or service quality. Large contracts from the car companies can be critical to the long-term future of suppliers and this can lead to poor margins as prices are cut to secure the contract. Alternatively, a company producing plastic products might find its supplier of petro-chemicals can increase the prices for its products but these higher costs cannot be passed on to the customer. This may reflect a very competitive market for the plastic products or the importance of very large customers such as the big DIY chains. In both these instances shareholders need to be aware that improving margins is likely to be difficult.

In the automotive supplier example, lower prices may have to be accepted given the purchasing power of the car maker. However, it may well be that significant R&D and other costs were essential to meet the order and provide goods of a satisfactory design and quality. If margins are too low, all this effort is failing to add value. In these circumstances a shareholder is, in effect, subsidizing the customer and is unlikely to make money from the investment.

Are margins so high they will attract new competition?

One of the potential dangers of high margins is that they encourage competitors to copy what you are doing. The ease with which people can do this will obviously vary, depending on the barriers to entry. An industry may have high barriers to entry due to patents or technical know-how, high capital costs, significant economies of scale, regulatory hurdles or a high level of brand recognition. Conversely, low barriers to entry are likely to characterize products/industries that are commodities by nature, have low set-up costs and few economies of scale.

If margins are high, is there little prospect for future growth?

A company that has hit a certain level of margin may find it very difficult to go beyond that point. This may mean there is little growth left in the business. There is also the risk of attracting competitors. This may be a warning sign and can be a good time to sell if the company's core business is ex growth. Attention should then turn to the management's strategy. The high margins will lead to the company being highly cash generative and if it has reached a 'natural' market share beyond which it is difficult to grow, the requirement for capital will be limited.

The dilemma at this point is whether the cash flow is returned to shareholders or used to find other avenues for growth. This carries a degree of risk subject to the transferability of the management's skills to other products or other regions. Merger and acquisition activity is a strong possibility in this situation, but whether this adds value is a moot point. (See pages 58–75 for an analysis of the risks and issues to be monitored in this area.)

Do the margins reflect the capital intensity of the business?

(See return on capital employed, right.) It is important to make sure that operating margins a company achieves reflect the capital employed in the business. In theory the higher the capital employed in the business, the higher the margins should be.

If a very capital-intensive business has low margins, returns on investment will be very low. So cement or chemical plants need to generate high margins to get a return on the big outlay involved in the plant. Conversely, it might be quite all right to have a low-margin business if it generates a high return on capital by using very little capital, or the capital is 'turned over' very quickly. For example, food retailers have margins of around 5 per cent but they use relatively little capital. Suppliers fund their working capital which they turn over quickly. Therefore, because they efficiently turn capital into sales, returns on capital can be very attractive.

Where are margins going in the future?

As with any investment issue we are concerned with the future trend and direction on margins. This is what will determine whether the company (and ultimately the shares) will make money. By bringing together the issues identified as being important in the margin equation you should have a good sense of the factors influencing margins.

Return on capital employed

The return on capital employed (ROCE) is a critical figure that tells you how well management is using shareholders' money.

There are a number of ways of calculating this. The simplest is to divide operating profit by shareholders' funds + net debt. If the level of debt moves sharply during the year you may want to think about the average level of debt employed. You can always look at the interest payments and divide these by the rate of interest the company pays (there will be some notes in the accounts that should help you). Net debt should also include any preference shares or convertible bonds that the company may have.

Shareholders' funds plus net debt effectively give you the amount of resources the company is using. To improve the ratio obviously requires an improvement in operating profit and/or a reduction in the amount of capital needed to produce it.

The level of returns is critical as the value of any asset depends on the amount of income it generates. Therefore high returns on capital are strongly linked with share price performance and valuation. The ratio, and more critically its future trend, is crucial for the performance of your investment.

The factors driving the operating margins (page 101), given that they drive operating profit, will also determine the return on capital. Again the influence of prices is crucial. As with high margins, a high return on capital employed may encourage new competition as competitors/new entrants seek out the profits available.

Example

Blogg's Cement

Take a fictional company, Blogg's Cement. We will assume it has invested £150m in a cement works. The works has the capacity to turn out 1.5m tonnes of cement a year, the cement sells at £60 per tonne, the operating margin is 10 per cent.

Blogg's Cement	
Investment in works	£150 m
Capacity	1.5 million tonnes
Price per tonne	£60
Revenue calculation	
Capacity × price	1.5 m × 60
Revenue	£90m
Operating margin	10%
Operating profit calculation	
Revenue × operating margin	90 m × 10
Operating profit	£9m
Return on capital calculation	
Operating profit/investment	9m/150m
Return on capital employed	6%

This shows us that the return on capital employed is 6 per cent.

Compare that with another fictional company, Joe's Widgets, which has also invested £150m and has the same operating profit margin of 10 per cent. It produces 3m widgets a year, which it sells at £50 each. This gives revenues of £150m a year.

This equals a return on capital employed of 10 per cent.

In both examples the margins are the same at 10 per cent, but the ROCE clearly shows that money invested in Joe's Widgets has generated a much better return than that invested in Blogg's Cement. This is because the revenue generated by the invested capital in Joe's Widgets is a lot greater than for the cement plant – £150m compared with £90m.

The relationship between margins and ROCE can be seen clearly from these figures. A 10 per cent operating margin from the cement investment generates a low return of 6 per cent. If we say the cost of capital (see pages 172–9) is 10 per cent, you can see this is a far from effective investment.

Joe's Widgets	
Investment in works	£150m
Capacity	3m
Price per widget	£50
Revenue calculation	
Capacity × price	3 m × 50
Revenue	£150m
Operating margin	10%
Operating profit calculation	
Revenue × operating margin	£150 m × 10 per cent
Operating profit	£15 million
Return on capital calculation	
Operating profit/investment	15m/150m
Return on capital employed	10%

An operating margin of 17 per cent would be needed to generate a return on capital of 10 per cent (£150m of investment @10 per cent is £15m. £15m/£90m is 16.7 per cent). Therefore much higher margins are needed to compensate for the capital that is needed in the business to generate the level of sales. (Alternatively, the prices charged are too low to generate the returns required. Whether they can be increased of course depends on market conditions and the market structure.)

Therefore, the greater the amount of capital/investment needed per £ of turnover, the higher the margins need to be to ensure an appropriate return.

In Blogg's case, each £ of turnover needs £1.67 of investment. However, Joe's Widgets needs only £1 of investment for each £ of turnover. A 10 per cent margin in both cases produces an acceptable return of 10 per cent on capital for Joe's Widgets but an unsatisfactory 6 per cent for Blogg's Cement.

Risk and returns

Investing in any enterprise clearly involves a degree of risk – how much will vary from industry to industry, company to company, and is likely to be different for different countries. Companies at an early stage of development are likely to have a higher risk profile than more established companies. Companies diversifying into new products or regions will be taking on higher levels of risk than those staying within their existing area of expertise.

Shareholders shoulder the risks of the business and therefore should be appropriately rewarded – the greater the risk you bear, the higher the returns you should receive. Being aware of the risks involved is important for you to assess the returns you want.

So if the ROCE is only, say, 6 per cent, you would have been better off putting your money in a high-interest deposit account. The return would be similar but without any risk. Another key problem with such a low return is that if the trading environment deteriorates, this could drop returns to extremely low levels. (The importance of risk is incorporated in the cost of capital where beta is used to reflect the volatility of an investment, see page 175.)

High returns

A high ROCE normally tells you that management is using your resources efficiently. This generates confidence that any investment programmes or acquisitions undertaken will reward shareholders. This improves the quality of the earnings and gives confidence in the longer-term growth outlook. The key is to evaluate the sustainability of those returns.

If returns are very high, there is a risk that potential competitors will be casting an envious eye at the company's market and looking to enter the industry/product segment to capture some of the returns. How easily they can do this will depend on the barriers to entry that exist. If relatively low, new entrants may trigger a battle for market share and lead to a significant erosion of return on capital.

Another potential problem if returns are very high is that there is no room for improvement. If the industry is mature, or the company has reached a market share that is difficult to expand upon, there may be concerns that the company is ex growth. Management may be tempted to raise the growth profile by acquisitions or moves into other business areas. These initiatives may increase the risk profile of the company and lead to a lower rate of return in the new areas.

Low returns

If ROCE is low, has it been low for a long time or fallen recently? This can be important when returns are low for a long period of time. The conclusion may be that these assets are considerably overstated in the balance sheet. This may lead to the company having to write down the value of these assets.

Alternatively, low returns may mean that poor management is under-utilizing the asset base. This may trigger a call to change the management or a hostile takeover if the considered view is that the asset value is right and the returns (through poor management) are wrong. This may lead to viewing the stock as a recovery or takeover story.

Is it poor management or poor industry?

If returns are consistently low, it is worth exploring the extent to which this is a feature of the industry in which the company operates. This is especially so if the returns are low even when the company is in an up-phase of an economic or industry cycle. If it appears that returns are indeed low but they are in line with the rest of the company's competitors, it is clearly an industry issue. This may well suggest that the shares, and indeed the sector, are best avoided.

To be a buyer of the shares you need to believe that something is about to happen that will raise returns – either for the company or across the industry – or that the shares are so lowly rated that the low-achieved returns are 'in the price' (see value stocks, page 212). Returns may be set to improve due to a significant increase in demand and/or firmer pricing. This may involve, for example, some capacity closure or mergers that improve the pricing power of companies in the sector. Such recoveries often fail to materialize and it is worth examining future prospects closely and realistically. The risks of investing in such a situation are high.

How much capital (and what type) is needed?

It is also worth considering how much capital is needed in the business. The valuation will depend on the amount of capital needed to grow. Some businesses may be capital intensive while others may be able to generate high levels of revenue growth on the back of relatively small investments. In some businesses that require a lot of working capital (stock, for example), it may be possible to use capital provided by suppliers. Food retailing is a good example of this. Here the capital required is relatively low as there is 'negative' working capital because suppliers fund this element of the business.

The relatively low level of capital employed in this instance leads to relatively low margins. Employing a lot of capital is not a bad thing per se –

it just has to generate an appropriate return. One would, therefore, expect to see in capital-intensive businesses higher operating margins, which then ensure that the all-important return on capital is high enough to add value.

In some industries the 'asset' base may be more people-oriented (e.g. service-related industries such as advertising). In this case there may be a high rate of return on capital, reflecting the fact that very little capital is employed. You will need to ensure operating margins are at healthy levels.

ROIC – assets written off the asset base

When looking at the return on capital figure it is important to ensure that the definition of assets is comprehensive. A company may have invested in an acquisition that necessitated a considerable write-off of goodwill (the amount paid for a business over and above its net assets). The total investment clearly needs to generate an appropriate return. However, the shareholders' funds figure will exclude the amount of goodwill written off and so flatter the ROCE (often calculated by adding debt to shareholders' funds) figure. The return on invested capital (ROIC) ratio, by adding back this goodwill, provides a more reliable guide to how management has been allocating resources. You will need to look in the notes to find the cumulative goodwill that has been written off. This needs to be added back to generate the invested capital.

Examining the numbers

To look at the difference that this can make to returns let us consider at the two companies A and B we discussed when examining quality of earnings (pages 86 and 91). From this example we know that company B is generating a greater proportion of profits from its core operations and has higher operating margins. We also know that Company A has preference capital as a preference dividend was deducted before arriving at earnings per share. This we will treat as debt and so it will form a part of capital employed.

We can see that Company A has written off goodwill of £90m in 2002 following an acquisition. We will assume that the acquisition was contributing from January 1 so there is a full year's contribution. Shareholders' funds are therefore reduced by a corresponding amount (the year-end figure is partially offset by retained profits in the year). You can see immediately that lower shareholder funds imply lower capital employed if we ignore goodwill. On a capital employed measure, the capital employed falls from £964.3m to £953m despite a £50m increase in debt. But this goodwill was an integral part of the money spent on the acquisition. Table 2.8 calculates the ROCE on the basis of shareholders' funds plus debt and ROIC where the goodwill written off is added back. We can see that the ROIC is much lower in 2002 at 13.6 per cent compared with the ROCE at 16.3 per cent. Clearly this makes an enormous difference when assessing the management's performance.

Table 2.8 Calculating the ROCE on the basis of shareholders' funds plus debt and ROIC including goodwill written off

	Company A	
Balance sheet data	**2001**	**2002E**
Equity shareholders' funds	575.4	510.0
Minority interests	68.9	68.9
Total shareholders' funds	**644.3**	**583.0**
Net debt	200.0	250.0
Preference capital	120.0	120.0
Capital employed	964.3	953.0
Goodwill written off	100.0	190.0
Invested capital	1064.3	1143.0
Gearing (%)	49.7	64.0
ROCE (%)	**14.0**	**16.3**
ROIC (%)	**12.7**	**13.6**
Post-tax ROCE (%)	9.8	11.4
Post-tax ROIC (%)	8.9	9.5
NAV (p)	118.2	106.9
No of shares (m)	545	545
	Company B	
Balance sheet data	**2001**	**2002E**
Equity shareholders' funds	575.4	620.0
Minority interests	–	–
Total shareholders' funds	**575.4**	**620.0**
Net debt	200.0	180.0
Capital employed	775.4	800.0
Goodwill written off	100.0	100.0
Invested capital	875.4	900.0
Gearing (%)	34.8%	29.0%
ROCE (%)	**20.6**	**22.5**
ROIC (%)	**18.3**	**20.0**
Post-tax ROCE (%)	14.42	15.75
Post-tax ROIC (%)	12.81	14.0
NAV (p)	105.6	113.8
No of shares (m)	545	545

Company B benefits from a higher operating contribution from its core business and does not have the investment and associate income distortions to its overall performance. Very importantly it also employs fewer assets to achieve that operating contribution. It does not have the preference capital or the level of goodwill employed by Company A in 2002. As a result in 2001 it is using invested assets of £875.4m to generate operating profit of £160m rather than A's use of £1064.3m to generate £135m of operating profit.

In 2002 the gap widens even further as the capital employed by Company A increases to reflect the goodwill increase following acquisition. Significantly, in year two B's cash generation leads to lower debt levels (which have fallen by £20m) and hence capital employed.

Pre or post tax?

The other issue is whether to use pre- or post-tax figures for the return on capital or invested capital calculation. In Table 2.8 I have included both, taxing the operating profit at 30 per cent. What is left for shareholders is clearly post tax and so this is perhaps the most useful way of computing the return. In addition, when looking to assess whether a company is adding value a post-tax return is used. This reflects the fact that the post-tax cost of capital is used for the debt figure. This is covered in more detail on the economic value added section, right, and when we look at the cost of capital in more detail when considering discounted cash flow valuations (page 168).

Return on equity

A similar and very important alternative to return on capital is to look at the return on equity. This is, in many ways, a more logical way of assessing the use to which shareholders' funds are put as it looks at what is left for shareholders in relation to what they have invested.

It is calculated by dividing the profit after tax and any deductions due to non-equity holders (for example minority charges or preference dividends) by the amount of ordinary shareholders' funds. Sometimes this is calculated by including any goodwill that has been written off because this has been deducted from ordinary shareholders' funds.

Again this provides an important way of assessing whether the company's management is using resources to best effect. If returns are low, the alternative would be to put the money in a (risk-free) deposit account.

Economic value added – exceeding cost of capital

Having looked at how to calculate ROIC and the factors that influence it, we are half way to assessing whether the company is adding value. Adding value refers to how the return on capital relates to the cost of that capital. This can appear complicated but is an extremely important concept to understand. In essence it is the minimum return you would expect from a business given the need to be compensated for the risks involved. It is also charging management a proper cost for all the resources they are using to ensure that they focus on exceeding this very real cost of doing business.

Adding value depends on the company's economic position, its efficiency and the returns generated by its assets and how these compare to the cost of capital. This in turn depends on the proportion of equity and debt capital as equity is more expensive than debt and does not have the same tax advantages. We have seen in analyzing the returns from acquisitions that economic value added is crucial for shareholders and helps reduce the emphasis that is commonly put on growth in earnings (or Ebitda). Whether a company is adding or destroying value will be a crucial driver for both valuation and share price performance. It is also crucial to give you a return that compensates for the risks you are taking.

Given the importance of the company's financial position in terms of the cost of capital and valuation of the company and the risks posed by poorly financed businesses, we now turn to examine how to assess the financial position of a company.

WHAT IS THE COMPANY'S FINANCIAL POSITION?

There are a number of key figures to look at when considering the financial health of a company:

- gearing
- cash flow
- interest cover.

Gearing

What is it?
Why is it important?
What to watch for

Gearing is the most common way of measuring a company's financial position. The normal way to derive this is to first work out the group's net debt. Net debt is the total debt a company has minus any cash it holds. You then divide that figure by shareholders' funds. Shareholders' funds are clearly listed on the balance sheet and are basically the book value of the company's assets at that point in time. This would include the value of buildings and plant, stock held and any profits retained over the years. A common definition of gearing is net debt/shareholders' funds, the latter including minorities (though some investors may exclude minorities which gives a more prudent view). Minorities are the portion of assets owned by outside shareholders when a company has a majority holding but does not own 100 per cent of a company.

You then multiply your answer by 100 to give you the gearing figure, expressed as a percentage. So if net debt is £100m and the company's shareholders funds are £200m, the company is said to have gearing of 50 per cent.

Gearing, then, is a measure of how much of the capital employed in the business is provided by shareholders' funds and how much by debt. A company with low gearing has a small proportion of its capital supplied by debt, whereas a highly geared company has a high proportion of its capital funded by debt.

Companies that are in sectors where there are few fixed assets or where assets tend to be 'intangible', such as the value of brand names – assets that are valuable but which cannot be physically touched – can be disadvantaged if you look just at gearing to evaluate their financial position. The same is true of highly acquisitive companies that write off a lot of goodwill on the 'assets' they acquire. These companies will tend to have a high level of gearing even if they have very little debt. In these cases a better guide to the companies' financial position would be to look at interest cover (see page 127).

There is no 'correct' level of gearing, but above 50 per cent is normally considered on the high side. A company operating in a stable industry, with a clear view of its revenues and little need for new investment in the business, will be able to live with a much higher level of gearing than a company in a cyclical business that has no visibility in its revenues (i.e. it is extremely difficult to predict the volumes and prices of the company's output) and needs a lot of cash to update a large factory or piece of equipment.

The main questions to ask are:

- How much cash is the company generating?
- How predictable is the revenue?
- Are the shareholders' funds realistically valued?
- Does the business need a lot of investment?
- Is the interest rate charged on the debt fixed or variable?
- Is the debt short or long term?

Example

Let us take another fictional company, Milk Pops, which produces breakfast cereal. We assume it has debt of £60m, shareholders' funds of £100m, so it would be said to have gearing of 60 per cent. Milk Pops has total sales per year of £200m and a 10 per cent operating profit margin, so its operating profit is £20m. One of the features of the business is the predictability of its sales, which have grown consistently at around 4 per cent per year even in periods of recession.

Milk Pops	
Debt	£60m
Shareholders' funds	£100m
Gearing calculation	
Debt/shareholder funds	60/100
Gearing	60%
Total sales	£200m
Operating profit margin	10%
Operating profit	£20m

Compare that with Full Stop, a fictional engineering group that makes brake units and sells them to a nearby large car manufacturer. Full Stop also has debt of £60m and shareholder funds of £100m and so like Milk Pops has ▶

gearing of 60 per cent. Its sales are currently £150m, having fallen from £200m last year. Its profit margin is 5 per cent, having fallen from 10 per cent last year. This year its operating profit is £7.5m.

Full Stop	
Debt	£60m
Shareholders' funds	£100m
Gearing calculation	
Debt/shareholder funds	60/100
Gearing	60%
Total sales	£150m
Operating profit margin	5%
Operating profit	£7.5m

A key feature of this business is that it is highly cyclical in nature (as demand for cars goes up and down with the business cycle). In addition it is vulnerable to the loss of one major contract with a car manufacturer. This raises uncertainty over its future performance.

While the two companies both have relatively high gearing it is evident that Milk Pops has a higher level of operating profit and a more stable performance than Full Stop. Full Stop has the same relatively high debt but makes less money, less consistently. This would be likely to cause concern for investors.

Efficient balance sheets

The increasing use of 'economic value added' approaches to investment analysis in the 1990s led to a lot of attention being focused on balance sheet efficiency. The argument is that debt is a cheaper form of finance than equity, so companies largely financed by debt enjoy lower costs of capital and this makes it easier to add value. The relative cost is also affected by the fact that interest payments are tax deductible. Therefore in the UK 30 per cent is taken off the cost of debt to reflect the tax advantage.

Adding value is defined as producing rates of return over and above the cost of capital. Companies with low levels of debt engage in share buy-backs to improve their cost of capital by increasing the proportion of debt in their financing mix. Gearing generally in the corporate sector has been on a rising trend, partially due to this drive for balance sheet efficiency. At the time of writing the average figure for the UK stock market was around 40 per cent.

It is also worth bearing in mind that capital was not only cheap in the 1990s it was widely available. This helped facilitate the move to higher gearing and encouraged companies to use debt finance. In the 2000s the environment is very different. Banks are much more cautious in their lending criteria, having seen many companies run into difficulties. The fashion has swung back towards low gearing.

Gearing and returns

The notion of efficient balance sheets highlights that gearing can be a good thing. It is much cheaper and more tax efficient to fund businesses with debt (the debt payments are deducted before arriving at pre-tax profits). This improves returns. In many cases it can be like the advantage of buying a property with a mortgage accounting for 100 per cent of the value of the property. Any increase in the value of the property then belongs entirely to the mortgage holder.

It can also be the case that the debt ensures that the business is run efficiently. There is the discipline of making sure the debt can be serviced and that there is extra left over for shareholders.

High gearing and volatile income to be avoided

A high level of financial gearing and a high level of operational gearing can be damaging in a downturn. If volume and/or prices fall in a business with high fixed costs, operating profits and cash flow will fall dramatically (see page 135). This might make it very difficult to service the company's debt and may well lead to the dividend being cut. In a prolonged downturn this may lead to a period of poor performance and conceivably bankruptcy. Of course an upturn in volumes and prices can see this impact working the other way.

The risks then are compounded if there is high financial and operational gearing. Indeed, one of the measures of risk (or volatility) – beta – very much depends on the combination of these two issues.

Short- and long-term debt

An important issue to bear in mind when looking at a company's financial position is the maturity structure of the debt as well as the overall level. If it is all short-term debt at variable rates of interest, profits will be hit hard if interest rates rise sharply. Also the banks may call in the debt, when it is up for renewal rather than extending the debt which could cause other lenders to panic. Longer-term debt at fixed rates will offer a more stable financial profile. The impact of changes in short-term interest rates would be minimized and there would be no need for constant refinancing. This would also allow for greater stability, liquidity and flexibility than shorter-term debt.

The other important thing to consider in terms of the time profile of the debt is the assets that the debt is used to finance. If the company has invested in factories and capital equipment that have a long economic life, it would be inappropriate to finance this with potentially volatile short-term debt. It is not dissimilar to buying a house: a mortgage over 25 years is infinitely more appropriate than an overdraft. You could argue that very long-term assets should be financed with equity.

Off-balance sheet debt

It always pays to make sure that the company has declared the full extent of its liabilities and that this is incorporated in the debt number. The company may have debt in a joint venture that is not consolidated in the overall debt numbers. This is referred to as off-balance sheet debt. Similarly, the company may have leasing obligations that are, in effect, debt.

The use of off-balance sheet debt was of course a major feature of the demise of Enron, the energy trader. The company flattered its balance sheet by parking debt off balance sheet in joint venture companies. These companies were set up specifically to conceal the debt. An important lesson from this saga was that the off-balance sheet companies had assets equivalent to their liabilities. These special-purpose entities therefore had gearing of 100 per cent. It can be difficult to unearth this information, but a close look through the notes to the report and accounts is crucial to try to find related party transactions and liabilities.

Convertible and preference shares – also debt?

When looking at the gearing ratio you should also consider whether the company has any convertible shares or preference shares that may be to all intents and purposes debt. This may be because the shares are redeemable or will never become equity. Many companies will exclude these from their gearing figures, which gives a much more flattering view of their financial position. Most analysts will treat these as debt and this will give a more conservative view of the financial position.

It is always worth taking a cautious view of overall indebtedness and being as comprehensive as possible in assessing the debt number.

The valuation of assets and shareholders' funds

When you have got to grips with the level of debt, you need to ensure that the value of shareholders' funds is appropriate. In most instances this should not be a problem. However, there are situations where the assets on the balance sheet might be considerably overvalued, such as where an acquisition has been bought at the top of the cycle at a very high price. If the industry then turns down and remains in the doldrums for some time, the value of the asset is likely to be overstated. If the performance of the business has fallen by 40 per cent and the likelihood for improvement is limited, in theory the value of the asset should be 40 per cent lower. It could of course be worth even less, subject to how overpriced the acquisition was in the first place.

Clearly in this case the shareholders' funds are considerably overvalued. Therefore let's take a situation where an acquisition accounted for 50 per cent of assets and those assets are deemed overvalued by 50 per cent (a 10 per cent overvaluation and 40 per cent permanent drop in returns from the business). This 50 per cent falls to 25 per cent, while the overall assets fall to 75 per cent. Gearing on this basis would rise dramatically. If the stated gearing is 60 per cent, then on the basis of the real value of the assets this rises to 80 per cent (60/75).

An obvious way of checking whether the assets are appropriately valued is to check the return on the assets (the assets are worth only what they are generating in terms of cash and returns on investment). So if the return on assets is 5 per cent and has been for some time, the assets are likely to be overvalued. This may apply to certain divisions or to the whole company.

The asset side of the equation is very important to the companies. Often there will be net asset covenants which stipulate that assets should not fall below a certain level or gearing must not exceed 100 per cent. In this situation the temptation is to maintain an asset base as high as possible. The reality of the worth of the assets is clearly very different. Therefore the asset side of the equation is very much worth taking on board.

Why high gearing may hurt the company and its share price

Generally speaking, a higher level of gearing suggests a higher level of risk. Below we detail some of the problems associated with high gearing and the adverse impact it may have on a company and its share price performance.

- *Higher risk.* An important aspect of the higher debt levels is that the risks are greater. This will put off potential investors who might have been interested in the situation if debt was at lower levels (i.e. they have low risk thresholds and may invest only in companies with low gearing). Clearly if interest rates are expected to rise, investors will be wary of getting involved.

- *Cash flow servicing debt – cannot invest.* This will undermine the valuation of the shares, especially when combined with the risk of a rights issue. A company with a high level of gearing may find that it cannot fund investment in maintaining the quality of assets or the growth of the business. This could be very dangerous competitively. Good commercial opportunities may be missed as the company takes too long to raise the money or cannot raise it all. This will undermine the valuation of the shares, especially when combined with the risk of a rights issue.

- *Business run for creditors not for shareholders.* One of the central problems if gearing is at very high levels is that the management will be taking decisions favoured by the bankers which may well not be in the interests of shareholders. Discretionary costs such as marketing and R&D are likely to be reduced and capital expenditure cut back. In addition, promising projects may have to be abandoned. Creditors anxious to get their money back may also sell off the most valuable assets. As a result shareholders may not be invested in what had attracted them to the company in the first place.

- *Risk of rights issue.* The higher the level of gearing and the weaker the cash flow, the much greater the risk of a company having a rights issue. This may be avoided by selling off assets, although that involves the risk that the most saleable assets are the most profitable. A rights issue in itself may not be a major depressant on a share price, but the laws of supply and demand suggest a lower share price. Importantly, rights issues that 'merely' pay down debt tend not to be well received by the market. Indeed, the performance of shares after rights issues generally tends to be disappointing.

- *Cost of debt.* Another problem for a company with high debt levels is that the cost of borrowing will tend to rise to reflect the higher risk of default. Bond issues by telecoms companies following their heavy investment in expansion in the late 1990s saw the cost of servicing their debt rise sharply as lenders, concerned about their poor financial position, demanded higher rates. This problem is compounded if much of the existing debt is at variable rates and interest rates are generally rising.

    Obviously if there are substantial amounts of debt, if the cost of that debt rises by three or four percentage points this will have a big impact on debt costs and hence reduce profits significantly. When this works through to earnings, the dividend is likely to be cut (especially as the trading environment is also likely to be difficult in these circumstances).

    The credit rating agencies have had a significant impact on this concern in recent years. Indeed, the ICI rights issue in 2001 was very much driven by debt ratings agencies warning of what would happen to the cost of debt if action was not taken to reduce debt. This led to a deeply discounted and underwritten rights issue. The downgrading of com-panies' credit ratings has a severe impact on share prices and again highlights the risks involved for shareholders.

- *Low dividend growth.* The need to service high debt levels will mean that the ability to grow the dividend is limited. This may be a deterrent for those investors that have a requirement for a growing income. This, combined with the inability to invest in the business, leaves the shares looking very unattractive.

- *Bankruptcy.* If the financial position deteriorates dramatically, ulti-mately a company may be forced into bankruptcy. If the business prospects are poor and it cannot service its existing debt, it will prove impossible to continue to fund the business on an ongoing basis. The fate of Marconi is salutary here – while it has not gone bankrupt, shareholders have ended up with a mere 0.5 per cent or so of the equity, as bondholders converted their bonds into shares.

Cash flow

What is it?
Why is it important?
What to look for

There is no one definition of cash flow. Nonetheless it is critical to monitor this aspect of corporate performance, for assessing both the operating health of a business and the valuation of the business.

Changes to cash flow within a business are a far more straightforward guide to the reality of its position than, say, earnings. As we have seen (pages 94–7) earnings can be very much influenced by the favourable interpretation of accounting policies and distortions such as the use of provisions (see earnings guide).

A commonly used measure of cash flow is Ebitda. This can be worked out by taking the operating profit (from the P&L account) and adding back the non-cash costs of the business, depreciation and amortization. However, as discussed on page 100, there is some dispute as to the usefulness of this number.

Gross cash flow comprises operating cash inflow (operating profit adjusted for the impact of the movement in working capital) with non-cash items, depreciation and amortization being added back. Net cash flow adjusts for the impact of tax and the cost of the dividends. This is sometimes used to generate a cash earnings per share number by dividing retained profit plus depreciation by the number of shares in issue.

Operating free cash flow is defined as net operating profit after tax plus depreciation and amortization, less maintenance capital expenditure (with an adjustment for any necessary movements in working capital). This recognizes that funds are needed to maintain the fabric and quality of the asset base and to meet the working capital requirements of higher turnover. This offsets one of the weaknesses of Ebitda in that it explicitly recognizes maintenance capital expenditure as a real cost of doing business. This is a definition we shall come back to when looking at discounted cash flow valuations (page 168).

While all these definitions may be used to analyze or value a company, it is worth bearing in mind what actually is left for shareholders will be after taxes have been paid and after the servicing of the capital within the business.

Why it is important

A healthy cash flow is crucial. At the very basic level a company will go bust without it. Cash enables a company to maintain and grow the business by providing funds to:

- maintain quality of assets
- invest for growth
- service debt
- pay a growing dividend.

If cash flow deteriorates sharply, this can have serious repercussions. This is particularly true if the company is highly geared. The ability to service the debt can diminish rapidly and can lead to a lot of uncertainty (and high risk) for equity holders. The cost of debt is likely to rise, possibly sharply leading to lower profits and earnings for equity holders. Assets may have to be sold to reduce the debt. This may result in a weakening of the business and its prospects. In addition, the price received for any assets may be low as the company is a forced seller. Remember, shareholders come bottom of the pecking order if a company runs into financial difficulties.

It is, therefore, very important to monitor this deterioration in cash flow and the financial position of the company. Sometimes the continued growth of earnings per share can conceal this deterioration. Earnings can be manipulated by accounting policies or adjustments; the cash flowing in or out of the business provides a more effective and straightforward guide to the real performance of the business.

It can also be true that a company is seeing heavy outflows of cash without it being a major concern. It may be investing aggressively for growth or be replacing a particularly large piece of plant and equipment. The important thing in this situation is that the capital expenditure can generate a return that is appropriate for the risks of the project.

You might want to consider the 'lumpiness' of the capital expenditure programme – is it one large item or a collection of small discrete items? – and the timescale – i.e. how long will it be before the investment generates a return? The longer the timescale, the greater the risk of a change in economic circumstances. A lumpy investment must be finished to have any value, while small incremental additions have the advantage that they can be curtailed in response to changing circumstances.

A worst case scenario might be a process plant which takes two to three years to build. It is started at the top of the cycle (when there is a shortage of capacity) but comes on stream when volumes and prices are dramatically lower at the bottom of the cycle. Clearly the returns on the investment are likely to disappoint, at least in the short term.

In terms of risk profile, the size of project in relation to the size of the company is worth bearing in mind. Large projects can be plagued by delays and overruns and this can have a material impact on the cash flow and earnings of a smaller company which a larger entity might accommodate more easily.

The higher expenditure will lead to a sharp increase in the depreciation charge which may limit earnings per share growth in the short term. This is not a problem in terms of cash generation. (This is one reason why many start-ups with high capital requirements are valued on an Ebitda basis.)

What to look for

When looking at the cash flow profile of a business it is important to see that the company is generating cash, where it is being generated and where it is being spent. Tracking the movement in net debt is one way of seeing whether the company is generating cash (making sure debt is not coming down due to one-off financing items such as disposals or share issues). It is always worth making sure that the cash is being generated from the ongoing business and not from, say, a one-off disposal of assets. Discarding peripheral or non-performing assets can be an important and sensible way of running the business, but it may also conceal a poor underlying performance and a response to deteriorating cash flows.

You also need to take into account the quality of earnings and the efficiency with which earnings convert into cash. This is particularly important if a high proportion of earnings comes from associates.

A fall in operating cash flow may come about because of money going into working capital (traditionally defined as stocks, plus trade debtors, minus trade creditors). This may not be a problem if it is to meet an anticipated expansion of the business. However, it may herald serious problems if stock is being accumulated involuntarily because of a sharp slowdown in demand.

A key driver of value

Cash flow is one of the (if not the) most important drivers of value – any asset is effectively worth the cash return it can generate. The ability to generate cash is critical for any business to be successful. It is no good growing rapidly and investing aggressively in a business if you are not generating cash – bankruptcy will inevitably follow.

Interest cover

Interest cover is a measure of how easily the company can pay interest on its debt. This is measured by taking the operating profit and dividing it by the annual interest payments. Both these items are listed in the P&L statement.

Example

Returning to the example of Milk Pops, its debt stands at £60m and its operating profit at £20m. Paying 5 per cent interest a year on its debt gives an annual interest payment of £3m. So, to calculate interest cover we take £20 million (operating profit) and divide by £3m (interest payment) to give a figure of 6.7. This means that the operating profit could pay the interest 6.7 times over . . . and it's expressed just like that, 6.7 ×.

This is a simple to calculate and widely used method of assessing a company's financial position. As a rule of thumb, figures below 3–4 × are viewed with caution, while those above are seen as safe. One of the advantages of using this measure is that it provides a much more reliable guide to a company's financial strength than conventional gearing (debt/shareholder funds) when a company has very few assets.

Where a company has few assets

The use of interest cover is particularly relevant in areas of the service economy where there are few assets ('people businesses') and situations where assets have been severely affected by the write-off of goodwill. Consumer products companies that have been involved in a series of acquisitions may have written off substantial amounts of goodwill (where the price paid for the deal considerably exceeds assets on the balance sheet). Diageo, the international drinks company, normally presents its financial position through the use of interest cover because a debt equity measure would be meaningless as considerable amounts of goodwill have been written off – i.e. shareholders' funds are relatively low, having been reduced significantly by goodwill written off.

How volatile are the operating profits?

As with debt/equity ratio, the degree of danger in any given ratio depends on the economic characteristics of the business. As the numerator is operating profit, the key to focus on is the sensitivity of operating profits to changes in prices and volumes (operational gearing, see page 135). If we consider the example of the engineering company Tin Can, we know from the characteristics of its markets – overcapacity, a commodity product and competition from imports – that prices are likely to be volatile. With turnover of £250m, a 5 per cent reduction in price will reduce turnover profits by £12.5m. With costs fixed, this then reduces profits by £12.5m (50 per cent) as well.

Similarly, its cost structure, given a high proportion of fixed costs, makes profits highly sensitive to changes in volume.

If we say that operating profits are £25m and interest payments are £5m, interest cover is $5\times$. However, on a 5 per cent price reduction, profits halve (from £25m to £12.5m) and accordingly interest cover falls to $2.5\times$. This is falling to dangerous levels. This deterioration is on an all too plausible assumption of a 5 per cent reduction in prices. If prices fell more than 5 per cent and a key contract was lost, the financial position would deteriorate even more sharply. A 10 per cent price reduction would eradicate profits and leave no interest cover at all.

By contrast, for Milk Pops (or Pink Tablet) a stable volume and pricing scenario suggests that the risks are much lower. Accordingly, interest cover ratios could be a lot lower and one would still be comfortable with the company's financial position.

The danger level for interest cover is around $2\times$

Companies with this sort of cover are in a difficult position, especially if operating profits are volatile as discussed above. At $2\times$ or below, the company's bankers will be keeping a close eye on its developments and indeed it may well be that debt covenants (agreements undertaken by the company with its banks) are being broken. This may lead to a downgrading of the company's credit status and force the company into disposals or a rights issue or quite possibly both. In an environment as difficult as the current one, it is likely to be only the best parts of the business that will attract buyers. Following the disposals, what is left of the company may not be what originally attracted you to invest. Therefore, when evaluating a potential investment idea, the risks attaching to a company with such a low level of interest cover are very high – it can cost you a lot of money. A simple and effective ratio, such as interest cover which can be quickly and easily computed, can help you avoid potential disasters.

Cash flow cover

A variant on interest cover calculated by using operating profit over interest payable is to compute a cash flow cover. This adds on depreciation and amortization to operating profit as they are non-cash costs. This obviously means that the cash coming into the business can also be used to meet the interest payments. However, the danger is that funds are diverted from replacement capital expenditure and investing to maintain competitiveness to servicing the interest. Nonetheless it may be that you wish to take into account the cash flow cover of interest payments.

An important feature to monitor in the calculation is that interest is not being capitalized and thus excluded from the interest payable figure. Interest may be capitalized when it is included in the cost of building plant or facilities for long-term use (the interest is treated as an important cost of the development and is therefore included in the total cost of the project, i.e. capitalized). Food retail outlets, property developers and hotels are some of the businesses that may capitalize interest. There is nothing necessarily wrong with this practice, but it is worth monitoring if the company is capitalizing interest and it is worth checking how much interest is being capitalized. The cover would then be calculated on the interest it actually pays to banks as opposed to the amount declared on the P&L.

Fixed charge cover

Also worthy of note is whether there are preference shareholders that have to be paid or other providers of debt to the company such as convertible bonds. The payments to these people effectively constitute interest or a fixed charge, where the providers of this money have a priority claim on funds before the shareholder. Some of these payments may occur 'below the line', i.e. after the profits figure has been struck. As a result, they may not feature in the interest line. Accordingly they should be added to the interest payments when calculating cover. Sometimes this is referred to as a fixed charge cover ratio.

Financial position summary

So, a company's financial strength can be examined by looking at its debt/equity (gearing) ratio, its interest cover and the degree to which the company is generating cash. In practice it is worthwhile considering all of them to provide a reliable picture of a company's financial position. They are clearly interrelated. If a company is highly cash generative, then a high gearing ratio may not be a major source of concern. Conversely, a high gearing ratio and a poor cash flow profile are a recipe for trouble.

The fashion changed considerably from the mid to late 1990s when the desire for balance sheet efficiency and cutting the cost of capital saw gearing levels rise (often as a result of share buybacks). However, the combination of a more difficult trading environment and uncertain equity markets has ensured that the fashion has swung back to low gearing and strong cash flow as the desirable financial attributes.

In considering gearing, ask yourself the following questions:

- How much cash is the company generating?
- What are the economic characteristics of the business?
- How predictable is the income?
- Are volumes likely to fluctuate?
- Are prices subject to severe competitive pressures?
- Are the shareholders' funds realistically valued?
- Does the business need a lot of investment?
- Is the interest rate charged on the debt fixed or variable?
- Is the debt short or long term?
- Are there off-balance sheet liabilities that need to be considered?
- Are there preference shares or convertible bonds that need to be included?

The dangers of high gearing include:

- higher risk
- it cannot fund investment in the business to maintain competitive position or grow
- the business is run for creditors not in the interests of shareholders
- increased cost of debt – higher interest payments
- risk of rights issue depresses share price
- no dividend growth
- risk of bankruptcy.

WHAT ARE PROFITS AND EARNINGS GOING TO DO?

The reason for getting to grips with the characteristics of the sector, the competitive and financial position of the company and appraising the performance of management is to establish a sense of what future profits and earnings the company might make. Gaining an understanding of the company, its track record, its operating and financial performance and financial position will be of great value.

The company's future profits 'simply' depend on the outlook for volumes, prices, costs and margins. However, as the whole spate of profit downgrades in recent years has testified, this is not as straightforward as we might like. This is a crucial driver of share prices and again getting a sense of what can go wrong is a critical part of the investment process.

The risks in forecasting

The stock market hates uncertainty and valuations/share prices will fall sharply to reflect the degree of uncertainty. In terms of forecasting operating profits, it is important to get a sense of perspective on the degree of uncertainty affecting the principal drivers of profit, volumes, prices and costs.

Volume

A large drop in investment and a cutback in discretionary expenditure by the corporate sector have driven the economic difficulties at the time of writing. This affects the types of company being hit by profits warnings. Therefore the slowdown in companies' spending on technology and software has caused great problems for the part of the technology sector serving those markets.

The increasing maturity of the market for mobile telephony is a good example of the concerns and uncertainty over future demand levels for this sector. The prospect of growth from 3G and the use of handsets for data as well as voice holds out the prospect for longer-term growth. This has changed the perception quite rapidly from its status as a key growth area into one where there is a lot of debate about short- and long-term prospects.

Similarly, with advertising being a discretionary item, cutting back on this can be done almost with immediate effect (helping the company to reduce costs and preserve cash). Again this has hit the media sector hard on a worldwide basis.

When considering the factors affecting the outlook for volume it is worth asking:

- How sensitive is demand to a slowdown in the economy?
- Is demand cyclical, mature or growth?
- Is it a capital good, i.e. part of companies' investment plans?
- Is it a consumer good?
- Is the government the main consumer?
- Is the purchase discretionary?
- Is it a 'high-ticket' item?
- Market share assumptions: is forecast volume growing more rapidly than the market?
- Is the company in an outperforming segment of the market?

Price

Prices have an enormous impact on profitability and margins. The slowdown in the economy has seen demand weaken which will tend to reduce prices of its own accord. In many areas there are also sector-specific reasons for price trends. This invariably depends on the market structure, how competitive the industry is, and the degree of overcapacity.

In many of the technology areas, investment during the late 1990s' boom saw capacity in many product areas increase dramatically. This causes all sorts of pricing problems in the downturn, especially given the extent of the sharp drop in demand. The elimination of industry overcapacity is fraught with difficulty and invariably takes longer than expected. Judging the robustness of pricing in such an environment is clearly very difficult.

The increasing globalization of markets and the use of technology (and especially the web) to enter into traditional markets has brought new competition into many areas of the economy. This again creates huge uncertainty over the pricing environment. The concern over deflation reflects precisely these sorts of factors. The impact of online retailers on the pricing of cars, books, travel, holidays, banking and financial products has been dramatic. With the help of the web consumers are increasingly better informed on pricing and able to negotiate a better deal.

Overoptimism on price is one of the major issues behind profit downgrades. When considering the factors affecting the outlook for price it is worth looking at the issues affecting both demand and supply:

- The economy – impact on demand?
- What is the industry structure and is it changing?
- Barriers to entry?
- Are there new forms of competition?
- Will globalization affect pricing?
- Is there industry overcapacity and if so how much?
- Are there fierce struggles for market share?
- How differentiated is the product or service?
- Are there changes in product mix affecting prices?
- If announced, why will price increases stick?
- What will the customer reaction be to those increases?
- What will be the competitor reaction and what are their objectives?

Costs

The cost side of the equation can be disrupted by a sudden increase in the price of a key raw material. This might be the price of fuel oil for an airline or haulage company. Energy and electricity price hikes can cause major cost pressures for many manufacturing-type operations, an issue which is affecting large parts of the US economy.

The proportion of costs that are variable will determine the impact on profits. The impact on profits will also be dependent upon the ability to pass on the increase in costs in the form of higher prices. This will vary enormously from industry to industry.

Costs associated with new projects or product launches have a notorious tendency to overrun and this can cause disappointment. However, by their very nature they tend to be one-off and would be expected to generate returns in the longer run.

When considering the factors affecting the outlook for costs the following should be considered:

- What is happening to raw material costs (variable costs) and what proportion of total costs are they?
- What is happening to the cost of bought-in goods and services generally?
- Are there costs associated with a new project or product launch?
- What is the cost structure, i.e. the relationship between fixed v variable costs?
- What is happening to labour/employee costs and what proportion are they of total costs?
- Is there a sharp increase or decrease in such discretionary costs such as marketing or R&D?

Profits

The outcome of all the issues affecting volume, price and costs is profits. Given the uncertainties and difficulties in forecasting all of these components, it is hardly surprising that forecasting profits can be such a hazardous exercise. Furthermore, there is a geared relationship between revenue and profits, operational gearing, where a small change in revenue can lead to a significant rise/fall in profits.

With any downgrade it is worth finding out whether the reduction has been driven by disappointing volumes, pricing or an adverse trend in costs. This may help form a view of the depth of the problems. If there is a small slippage in demand for easily understandable reasons, this may not pose too much of a long-term threat. Falling volumes, significant price erosion and industry overcapacity suggest much deeper concerns and a high degree of uncertainty.

The complexity of these factors and the difficulty in quantifying the extent of the profits fall lead companies and analysts to underestimate the seriousness of the downgrade required. This so often leads to a whole series of downgrades occurring – undermining confidence in the company and its ability to read what is happening in its markets.

There is always a danger of hope springing eternal. Optimism rather than hard analysis may be determining the following year's forecast. Hence the health warning that accompanies all forecasts.

Operational gearing

Impact of percentage change in revenue on profits
Volume gearing
Price gearing

This describes the extent to which profits move on changes in turnover. It very much depends on the cost structure of the business. The higher the fixed costs of a business as a percentage of turnover, the bigger the rise or fall in profit for any given change in turnover.

Therefore when companies revise down their sales expectations by an apparently modest amount, profits and earnings expectations can fall alarmingly. For highly operationally geared businesses, a 5 per cent reduction in revenues can translate into anywhere between 30 per cent and 80 per cent+. The effect is greater if the revenue reductions are driven by price rather than volume falls as these come straight off profits – there is little that can be done about it.

To illustrate this, let us take a company with high fixed costs and one with high variable costs and see what happens when volumes and price falls by 10 per cent. As Table 2.9 demonstrates, a business where 70 per cent of costs are fixed with an operating margin of 10 per cent will see an 80 per cent fall in operating profit for a 10 per cent fall in turnover caused by falling volumes. Variable costs of 20 per cent will fall by 2 per cent (i.e. 10 per cent), reflecting the drop in volumes. As a result of the fixed costs remaining at 70 per cent, operating profit falls from £10m to £2m – a fall of

80 per cent. Therefore a 10 per cent fall in volumes leads to an 80 per cent reduction in profit. This means that the operational gearing is very high. Each 1 per cent move in volumes has an 8 per cent impact on profit. This works on the upside as well. A 10 per cent uplift in volumes would lead to an 80 per cent uplift in profit.

Table 2.9   A company with high fixed costs

		−10% V	−10% P
Volume	50	45	50
Price	2	2	1.8
Revenue	100	90	90
Fixed costs	**70**	**70**	**70**
Variable costs	20	18	20
Operating profit	10	2	0
Operating margin	10%	2.2%	0

The gearing effect is greater if the falling turnover is driven by price decreases. As Table 2.10 shows, a 10 per cent reduction in prices leads to a 100 per cent reduction in profits in this case. The variable costs are tied to volumes and thus they will not reduce with falling prices. So a 10 per cent reduction in price eradicates profits.

Table 2.10   A company with high variable costs

		−10% V	−10% P
Volume	50	45	50
Price	2	2	1.8
Revenue	100	90	90
Fixed costs	20	20	20
Variable costs	**70**	**63**	**70**
Operating profit	10	7	0
Operating margin	10%	7%	0

Conversely, where variable costs are high, the operational gearing effect as a result of falling volumes is more limited. With variable costs at 70 per cent of revenues, a fall of 10 per cent in volumes leads to a 30 per cent fall. Variable costs fall 10 per cent in line with the drop in volumes. Therefore operational gearing is much lower with each 1 percentage point drop in volume, leading to a 0.3 per cent fall in profit.

Importantly, with falling prices the effect is the same as with high fixed costs as nothing can be done about costs. The 10 per cent drop in price again leads to profits being eliminated.

This geared way in which profits respond to changes in turnover explains why profits can be downgraded so severely if turnover falls short of expectations. The effect is greater if the fall in turnover is driven by falling prices. This can cause major share price weakness.

You can get a quick gauge to the operational gearing by always looking at the relationship between turnover and operating profits when looking at results announcements, press reports or through reports and accounts. Of course this is slightly simplistic as there may be other factors affecting the numbers, such as one-off costs or currency movements. However, it is a useful way of getting used to the relationships involved.

This will help in your assessment of future profits and how they might be impacted by future volumes and prices. It may also put you in a stronger position to sell quickly if you become worried about pricing and hence the direction of future profits. (For companies with a number of divisions you may want to get a feel for each of the divisions if the company provides a detailed divisional breakdown.)

Therefore a major difficulty in forecasting and where things invariably go wrong is in the understanding of the relationship between falling volumes and prices. When trading volumes and prices start to fall it is often the case that the initial downgrade does not fully reflect the full impact on profits – the impact is often severely underestimated. This partly reflects overoptimism and partly perhaps a reluctance to face up to the full and dramatic extent of the profit downgrade required. Accordingly there is a familiar pattern of profit downgrades occurring in a series, with three or more downgrades often being required. Hence the stock market adage of selling on the first downgrade.

Forecasting operating margins

A good check on your forecasts for volumes, prices and costs is to make sure that the implicit resultant margin makes sense. Operating margins are an important way of evaluating both the performance of the company (see page 101) and valuing the shares (see page 196).

This overoptimism is often reflected in the difference between the top-down forecasts for company profits provided by market strategists compared with the bottom-up forecasts of the analyst. These can often diverge quite dramatically. The top-down view tends to be a far more reliable guide to profit and earnings trends than the bottom-up projections of analysts. For example, top-down forecasts for 2003 seemed to be for earnings growth of around 7 per cent. Given the uncertainty over economic activity, concerns over deflation and pricing pressure in many sectors of the market, this appears sensible. Bottom-up forecasts on the other hand seem to be around 15 per cent+.

The implication for your decision is very important. If you can find top-down projections from the financial pages of the press or brokers' research, it is worth having this figure in mind when assessing the future profits of any individual share in which you are considering investing. If profits for the economy are going to rise only 7 per cent, should you believe forecasts of, say, 15 per cent for a company you are looking at? Analysts always tend to offer important reasons why the company can outperform the top-down view. The reality may be significant downgrades during the course of the year. This will be because volumes and prices will have been weaker than hoped and this has a big impact through operational gearing on profits and earnings. In the current environment, with concerns over gross national product (GNP), the impact of deflation, increasingly global (and hence competitive) markets and overcapacity in many areas combine to suggest that caution is needed.

Some of the factors that determine why forecasts tend to prove all too fallible include:

- overoptimism on volumes, prices and costs
- falling volumes and prices picked up with a lag or not spotted
- impact of falling volumes and prices underestimated
- impact of rising volumes and prices underestimated
- cost reductions will all feed through to the bottom line – not if prices and volumes continue to fall (operational gearing)
- not realizing just how bad things are within the company, e.g. losing more market share than realized or finances (especially cash flow) much weaker than appreciated
- previous results achieved through one-off benefits or use of provisions

that run out. In this case the past performance has been distorted and overstated and is therefore an inappropriate benchmark for forecasting.

Sanity checks

Given how many downgrades tend to feature in market conditions at the time of writing it is worth imposing the discipline of a series of sanity checks to make sure you are happy with the forecasts for the company. This will be a crucial determinant of the performance of the shares and so is well worth spending some time on.

You may be using consensus forecasts available from some websites and so think about whether the percentage profit uplift makes sense in the context of the following.

- What is the top-down forecast compared with the bottom-up?
- What are the broader trends in the economy and how does this affect the company?
- What sort of volume growth is realistic given trends in the overall product market?
- Is the volume growth based on market share gains and how will competitors react?
- Where are we in the cycle?
- Are there structural factors that will exacerbate the cycle (for example too much capacity and customers in a weakened financial state)?
- Are there new entrants or competition from other areas?
- What are the trends in overseas markets?
- Beware of straight line forecasting!
- Beware of phrases such as 'this time it's different'.
- Longer-term assumptions: beware of extrapolating too far into the future.

COMPANY PROSPECTS CHECKLIST

This section has detailed what to consider when evaluating the company you are investigating. Here are some of the key considerations.

The business

- Strong market position
- Strong brand
- Pricing power
- High barriers to entry
- Efficient cost base

The management

- A good management with a strong track record
- Quality and integrity
- A management driven by delivering appropriate returns for shareholders

The numbers

- Clean accounting and quality of earnings
- Good performance – return on sales
- Return on capital
- Compensating shareholders for risk – adding value

Financial position

- Good financial position
- Manageable debt and strong cash flow

Prospects and outlook

- Good outlook for volumes and prices
- Confidence in forecast?

3

Valuation

The valuation of a company is driven by the factors discussed in the earlier section on the prospects for the company:

- management and strategy
- performance and returns
- financial position
- outlook and prospects.

These factors can be used to assess why one company's valuation differs from another. It may be that one company is perceived to have a much better management team with a compelling strategy and, as a result, is valued more highly even though all the other factors are similar. Alternatively, the performance and returns may be much weaker, with no real probability of a sustainable recovery – as a result the valuation will be much lower. This matrix provides a useful way of diagnosing the factors affecting the relative valuation.

There are a number of ways to measure the value of a company. This in turn should give an indication of whether the shares are priced correctly. In practice analysts use a number of measures and then take a 'blended' view.

We will explore the following methods of valuation:

- price/earnings ratio
- price/earnings ratio relative
- peg ratio
- yield
- discounted cash flow
- EV/Ebitda
- EV/sales
- price to assets.

▮▮▮ EARNINGS

Price/earnings ratio

This is one of the simplest and often a very effective way of establishing the value of a share. The P/E ratio is simply the share price divided by the earnings per share of the company. This tells you how many years the company would take, with profits at current levels, to make enough money to cover the cost of all the shares in issue. The P/E (and indeed other valuation measures) is often referred to as the stock's 'multiple' or 'rating'.

Be aware that there are some companies for which P/E is completely inappropriate (see 'When not to use P/Es', page 158).

Earnings per share is calculated by dividing post-tax profit by the number of shares in issue.

Example

Let us return to fictional brake-unit manufacturer Full Stop. This company has operating profits of £7.5m. Let us assume that interest costs are £2.5m, so deducting that from the operating profits gives a pre-tax profit of £5m. If the standard tax rate of 30 per cent is applied, post-tax profits are £3.5m. Assume there are 30.5m shares in issue. This gives earnings per share of 11.5 pence (3.5m divided by 30.5m). If the share price is currently 115 pence, you divide that by the earnings per share to give a P/E of 10× (ten times).

For a more detailed analysis of calculating EPS see page 79. The section on earnings is crucial to understand, as this is what the P/E is attempting to value.

So far this measure is based on historic information: the earnings per share from the last set of figures. However, P/E becomes much more useful to investors if a forecast of EPS is used. This, if you like, is shorthand for all the factors analysts believe are relevant to the profit outlook – demand, prices and costs. The analysts should have factored all these into their EPS forecast.

If analysts predict earnings per share rising gently over the next three or four years it tells us they think things are going well. A falling forecast for earnings per share (especially a rapidly falling EPS) tells us that a great deal is going wrong.

In essence the P/E (and the P/E relative) is driven by a combination of

- growth of earnings
- quality of earnings.

It is wrong to focus on one of these in isolation when assessing whether the shares are attractive. As we discussed on pages 86–92 when exploring the quality of earnings, not all earnings growth is going to be valued equally. It depends on where the growth has come from and whether it is sustainable or due to one-off factors. These one-off factors may be property disposals or a reduction in discretionary spending, such as marketing or R&D, that has delivered the growth. Growth needs to be generated by a good performance of the underlying business (strong volumes and prices and a close attention to cost control) if it is to command a high valuation. On the face of it a low P/E is going to be more attractive than a high P/E. But this may not always be the case. There are a number of situations that commonly produce low P/Es but may not mean the shares are cheap. The main factors will revolve around the valuation matrix we identified above.

Why a low P/E may not mean a share is attractive (or 'cheap') may reflect a combination of:

- uncertainty over a company's prospects for earnings
- a highly cyclical sector – again giving a high level of uncertainty
- company serving volatile markets
- a sector with overcapacity and weak pricing power
- a sector or company with consistently low returns (operating profit margins and/or ROIC) and not adding economic value
- a mature sector, with little prospect of growth
- a company which is ex growth
- poor management
- a management with no convincing strategy for growth
- poor cash generation
- weak balance sheet.

The first four factors mean it is difficult to forecast earnings with any accuracy; they have low quality of earnings (as discussed on pages 86–92). This volatility suggests a low P/E. If the earnings are revised down, the shares become a lot more expensive. Indeed, the low P/E may be 'discounting' or anticipating just such a downgrade.

Importantly, the factors in the valuation matrix are clearly interrelated. Furthermore, they tend to reinforce one another. So, for example, a poor profits outlook due to weak pricing as a result of overcapacity would lead to weak returns – low margins and returns on capital employed. This in turn leads to weak cash generation (the higher the margin, the greater the cash generation) and a poor financial position. This puts pressure on the company's plans for investing in the business to generate higher returns and growth.

This 'vicious circle' obviously makes it extremely difficult for the company, and hence the shares, to make money.

There may be instances where the company is actually doing reasonably well but where there is little prospect of further growth, perhaps due to the company dominating its market and/or having good margins, but with no clear strategy for generating growth. The company is effectively ex growth. Again this would lead to a low P/E. If there is not a convincing strategy for value-generating growth, there will be pressure on the management to distribute the cash it generates (or indeed any surplus cash on the balance sheet) to shareholders. The shares would then be attractive on yield grounds but the lack of growth leads to a low P/E.

Conversely, there are a number of situations that commonly produce a high P/E but which may not mean the shares are expensive. These tend to be the mirror image of those driving low valuations and include:

- companies with an excellent growth record and prospects for growth
- a high-growth sector
- high confidence in the company's forecasts
- predictable/stable revenues
- strong market share
- high barriers to entry
- companies that have strong pricing power
- companies that have high margins and produce excellent ROCE and add value
- strong cash generation
- strong balance sheet
- excellent growth strategy.

The first two factors mean the company is seen as a growth investment. As a result of the strong earnings growth, the P/E is likely to be high. The confidence in forecasts and the predictability of revenues suggest that the quality of earnings is high – again a characteristic that will command a higher rating.

The economic characteristics such as high market share, strong barriers to entry and strong pricing power are all likely to translate into high returns on both sales and capital. A good management track record would also suggest that the cost base is being managed well and that the company is focused on the market and takes customer care very seriously. Again these characteristics will lead to a higher valuation.

As mentioned with the 'vicious circle' earlier, the factors here are also closely interrelated. A 'virtuous circle' of growth and high returns will lead to strong cash generation. This will enable the company to fund its own growth strategy without recourse to shareholders. Invested properly, this cash flow will generate even higher growth in the long term. This is dependent on the management having in place an effective and credible strategy for growth.

Re-ratings and de-ratings

When looking at the company you may conclude that the P/E is too low, with respect to both the outlook for earnings and the quality of those earnings. The company is a better business with better prospects than the rating is allowing for. If this is the case, the shares will benefit from what is referred to as a re-rating. This can make for very profitable investing. If the P/E stands on a modest $8 \times$ earnings but actually the business deserves a $10 \times$ rating, this represents a considerable 25 per cent upside. You need to be confident of the assessment you have made to buy the shares on this basis and you should have a sense of what will act as the catalyst to prompt the re-rating.

Some of the factors that might trigger a reassessment of the company's valuation might include:

- results that comfortably beat market expectations
- the market the company operates in performs more strongly than anticipated
- the company continues to gain market share
- a disposal of a business that has been holding back the main business

- a disposal or deal which transforms the balance sheet
- the cash flow profile is far more attractive than originally thought
- a new CEO or management team
- takeover and consolidation activity among similar companies
- improved industry pricing as a result of consolidation.

While there may well be a good case for a re-rating, it often happens that without a catalyst, the shares continue to languish at low valuations. Therefore care needs to be taken.

Conversely, shares that disappoint expectations can undergo a severe de-rating. If the growth expectations that justify the high rating are not fulfilled, the P/E will fall dramatically. As well as the growth being disappointing, the downgrade is likely to flag up risks and issues that were previously thought to be unimportant.

A de-rating might result from factors that cause the earnings to disappoint and lead the growth assumptions to be questioned, such as:

- a new entrant has taken market share
- extra competition from a new product or service
- pricing disappoints
- demand proves to be susceptible to economic slowdowns when it was previously thought to be recession proof
- costs go out of control
- a poor acquisition or strategic decision is made.

The last factor is more a case of management disappointing rather than the growth of the business falling below expectations. Nonetheless, it can be an important trigger for reassessing the company's rating.

The issues of re-ratings and de-ratings tend to affect value stocks and growth stocks respectively. We will explore these investment styles in more detail on page 211.

The advantages and disadvantages of using P/Es

The case for using P/Es is very much linked to the analysis of earnings as a performance number. We saw that accounting issues, the manipulation of earnings and the relationship between earnings and cash were real concerns. However, by focusing on the quality of earnings, we can try to side-step some of these problems.

Given the widespread use of the P/E, it is vital to get to grips with the pros and cons of this valuation measure.

As a performance metric, earnings are an effective shorthand for the issues driving price, volume and costs. The performance of these variables is what will determine the success of the company and the share price. This is corroborated by the attention that is given to consensus earning numbers and when results are announced the relationship between earnings and market expectations. Therefore it is a key number to understand and follow.

The advantages of using the P/E are that:

● it is easy to compute

● it is conventionally and widely used

● it takes forecasts into account

● earnings is a measure of what is generated for shareholders.

The widespread use of the P/E makes it a valuation measure that needs to be understood. For many private investors it also has the advantage of being simple to understand and to calculate. In addition, a lot of information on earnings forecasts is available on the web. Earnings have the advantage of being what is left to shareholders after all other claims on the company's income have been satisfied.

However, even with these genuine attractions, when using a P/E it is important to be aware of the potential pitfalls that attach to it as a valuation measure. This is not an attempt to undermine its effectiveness, but to ensure that great care is taken.

The disadvantages or problems with using the P/E include the following:

● it does not take debt/financial structure into account

● gearing up/share buy-backs increase earnings – but it may be a one-off effect and achieved at the cost of increased risk

● comparisons are undermined by different accounting policies across companies and countries (depreciation, amortization, tax, etc.)

● earnings are particularly prone to manipulation

● targeting earnings may lead to decisions that disadvantage the business

● it cannot be used to value loss-making early-stage growth or cyclical businesses

- it does not take cash generation into account
- it does not take investment returns into account
- growth of earnings may take place at the expense of ROIC (see impact of M&A, page 64)
- growth of earnings may take place at the expense of net asset value (exceptional provisions or provisions set up on acquisition are written off shareholders' funds but allow earnings to grow)
- it presents difficulties in assessing quality of earnings.

One of the difficulties with earnings is when valuing cyclical businesses. Here the logic is often inverted – you buy on a high P/E and sell on a low P/E. This is because earnings are depressed or non-existent at the bottom of the cycle. If earnings are low, the P/E will be very high. If we are indeed at the bottom of the cycle, things can be expected to improve. Investors may want to buy for the recovery and so will take the very high P/E as indicating that we are at, or approaching, the bottom. Conversely, when we come to the top of the cycle, earnings will have recovered substantially, reducing the P/E. Concerns that the cycle will turn down do not make the low P/E attractive.

We have covered the growth of earnings at the expense of returns or assets in the earnings section and when looking at M&A activity. However, it is crucial to ensure that earnings growth is not being achieved by deals or exceptional charges that flatter earnings while returns and assets fall. Similarly, earnings growth that is achieved through increasing the risk profile also needs to be treated with caution.

We explored the benefit of using debt rather than equity and its impact on earnings when looking at acquisition activity on page 64. Here we saw that the tax advantages of using the all-debt option resulted in a massive boost to earnings of the deal. However, the subsequent fall in interest cover illustrated the greater degree of risk involved in this option.

It is interesting to note here the difficulty in valuing the earnings generated by this gearing-up given the higher risk attaching to this strategy. A company that used a combination of debt and equity would have a lower boost to earnings but a much lower risk profile. The problem of considering the whole capital structure and valuation is corrected by looking at a company's enterprise value, which we shall discuss on page 190. The use of discounted cash flow analysis also takes the whole funding structure into account and we shall look at this in detail on page 168.

Price/earnings ratio relative

Once you have established a company's P/E there is a slightly more sophisticated equation that helps to tell whether its shares are cheap or expensive. This compares the P/E of the company to the P/E of the stock market as a whole. The P/E of the stock market and of individual sectors is listed, among other places, in the *Financial Times* on the back page of the Companies section in a table entitled FTSE Actuaries Share Indices. For industrial companies the figure to use is the P/E for 'non financials' (see 'When not to use P/Es', page 158).

If, for example, the stock market trades on a P/E of 20×, a company that trades on 15× is said to have a P/E relative of 75 per cent (15 being 75 per cent of 20). Conversely a stock trading on 30× compared to a market trading at 20× is said to be on a relative of 150 per cent.

The great advantage of using the P/E relative is that it takes into account how the company is valued compared with the stock market overall. In particular it factors in the performance of the company relative to the market in terms of earnings growth. There is an obvious difficulty here if the whole stock market is overvalued – you may be in a company in a better relative position than the market overall, but the absolute level may not be correct.

The same analysis can be carried out for the appropriate sector to see whether the company is cheaper or dearer than its sector peers.

As with the P/E, the P/E relative is driven by a combination of:

- growth of earnings relative to the market
- the quality of earnings.

Clearly companies that have a P/E relative above 100 per cent are those that are perceived to have better growth prospects and better-quality earnings than the market average.

The pros and cons for the P/E apply equally to the P/E relative. The danger of accounting differences between companies creates a particular problem given that the valuation is conducted relative to the market or relevant sector.

What determines the extent of the premium?

The extent of the premium will depend on how long the earnings growth is expected to continue at a high rate and the visibility (quality) of that growth. If we take an example of a company growing at 20 per cent over the next five years while the stock market overall is expected to grow at 8 per cent, then you would expect the premium to be:

$$(1.20/1.08)^5 = 69 \text{ per cent}$$

So a stock delivering this sort of growth would stand on a premium of 69 per cent. In relative terms the stock would be on a P/E relative of 169.

P/Es and P/E relatives

We will now look at examples of both the P/E and P/E relative working in practice.

Example

Pink Tablet

Let us take a fictitious pharmaceutical company Pink Tablet. It has a reliable income stream from a range of drugs including a popular and well-established anti-asthma drug. It also has excellent growth potential from three new drugs which have begun to sell well and from some exciting drug development work which is expected to bring new products to market in the near future. Pink Tablet, therefore, combines a reliable profit stream (quality earnings) with excellent growth prospects. These two factors are reflected in the profits forecasts which, as can be seen in the table below, grow rapidly. Note that today's share price is used for the calculations. The example also assumes that overall the market is forecast to grow at 10 per cent per year.

The table tells us a number of things.

- The P/E at 34.5× in Year 1, on first viewing, suggests that the shares are quite expensive. It would take 34.5 years for the company to make enough money to buy back all its shares at today's price. However, as we know that Pink Tablet has a high-quality earnings stream and good growth prospects, this is not a surprise.

- Looking at the P/E for Year 2 and Year 3 shows us that once the rapid growth in earnings is factored in at today's price, the shares are beginning to look cheaper.

Share price today 875p

Pink Tablet	Year 1 forecast	Year 2 forecast	Year 3 forecast
Pre-tax profit	£100m	£125m	£155m
Tax	30%	30%	30%
Earnings (after tax)	£70m	£87.5m	£108.5m
Number of shares	276m	276m	276m
EPS	25.4p	31.7p	39.3p
P/E calculation	875/25.4	875/31.7	875/39.3
P/E	34.5×	27.6×	22.3×
Market P/E	20×	18×	16×
P/E relative calculation	34.5/20 × 100	27.6/18 ×100	22.3/16 ×100
P/E relative	173%	153%	139%

- The P/E relative at 173 per cent in Year 1 tells us that these shares are much more expensive than the average for the market. With earnings growth at 25 per cent compared with a market growing at 10 per cent, the extent of the premium would be determined by the length of time this differential growth was expected to continue. If it was for, say, four years, you might say that as $(1.25/1.1)^4$ suggests a P/E premium of 67 per cent – not far from its actual rating.

- Similarly, the falling P/E relative for Year 2 and Year 3 tells us that the shares begin to look cheaper relative to the market when the higher earnings growth is factored in.

- The key problem is determining the extent to which the earnings growth and quality are already reflected in the share price. To the extent that the share price is factoring in the 25 per cent growth relative to a market growing at 10 per cent over the next four years, if this is how it turns out, you will not necessarily make money. For the share price to perform it may need growth to be even higher or a new drug to do even better than hoped.

Tin Can

A rather different example is the fictitious company Tin Can. It produces tin cans, which are steadily going out of fashion. A high proportion of its costs are determined by the price of raw materials, which have been volatile over the past few years. There is intense competition, and Tin Can is dependent on a few large contracts with food producers which can easily change suppliers. This is therefore a commodity business (it is very easy to make these cans), costs are difficult to forecast, it is operating in a mature market and there is a high risk that revenues could be affected by the loss of an important contract. It has low-quality earnings (they are unpredictable) and no growth prospects. Both these factors will be reflected in today's share price.

Share price today 100p

Tin Can			
	Year 1 forecast	Year 2 forecast	Year 3 forecast
Pre-tax profit	£20m	£18m	£20m
Tax	30%	30%	30%
Earnings (after tax)	£14.0m	£12.6m	£14.0m
Number of shares	138m	138m	138m
EPS	10.1p	9.1p	10.1p
P/E calculation	100/10.1	100/9.1	100/10.1
P/E	9.9×	11×	9.9×
Market P/E	20×	18×	16×
P/E relative calculation	9.9/20 × 100	11/18 × 100	9.9/16 × 100
P/E relative	50%	61%	62%

The table tells us a number of things.

- The P/E at 9.9× in Year 1, on first viewing, suggests that the shares are quite cheap. It would take only ten years for the company to make enough money to buy back all its shares at today's price. However, as we know that Tin Can has a low-quality earnings stream (i.e. the forecasts are not likely to be accurate) and no growth prospects, this is not a surprise.

- Looking at the P/E for Year 2 and Year 3 illustrates that as there is no earnings growth the P/E remains pretty much the same.

- The P/E relative at 50 per cent in Year 1 tells us that these shares are much cheaper than the average for the market.

- The rising P/E relative for Year 2 and Year 3 tells us that the shares are becoming more expensive relative to the market as other companies in the market grow their earnings more rapidly than Tin Can.

This example shows how useful the P/E relative is when assessing how cheap or expensive a share might be compared with the stock market overall.

If Tin Can were to lose a key contract, which reduced profits by £5m in Year 3, the picture would be very different.

Tin Can	Year 1 forecast	Year 2 forecast	Year 3 forecast
Pre-tax profit	**£20m**	**£18m**	**£15m**
Tax	30%	30%	30%
Earnings (after tax)	£14m	£12.6m	£10.5m
Number of shares	138m	138m	138m
EPS	**10.1p**	**9.1p**	**7.6p**
P/E calculation	100/10.1	100/9.1	100/7.6
P/E	**9.9×**	**11×**	**13.2×**
Market P/E	20×	18×	16×
P/E relative calculation	9.9/20 × 100	11/18 × 100	13.2/16 × 100
P/E relative	**50%**	**61%**	**83%**

Here we see that the risks to forecasts can quickly convert an apparently cheap share into looking horribly expensive. This company, despite all its problems, is trading at only 17 per cent discount to the market as a whole. For such low-quality earnings and no growth prospects, this discount needs to be much greater to represent good value.

Given the background market characteristics that Tin Can faces, we can also see what happens to the P/E if prices fall 5 per cent. Let's say prices fall 5 per cent at the end of Year 1. Revenues are £250m. Therefore, a 5 per cent reduction in prices takes 5 per cent off revenue, i.e. £12.5m. With costs unchanged, operating profits are reduced by £12.5m – from £25m to £12.5m. This illustrates the impact of operational gearing. With interest costs fixed at £5m, the pre-tax profit falls to £7.5m. The table below demonstrates the effect on earnings.

This fall in profits also leads to a weaker cash flow. We have effectively lost £12.5m of operating profit. While this will also reduce the tax charge by 30 per cent, let's assume that with tax of 30 per cent, the net loss is £8.75m. With interest costing, say, 7.5 per cent, this reduces profits by £0.65m.

So if we assume that the lower prices prevail for Year 3 and all other things remain equal (highly unlikely but it illustrates the point), Year 3 forecasts are reduced due to the higher interest costs.

Tin Can			
	Year 1 forecast	*Year 2 forecast*	*Year 3 forecast*
Pre-tax profit	**£20m**	**£7.5m**	**£6.8m**
Tax	30%	30%	30%
Earnings (after tax)	£14m	£5.3m	£4.8m
Number of shares	138m	138m	138m
EPS	**10.1p**	**3.8p**	**3.5p**
P/E calculation	100/10.1	100/3.8	100/3.5
P/E	**9.9×**	**26.3×**	**28.6×**
Market P/E	20×	18×	16×
P/E relative			
calculation	9.9/20 × 100	26.3/18 × 100	28.6/16 × 100
P/E relative	**50%**	**146%**	**178%**

Therefore, these modest changes to pricing assumptions have dramatically changed the valuation. The P/E relative of 61 in Year 2 is transformed to a P/E of 26.3 × and a relative of 146 per cent. Given the low quality of earnings and the fact that earnings are falling while the market is growing, the shares become progressively more expensive against the market.

Clearly the share price looks unsustainable on this basis. The question is then, how far might the share price fall?

If the shares fall back to a P/E relative of, say, 70 for Year 3, the P/E will fall to 16 × 0.7, which is a P/E of 11.2. Multiplying this by 3.5p of earnings suggests a price of around 40p. This represents a fall of 60 per cent. It is contentious whether 70 would be an appropriate P/E relative in these circumstances. The previous relative of 50 or 60 might be more appropriate. However, there might be some sense that the earnings have been hit so hard that they are due to bounce. This may well be the triumph of hope over experience. To a certain extent this is academic – the shares will lose at least 60 per cent of their value.

When not to use P/Es

The use of P/Es may not be appropriate in certain circumstances or for certain sectors/industries. The reasons for this include:

- no earnings
- financial companies such as insurance, banks or property.

No earnings

This may reflect a highly cyclical company where operating profits have fallen into losses. This obviously makes a P/E inappropriate. If profits have fallen to very low levels (but remain positive) the P/E will be so high that it is not meaningful. Alternatively the absence of earnings may reflect a company that is in a 'start-up' phase. The costs associated with developing the business mean that earnings are negative.

In these instances EV/sales or EV/Ebitda measures may be used. We will come on to explore the advantages and disadvantages of these valuation methods.

Financial companies

These are valued on asset values rather than earnings. For example, an insurance company is commonly assessed on how much money is left in its pot of investments after it has paid out all projected liabilities. The equivalent of earnings per share in this case is the money left in the pot divided by how many shares are in existence. Similarly, a property company is commonly assessed on the value of its bricks and mortar, with the equivalent of earnings per share being that value divided by the number of shares in existence. This is called net asset value (NAV).

Peg ratio

This is a measure of value that combines a company's P/E and its rate of earnings growth. It is calculated by dividing the P/E by the growth rate. So for example a stock on a P/E of $20\times$ growing at 10 per cent would be on a peg ratio of $2\times$. The P/E is in theory what investors are prepared to pay for growth and so it should be correlated with growth.

A lower peg value indicates that investors are paying a low price for future earnings growth. Conversely, a high peg value tells us that you are paying a relatively high price for future growth.

This method of valuation is most commonly used for valuing companies that are good growth prospects with good earnings quality. The peg ratio approach to valuing shares has been publicized by investment guru Jim Slater. He suggests that shares are attractive when the peg ratio is somewhere between 0.6 and 0.8. It is often associated with an investment style called 'growth at a reasonable price'.

So let us see what this method would do to our pharmaceutical company Pink Tablet. Its earnings are forecast to grow 25 per cent a year over the three-year period considered above. Let's take year 1, where the P/E is $35 \times$.

$$35/25 = 1.4$$

Some analysts would suggest that a peg ratio of 1.4 was much too high, indicating that the share was already overvalued: others, however, would take the view that the strong and consistent earnings growth and high-quality earnings were worth paying for. Again it depends whether you take earnings growth over one year or whether you take a longer-term view.

Interestingly, the engineering company has falling earnings in Year 1 but rising earnings of 11 per cent in Year 2. This makes the first year peg ratio meaningless while in Year 2 it is $0.9 \times$.

This raises a central problem for the peg ratio – it works far less well for cyclical or volatile earnings patterns. If earnings have collapsed, the next year may show a sharp bounce but from such a depressed level as to make the degree of growth meaningless. The growth over one year is high, but the earnings may just be catching up on where they were two or three years previously. After this recovery they may well fall back again, suggesting that medium-term growth is very low. However, one has to be careful about what the peg ratio is telling you.

As with low PEs, a low peg ratio may be telling you a number of things that may mean the shares are not necessarily cheap.

● High risk and high beta . . . volatile finances and operating gearing?

● There is high risk attaching to earnings forecasts which argues for lower peg.

● Profits will not hit growth targets.

● The quality of earnings is low.

● The projects driving the growth are expected to produce a low return on invested capital.

The peg may also transmit the wrong message if growth is being depressed by revenue investments in marketing, R&D or other longer-term projects, all of which are improving the longer-term growth capability. In this case the peg is not taking a sufficiently long-term view of things.

The message as ever is the need to look at other aspects of the business performance apart from earnings growth, and in particular returns on invested capital, whether value is being added and whether cash is being generated.

INCOME

Yield – investing for income

Another way to assess the value of a share is to look at the income the investor receives from holding the shares. This is calculated by dividing the full year dividend by the share price. The advantage of this method is that it is very simple and can be very effective.

$$\text{Dividend yield} \quad = \frac{\text{Dividends per share}}{\text{Share price}} \times 100\%$$

So assuming a share price of 100p and a dividend of 5p, the yield is 5 per cent. Stock market average yield in 2002 was around 3.3 per cent so such a stock may be attractive if you are looking for income.

Dividends normally consist of two payments: an interim and a final. The interim dividend tends to be around 25–40 per cent of the full year total, while the final typically represents between 60 per cent and 75 per cent. This is because the interim dividend declared at the halfway stage is based on unaudited numbers with only half the year gone and carries more risk. The declaration of the full year dividend will be on audited figures, with not only the full year performance under the belt but also a good sense of how the current financial year has started.

Income can be an important requirement for many investors. A high yield may be attractive on income grounds. However, as with companies on a low P/E, it may reflect poor-quality earnings and low growth. This will mean the shares will find it difficult to increase in capital value. Therefore you may be sacrificing capital growth for income.

Importantly, as we discussed with earnings, it is the future direction of dividends, not their historic level, that is important. Growth of income, as well as initial income, can be an extremely important aspect of the income equation. For example, if you take the last full year dividend of Tin Can, which we will assume was 5p, and divide this by the share price of 100p, it gives a yield of 5 per cent. This compares with a market yield of 3.3 per cent, making it an attractive income stock. The yield relative to the market is therefore 5 per cent/3.3 or 152 per cent.

But bearing in mind some of the problems of Tin Can's business and its limited growth potential, the share price may well fall, wiping out the advantage of the dividend income. Moreover, it is worth noting in this case that as the earnings cover the dividend only two times (i.e. EPS of 10p and dividend of 5p), and earnings are forecast to be flat, there is no realistic prospect of that dividend being increased.

Another factor to be aware of with high-yield stocks is that they are paying out to shareholders a large proportion of their profits. This means that there is relatively little left to be reinvested in the business. This, in turn, may mean that the management is not maintaining the quality of the assets, which may affect its competitive position. In businesses which are relatively asset intensive and where keeping the quality of assets up to scratch is crucial for the competitive position of the company this could be very damaging. As well as a weakening of competitive position, the lack of investment will limit potential growth. Share price weakness of Pizza Express during 2000 was attributed to a lack of investment in the core restaurant chain leading to its premises and service offering being less attractive in a competitive restaurant sector. If the restaurants need a huge investment to be refurbished to an appropriate standard, this could put pressure on the dividend.

Alternatively the high payout ratio may reflect the fact that there are few opportunities open to management for profitable, value-added investment – in this context returning funds to shareholders makes eminent sense. The issue then is to what extent the lack of profitable investment opportunities means, with the company effectively ex growth, the share price will show little capital growth. Remembering that 'total return' is what drives investors (i.e. income and capital growth), this can make for a very poor investment.

Dividend cover and dividend policy

Dividend cover is a measure of the affordability of a company's dividend. It is defined as the company's earnings per share divided by its dividend per share and is normally expressed as a multiple. The higher the cover, the easier it is for the company to pay the dividend and also the greater the scope for growth in that dividend.

Factors affecting security and growth of dividend include:

- level of dividend cover
- financial position – cash flow and gearing
- prospects for the business – the outlook for earnings growth
- investment needed in the business
- returns that can be generated by investment.

A higher level of dividend cover also allows for the dividend to grow in the future. The growth in the dividend will normally be determined by the performance of the company and how this translates into earnings growth. Clearly other criteria will come into play. The need for capital for investment for example will affect dividend policy, as will the indebtedness of the company (gearing). This highlights that the level of the dividend is effectively a capital allocation decision.

Another key issue determining the dividend decision will be the outlook for the company and the confidence the management team has in those prospects. Often a big increase in the dividend is regarded as a bullish signal by investors as it conveys a high degree of confidence by a management team in its future. Conversely, a good set of results that is accompanied by a very small dividend increase may be a cautious message from the management team as to how it sees the future.

While the dividend cover is expressed as earnings/dividends, it has to be paid out of hard cash. Accordingly the cash flow profile of the business needs to be watched when assessing a company's ability to service/grow the dividend.

The stability of the company's earnings and cash flow profile are clearly important in this regard. A low level of cover may be of less concern for a utility that has predictable revenue and earnings streams than for, say, a bulk chemical company where earnings are hugely sensitive to relatively modest movements in demand and pricing (see operational gearing on page 135).

Example

To illustrate the issues involved let's consider two very different companies that might appear attractive on yield grounds. Company A is a utility with visible revenue streams. It has a dividend covered 1.5×, gearing of 65 per cent and stands on a yield relative of 160 (i.e. the yield is 60 per cent greater than the yield of the overall market). Our bulk chemical company, Company B, is in an internationally competitive market that is both cyclical and prone to over-capacity and severe price competition. Gearing is 50 per cent, the dividend is covered 2× and the yield relative is 225.

On the face of it Company B would be more attractive on dividend grounds. The yield is much higher and gearing is lower. However, the utility would be more attractive on the grounds that the revenues and cash flows are highly visible when compared with those of the engineering company. This means its debt/equity profile and its dividend payments are far more manageable. So although the yield relative is lower, the income is far more secure.

Conversely, the level of dividend cover given the business risks facing Company B raises serious issues as to how sustainable this dividend is. A sharp fall in prices would see operating profits drop dramatically. This would see the dividend cover (and interest cover) fall to unsustainable levels and hence the very high possibility of a cut in the dividend.

Cuts in dividend

In the UK the dividend being cut is normally seen as an extreme measure – often in response to a company being in a crisis situation. BT, Marconi and Marks & Spencer are recent examples. This also serves to highlight that the size of a company is no defence when it comes to the security of the dividend. Obviously the cut can be damaging in income terms, but also in capital terms. Having said that, the share price may have been falling for some time in anticipation of the cut and it may not fall further on the announcement.

High yields and dividend cuts

When a stock is yielding (on its historic dividend) substantially above the market yield, say over 8–9 per cent, the market is anticipating that the dividend will be cut. The share price is being based on what the market believes is a sustainable dividend and hence income level. The dividend is therefore likely to be cut the next time the company reports its results.

Given that the share price may well have fallen quite sharply and be in a 'crisis' situation, it is a difficult call as to what you should do with the shares. They may be a 'buy for recovery' as the cutting of the dividend conveys to the market that the company has fully grasped the seriousness of the situation and this will presage a turnaround. Clearly in this situation a whole range of initiatives will be required (not just the dividend cut) to convince investors that there is a strong chance of the company's fortunes being restored.

High yields and low growth

High yields can also be an indication that there is little prospect for capital growth. This may signal a mature phase in a company's development or that the company operates in a low-growth part of the economy (e.g. a utility).

If investors are expecting little capital growth they need a high income to compensate. Also, with a mature business, the management may be faced with the dilemma of whether to invest in new product or geographic areas for growth. If the management has a good record in generating high returns from its investments, investors may well be prepared to allow this. If, however, investors are wary of the returns that any investment may generate (perhaps feeling that the track record is far from encouraging or that funds are being used outside the management's area of competence), the best thing to do is to distribute funds to shareholders through higher dividends. Investors can then choose for themselves where to invest for higher returns. The past ten years or so have seen an increasing emphasis on companies remaining focused, with diversification being achieved by fund managers/investors.

Low yields and high growth

Conversely, a high-growth company will require all available resources to invest in the business. A low yield in this situation is not deemed a problem, as investors will be rewarded with capital growth. If the money invested in the business is capable of generating a much higher return than is generally available to shareholders, it is clearly beneficial for cash to be retained within the business. Again it is worth scrutinizing the management's track record as well as examining the prospects for the markets within which the business is operating. Does the investment make sense? Are the anticipated returns realistic? How will competitors react?

Special dividends and buy-backs

Companies occasionally pay what is called a 'special dividend'. This is, as the name implies, a one-off dividend to shareholders. It is normally done when the company is sitting on a lot of cash for which there is no immediate requirement. The cash on the balance sheet may be the result of the company having disposed of non-core operations. The alternative to a special dividend would be to mount a share buy-back. There may be tax reasons for share buy-backs being preferred. Where there is a 'double taxation' of dividends, i.e. the company pays tax and then shareholders are also taxed on their dividends, buy-backs may be more efficient. The buy-back may also favour investors if it triggers capital gains tax rather than perhaps higher rates of income tax that a dividend might attract. Where this double taxation exists there may be a tendency to minimize dividends and keep the cash within the business. This is not a problem provided it is used effectively. With debt attracting tax relief, this may also lead a company to have a preference for debt rather than equity.

As discussed above it may also be that the market is sceptical as to the management's ability to use the funds effectively in a strategic move such as an acquisition. It may be felt that the return on the money invested, taking into account the risks involved, would be lower than investors could generate in other companies. Accordingly the cash will be distributed to shareholders.

This payment is normally a one-off and it is important to note whether the trend in dividends includes this one-off payment. This is because it might appear that the dividend has been cut when in fact the comparative dividend includes the one-off payment.

Yields back in favour

Out of favour in the mid to late 1990s, yields were deemed a relatively unimportant element of the investment decision. With such strong capital growth the income element of total return was negligible. The fall in capital values since the end of 1999 and the uncertainty attaching to future profit levels (and hence where share prices are going) has seen the importance of dividends increase dramatically. Consensus expectations of total returns (capital growth and income) have fallen back to a level of around 7–8 per cent. With yields in the UK of 3.5 per cent this accounts for half of the expected total return from equities.

However, as we have discussed, ensuring the security of the dividend is crucial. High yields may signal a company in trouble and not an attractive source of income. Related to this, some studies suggest that it is companies that grow the dividend that prove the better long-term investment. Therefore an attractive yield, with a secure and growing dividend, is likely to offer a better total return.

DIVIDEND CHECKLIST

- What are the economic characteristics of the business? How certain are volumes and prices?
- What is the financial profile of the company in terms of debt (gearing) and cash flow?
- How many times is the dividend covered?
- If EPS is manipulated through flexible accounting policies, the cover will be distorted – it will not be a true measure of ability to pay.
- Cash not earnings pays the dividend.
- Is the company underspending on maintaining the fabric of the business (capex) to sustain a dividend?
- Has there been an erosion of competitive position due to underspending?
- If the money is needed in the business, what return would it generate?
- If the dividend is uncovered, the dividend is effectively being paid out of reserves, thus reducing shareholder assets – are you any better off?

CASH FLOW

This is one of the most important drivers of value – the ability to generate cash is critical for any business to be successful. Accounting policies can often be used to flatter the profits and earnings of a business, but it is much more difficult to mislead investors on the cash flow of the company. There may well be year-end window dressing to flatter the debt position, but on a long-term basis the debt position will deteriorate rapidly if the company is not generating real cash.

With cash a key measure of value, we shall look at:

- discounted cash flow
- EV/Ebitda.

Discounted cash flow (DCF) valuation

The calculation

For those not familiar with the maths and the process of 'discounting', a DCF approach can appear a little daunting. But understanding the key concepts is important and straightforward. In particular it is crucial to be aware of the disadvantages of using DCF as a method of valuation. Shares that have been promoted on the basis of looking attractive on a DCF basis have frequently been a disaster. Eurotunnel, Telewest (and other cable companies) and a number of the high-growth stocks of the boom years were all sold on the basis of DCF forecasts. In fairness there were few other ways of doing it – the profits and returns were a long way off and significant amounts of capital were needed to get the projects finished. Nonetheless, being aware of the dangers implicit in this method will help you have the correct degree of circumspection when looking at stocks that are deemed attractive on this basis.

Essentially there are five elements to the process:

1. defining operating free cash flow
2. forecasting the company's operating free cash flows over the initial growth period
3. establishing at the end of this forecast period the 'terminal value'
4. determining the 'discount rate' by calculating the weighted average cost of capital
5. the calculation.

1. Defining operating free cash flow

So what is operating free cash flow? This is normally defined as:

Net operating profit after tax (NOPAT)

+ depreciation

+ amortization

– (maintenance) capital expenditure

– working capital requirements

= operating free cash flow

Depreciation and amortization are added back as they are what are called 'non-cash costs'. This means that while the amounts are deducted to arrive at a profit number, they do not involve an outflow of cash.

Capital expenditure explicitly recognizes that this is a critical component of the company achieving the forecast growth targets. Maintenance capital expenditure is often used in more slowly growing environments or phases of a company's development. This ensures that the fabric of the business is protected, recognizing that maintenance expenditure is a real cost of doing business (a weakness discussed when considering Ebitda as a valuation number).

Similarly, working capital is required as the higher sales over the growth period will require cash to fund the expansion of working capital.

Things to watch

- *Is cash coming from the underlying business and is it sustainable?* While this seems an obvious point, it is always worth ensuring that the cash is coming from the business and is sustainable. A one-off movement in working capital that improves the cash flow profile may unwind in another year.

- *How much is from one-offs, e.g. asset disposals?* There may be one-offs coming from asset or business disposals which again need to be excluded or considered separately.

- *Associate income.* As we discussed when exploring earnings quality and cash flows, it is important that associate income is excluded. In cash flow terms this generates a dividend. Often it is best to exclude this contribution and deduct a value for the associate from the enterprise value (treating it as a 'peripheral asset', see page 192).

- *Minorities*. Again as discussed under earnings, if a part of the business is owned by outside shareholders this also needs to be considered.

2. Forecasting cash flow

The initial period of forecasting is typically between five and ten years. The key variables driving operating cash flow, prices and volumes (which drive revenues) and costs need to be forecast. As the section on the difficulties of forecasting made clear (page 138), this is a hazardous process fraught with difficulties even in the short term, let alone the long term.

The frequency and extent of profits downgrades that have afflicted the stock market since the market peak in 2000 clearly demonstrate the risks and difficulties in forecasting. Interestingly, many of these downgrades have been in perceived growth stocks (e.g. telecommunications or technology) where DCF may well have been used to justify their share price/value. For a highly cyclical business this situation is more complex and in theory one should forecast over a complete cycle of its activity.

Therefore, when forecasting this initial period, care needs to be taken with the following.

- *Forecasting volumes, prices and costs*. As these are the key drivers of cash, great care must be taken arriving at the forecasts. The section on the difficulties of forecasting volumes, prices and costs (page 138) explores the issues and problems at the heart of this element of a discounted cash flow valuation. The impact of operational gearing and the sensitivity of profits and cash flow to changes in price are especially crucial.

- *'Sanity checks' – do the forecasts make sense?* The level of volumes, prices and costs should be subject to a 'sanity check' so that any overoptimistic assumptions are reined in. Are the volume forecasts predicated on taking a degree of market share that will inevitably cause a price war? Are volume assumptions extrapolated on the back of high and unsustainable current levels? Are prices likely to come under pressure from new entrants or customers with strong bargaining power? Are the operating margins realistic in the context of the economics of the industry? Again, it is important to be sceptical of any forecasts used.

- *How long is the growth period?* Over the initial forecast period the company is often in a high-growth phase. This period of high growth and high returns will tend to decay as the company becomes more established. At some stage demand growth slows and increasingly competitive conditions arise affecting growth and returns. The length of this initial period of strong growth and returns is of course subject to considerable uncertainty. In many new industries the growth periods may be a lot shorter than hoped for as maturity quickly follows a period of exceptional growth. Clearly if the industry matures in Year 5 and the forecasts of exceptional growth go out to Year 8, the valuation will fall sharply.

In theory, at the end of the initial growth period returns will fall until the cost of capital is covered. When the company has arrived at this phase of its development, at the end of the initial forecast period, the valuation process turns to the terminal value phase.

3. Terminal value

The terminal value is often 50–60 per cent of the total value of the company. Making appropriate assumptions at this stage of the company's development is therefore crucial. Indeed, flexing the assumptions at this stage can be used to generate a very different result. (see page 186)

There are two ways of determining the terminal value. First, a multiple of the operating profits or operating free cash flow can be used. Alternatively a 'steady state growth' approach can be used.

- *A multiple approach.* With a multiple approach you would take (say) the operating profits at this stage and apply a multiple. Let's say the company is forecast to be generating operating profits of £50m. Having looked at similar companies with these characteristics and growth profile, you find they are trading on 7 × operating profit. You simply multiply the £50m by 7 to generate the terminal value of £350m. This then has to be discounted back to the current value. If the terminal value occurs in, say, Year 7, you would discount back from Year 7.

  The danger, arguably, of using the multiple method is that the absolute nature of using the DCF approach is compromised by using the relative valuation implied by the multiple. It raises questions as to what multiple should be used given the low growth scenario at this stage of the company's development.

- *Steady state growth.* The 'steady state' refers to the maturity of the business and implicitly relatively low growth assumptions should be used. When projecting growth at the terminal phase in a steady state approach, it may be sensible to tie the assumptions to the long-term trend in GDP growth.

There is a formula that can be used to determine the terminal value based on something called the 'Gordon growth model". We will not go into the basis for this here but the formula is really useful.

Terminal value = operating free cash flow/WACC – growth rate

In this case the drivers of value are the cost of capital and the assumed growth rates. The higher the growth rate, the greater the value as you are dividing the operating profit by a much lower figure.

The sum generated by this formula is then discounted back from the last forecast period. So again if you have forecast out to Year 7, the terminal value will be discounted back from Year 7.

We now need to assess the cost of capital and how to derive the weighted average cost of capital.

4. The weighted average cost of capital

Having decided upon the forecasts for the initial growth phase and the assumptions used for the terminal value phase, the cash flows need to be 'discounted'. This means that the future value of the cash is brought back to a current value – the longer away the cash, the less valuable it is.

The cost of capital is determined by the structure of the company's funding – the balance between debt and shares. It is affected by:

- mixture of debt and equity
- debt cheaper than equity
- tax treatment of debt.

The relative cost – debt

The cost of the debt is straightforward to appreciate and to calculate. If the company can borrow from the bank or in the debt markets for, say, 8 per cent, this tells you the cost of servicing the company's debt. Importantly, the interest payments are tax deductible, which makes the debt even cheaper relative to equity. So in this case the cost of debt would be 8 per cent × 0.7 or 5.6 per cent (i.e. deducting the 30 per cent tax charge).

The company's cost of debt will depend on its financial position, as discussed on pages 115–131. The debt rating will have a big impact on the cost of debt. The rating is normally provided by a credit rating agency and is expressed in terms of the rating being AAA or Bb1. The lower the rating, the more expensive the debt. In addition, when an agency downgrades the credit rating, not only does the cost of debt rise but the company's share price normally falls dramatically.

Cost of equity

The cost of equity is more complex and it is important to think about the issues involved. Essentially, the cost of equity must reflect what rate of return an investor requires to compensate for the risks attaching both to shares in general and to a particular company (which may be riskier than the stock market overall).

Reflecting these considerations, it is calculated by reference to:

- the risk-free rate of borrowing
- an equity risk premium to allow for the risks associated with investing in shares
- the volatility of the individual share which is measured by its beta.

The risk-free rate of borrowing is normally based on the interest on a long-term government bond and reflects the 'opportunity cost' of investing in shares: the return you can get without risk. The use of a long-term government bond also ties in with the fact that it is the company's long-term cash flow projections that are being discounted.

The equity risk premium is the return required by share investors over and above the return on risk-free government bonds to compensate for the additional risks involved in equity investment. This is normally calculated by looking at the historic return of equities compared with government bonds, with the difference being deemed the premium required for investing in shares.

However, the use of historic data to determine the equity risk premium immediately creates a problem as investing in shares is a forward-looking activity. Generally the equity risk premium is thought to be between 3 per cent and 6 per cent. Controversy has raged over the past few years as to what exactly the level of this risk premium is. The recent bear market has seen the premium rise significantly as investors have become very aware of the risks involved in shares. During the strong markets of the late 1990s many people argued that the risk premium was negligible – the risk was being out of shares.

The beta measures the degree of volatility a share displays against the overall market and is discussed in much greater detail below.

Taking these three components into account, the cost of equity is then the:

Risk-free rate + (equity risk premium × beta)

If the risk-free rate is 6 per cent and the equity risk premium is 4 per cent, a stock with a beta of 1.2 would have a cost of equity of:

$$6 + (4 \times 1.2) = 10.8 \text{ per cent}$$

As this example shows, the cost of equity is significantly higher than the cost of debt – essentially reflecting the higher risks associated with issuing shares and the tax advantages that debt enjoys.

The importance of beta and the risk premium can be seen by looking at a higher-risk premium and differing betas. If we use an equity-risk premium, of say 6 per cent, and high beta, say 1.5, the cost of equity becomes:

$$6 + (6 \times 1.5) = 15 \text{ per cent}$$

We can see that the cost of equity increases dramatically on this basis. Conversely, if we have the same risk premium (6 per cent) and a company with a low beta (0.5), the cost of equity becomes:

$$6 + (6 \times 0.5) = 9 \text{ per cent}$$

Therefore we can see how sensitive the cost of equity is to assumptions about the equity risk premium and the dramatic difference in the cost of equity for a company with a low beta compared with a company with a high beta. Given this it is worth having a better sense of what beta is and the factors that determine whether it is a high or low number. It is also worth debating whether it is in fact a sensible way of looking at risk.

Beta – what is it?

- *Beta is a measure of how volatile an individual stock is against the market.*

If the overall market rises 10 per cent and a stock rises 12 per cent, the beta would be 1.2. Conversely, if in a market that rises 10 per cent the stock rises only 8 per cent, the beta would be 0.8. The situation would be reversed in a falling market, with the stock on a beta of 0.8 falling 8 per cent in a market that falls 10 per cent.

To derive beta, the stock returns on a monthly basis are recorded normally over a five-year period. This can cause problems for stocks new to the market, but here a comparable company or looking at the company's characteristics can provide a proxy. In the academic theory beta is predictive, i.e. forward looking, and over time will trend towards 1 (i.e. the share ultimately moves in line with the market). This sounds complicated and indeed is . . . different methods and different providers of statistical data can and do provide different betas. This can affect the cost of capital materially.

Again in the technical jargon the 'stock specific risk' of the shares is not included in this calculation. This is because the stock specific risk can be diversified away by holding a portfolio of shares. Equity market risk and volatility against the market is what is being used to determine the cost of capital.

Beta and risk – what determines it?

- *Beta will vary across stocks and sectors.*

Essentially the more cyclical a sector, the higher the beta is going to be. This is because the individual shares will be more volatile than the market overall. Table 3.1 highlights the range across three very different sectors.

Table 3.1 Beta across different sectors

Sector	Stocks	Beta
Defensive	Unilever	0.5
Cyclical	Corus	1.3
Growth	Logica	1.9

Clearly in markets that are going through nervous times, the defensive, lower-risk characteristics of Unilever, the international branded food manufacturer, are going to be something of a 'safe haven'. However, as and when the stock market develops into a more positive mood, this may turn into a disadvantage.

- *High operational gearing v low operational gearing (profit sensitivity).*

Again high operational gearing (see page 135) is likely to see greater volatility, which will see a higher beta accorded. Here for any given change in revenues a much greater change in operating profits will be recorded.

- *High financial gearing v low financial gearing (profit volatility).*

Again, a company that is heavily indebted is a higher risk and will see its profits fall (rise) more dramatically if there is a significant rise (fall) in interest rates.

Beta as a measure of risk?

- *Volatility not risk?*

It can be argued that beta as a measure of risk is not a reliable gauge. It measures volatility which may, or may not, be the same thing as risk. A fundamentally sound, quality company which represents good value may have a higher beta than one which has a weaker market position and poorer prospects.

Warren Buffett has an extremely effective risk assessment procedure. His approach, detailed in his 1993 letter to shareholders, focuses on the following:

- Evaluating long-term economic characteristics of the business – how certain are they?
- Management: are they running existing assets properly? Will they use cash flows properly? Is management working for shareholders or for itself?
- Inflation and taxes – long-term impact on purchasing power.
- Purchase price.

This very much ties in with the approach proposed in Chapter 2 of getting to understand the qualities and performance of the company before going on to assess its value. And as ever when put by Buffett it looks wonderfully sensible and easy. Certainly shareholders in any of the fallen stars of Wall Street (Enron, World Com, Global Crossing, et al) would have been much better scrutinizing the Buffett list rather than worrying about betas. Focusing on the economic characteristics of the business and management represents the key fundamental issues.

The use of purchase price in Buffett's list is interesting. His argument is that if you have done your homework on management and the economics of the business, if the price falls (due to volatility) then do not worry about the volatility but buy more shares at an even cheaper price.

For those who are not algebraically inclined, the following is a source of reassurance.

> Read Ben Graham and Phil Fisher, read annual reports, but don't do equations with Greek letters in them. (Warren Buffett in Janet C. Lowe, *Warren Buffett Speaks*, Wiley, New York, 1997)

Much of this discussion on the cost of capital may feel unnecessarily arcane and obscure. To some extent the Buffett quote has great validity and focuses attention on getting to grips with the company's competitive position and its management quality. Nonetheless, the idea behind the cost of capital is crucial and the principle is quite straightforward. It is essentially saying that you as an investor need to be compensated for supplying risk capital. Importantly this is the cost you want to charge to the company (and its management) for using your money.

You can always adopt your own rule of thumb by assessing the risks in the business as discussed by Buffett and in the section on what drives the beta (i.e. the combination of operational and financial gearing). If there are a number of risks you may want to use a cost of capital of, say, 15 per cent, i.e. this is the return you want from the shares. For less risky and less volatile situations you may feel that (say) a 10 per cent cost of capital is more appropriate. For emerging companies you may feel that 20 per cent is the sort of return you need to compensate for the greater risks you are undertaking.

This then puts an explicit cost on the management for using your money. Can it generate returns that exceed the cost of capital to provide you with a positive return? This is one of the fundamental tenets of equity investment. Again while you may not wish to use the jargon it is important to be aware of the concept. We explored the importance of value added when trying to assess mergers and acquisitions. It is at the heart of many of the debates on corporate governance. A management team may well be excellent at delivering growth and remunerated accordingly. However, if this is at the expense of value added, you as the investor are losing out.

Cost of capital – WACC calculation

Having worked out the way to calculate the cost of debt and the cost of equity we can now compute the weighted average cost of capital.

$$\left(\frac{\text{Market cap}}{\text{market cap} + \text{debt}}\right) \times \text{ cost of equity } + \left(\frac{\text{debt}}{\text{market cap} + \text{debt}}\right) \times \text{ post tax cost of debt}$$

5. The calculation

To illustrate the way in which the discounted cash flow process works we return to our two fictional companies, pharmaceutical stock Pink Tablet and engineer Tin Can. We shall explore the mechanics of the DCF valuation and assess how this valuation method compares with the others.

The operating forecasts are detailed in Tables 3.2 and 3.3.

Table 3.2 Pink Tablet operating forecasts

	Year 1	Year 2	Year 3	Year 4	Steady state
Operating profit	105	130	160	180	200
Tax	30%	30%	30%	30%	30%
Nopat	73.5	91	112	126	140
Depreciation	21	25	28	31	34
Capex	(40)	(45)	(50)	(50)	(55)
Working capital	(15)	(18)	(20)	(20)	(20)
Operating free cash flow	39.5	53	70	87	99
WACC	8.9%				
NPV calculation	39.5/1.089	53/1.19	70/1.29	87/1.41	2912/1.41
NPV	36.3	44.5	54.3	61.7	2065.2
Total	£2262m				

The process:

1. Defining operating free cash flow.
2. Initial growth period.
3. Terminal value.
4. Cost of capital.
5. The calculation.

Operating free cash flow

Table 3.2 lays out the components of operating free cash flow for Pink Tablet. The operating profit is taxed at 30 per cent. Depreciation as a non-cash cost is added back on. We then have to deduct the amount spent on capital expenditure. In this case it is relatively modest as, for pharmaceutical companies, it is the R&D budget that is the major area of investment

The boom years saw a peak in operating margins in some sectors which we are never likely to see again. A combination of strong volumes and pricing enabled margins to expand to very attractive levels. We are also still digesting the extent to which margins were inflated by creative accounting policies.

If prices have fallen dramatically, with no convincing reason why they should recover, it is extremely unlikely that margins will get back to anywhere near their peak level. In the case of sectors exposed to the trends driving deflation, margin forecasts need to be very cautious.

In addition to the factors driving volumes, prices and costs that determine margins, it is worth examining the following:

- What margins are appropriate to reflect the capital intensity of the business?

- When and where was the last peak?

- What has happened to prices since the peak?

- What has happened to costs since the peak?

- Why should they ever get back to peak margins?

- What are margins among competitors?

- Is there new competition?

- Will cost cutting offset poor pricing trends?

Forecasting – common mistakes

Since 2000 there has been a phase of a massive downgrade to earnings expectations which has obviously made it difficult for the overall stock market to progress. This reflects the market's experience that the first downgrade for a company is seldom the last – they tend to come in threes. (This is discussed under the Momentum element of the investment style guide on page 218.)

Why is this and why does it take three or more goes to get earnings expectations back to a reasonable level? Partly it is the hope springs eternal school of forecasting, based more on hope than on cold-headed analysis. This can be the responsibility of an overoptimistic management team or analysts not following the logic of pricing and volume trends and perhaps listening to the management's overoptimism.

and this is charged to costs as a revenue item. Then working capital requirements are deducted. This leaves us with the operational free cash flow.

Initial growth period

We have forecast operating profits out for the first four years. The growth rate is very high in the first two years in particular, with operating profit growing at 23 per cent p.a. This reflects the success of drugs that have reached the market in Year 1 and built up sales in their first two years. This slows down in Year 4. For the sake of illustration we have restricted this initial growth period to the first four years. It will often be the case that the initial period will be for the first seven to ten years. Obviously the risks attaching to the numbers when forecasting out so far increase dramatically.

Terminal value – steady state growth phase

At the end of Year 4 it is assumed that the steady state growth rate slows considerably. The steady state represents an 11 per cent uplift on Year 4. Thereafter it is assumed that the growth rate at this stage falls to 5.5 per cent. This is considerably above the growth rate of the economy (which for the sake of argument grows at a long-term rate of 2.5 per cent).

We will use the formula:

Terminal value = steady state cash flow/ (WACC – growth rate)

We then need to establish the weighted average cost of capital.

Weighted average cost of capital

Cost of debt: we already know that Pink Tablet is very low geared and highly cash generative. As a result it can borrow money very cheaply. We will assume that it pays 6.5 per cent on its debt. Given that interest payments are tax deductible, the net cost of debt is 70 per cent of 6.5 per cent – or 4.6 per cent.

Cost of equity: we know that for a pharmaceutical company the impact of the economy on operating results is relatively low, the operational gearing is relatively low and the company is very low geared (it has little debt). The impact of the economy on operating results is relatively low. As a result the beta of the shares is going to be low. We will use 0.7 – consistent with pharmaceutical shares in the market.

If we take the risk-free rate on a long-term government bond as being 5.5 per cent and a relatively high equity risk premium of 5 per cent given the uncertainty of the current environment then: cost of equity is:

Risk-free rate + (equity risk premium × beta) =
5.5 per cent + (5 × 0.7) = 9 per cent

The mix of equity and debt is very much skewed towards equity. The market capitalization is £2415m, while there is debt of £50m. This gives a business 98 per cent funded by equity and 2 per cent by debt.

Therefore the weighted average cost of capital is:

0.98 × 9 + 0.02 × 4.6 = 8.9 per cent

The calculation
We are now in a position to calculate the DCF of Pink Tablet. The discounting process works as we have seen by dividing the operating cash flow by one plus the weighted average cost of capital with this factored by the relevant number of years.

The formula is normally expressed:

$$\text{OPFCF}/(1+\text{WACC}) + \text{OPFCF2}/(1+\text{WACC})^2 + \text{OPFCF 3}/(1+\text{WACC})^3 \dots \dots \dots \text{OPFCFN}/(i+\text{WACC})^n$$

Table 3.2 demonstrates how the numbers are put together. The series for the initial growth period runs:

$$39.5/1.089 + 53/(1.089)^2 + 70/(1.089)^3 + 87/(1.089)^4$$

Using the formula, the terminal value is 99/ (8.9 per cent – 5.5 per cent) = 2912. As this is the value at the end of Year 4 we then have to discount this back to obtain a net present value. Discounting this back from the end of Year 4, i.e. £2912m/ $(1.089)^{4*}$, gives us £2065.2m (* rounded to 1.41).

The total sum is then £2262m.

This value is the value of the whole business, the enterprise value. To arrive at the value of the shares we have to take the debt off this amount to generate the equity value. Therefore on this basis the equity value is £2262m – £50m = £2212m.

From the market capitalization, we know that the stock market values the shares at £2415m. Therefore we can say that the DCF is producing a value 8.5 per cent below that of the company's stock market value. On this basis, if we believe all our numbers and projections, we would conclude that the shares are overvalued. Alternatively, we can argue that the stock market is making more optimistic assumptions than our central case.

To illustrate the sensitivities involved, if we flex the terminal growth assumption to 6 per cent (feasible given the growth profile of a drug company), the terminal value becomes £3414m; discounted back this is £2421.2m – a £356m uplift on the original valuation. This gives an equity value of £2568m, 6 per cent more than the price of the shares.

Flexing the steady state growth assumption by 0.5 per cent equates to the shares going from being 8.5 per cent dear to 6 per cent cheap.

Table 3.3 Tin Can operating forecasts

	Year 1	Year 2	Year 3	Year 4	Steady state*
Operating profit	25	23	25	22	22
Tax	30%	30%	30%	30%	30%
Nopat	17.5	16.1	17.5	15.4	15.4
Depreciation	20	22	23	24	24
Capex	(20)	(15)	(20)	(15)	(15)
Working capital	(12)	(12)	(15)	(12)	(12)
Free cash flow	5.5	11.1	5.5	12.4	12.4
WACC	10%				
NPV calculation	5.5/1.102	11.1/1.21	5.5/1.34	12.4/1.47	151.2/1.47
NPV	5	9.2	4.1	8.4	102.9
Total	129.6				

The process:

1. defining operating free cash flow
2. initial growth period
3. terminal value
4. cost of capital
5. the calculation.

Operating free cash flow

Table 3.3 lays out the components of operating free cash flow for Tin Can. The operating profit is taxed at 30 per cent. Depreciation as a non-cash cost is added back on. We then have to deduct the amount spent on capital expenditure. In this case we have assumed that maintenance capital expenditure is £15m, £5m below depreciation.

Initial growth period

We have forecast operating profits out for the first four years. For the sake of illustration, we have restricted this initial growth period to the first four years. It will often be the case that the initial period will be for the first seven to ten years. Obviously the risks attaching to the numbers when forecasting out so far increase dramatically.

The forecasts reflect the cyclicality of its markets and the non-existent growth prospects.

Terminal value – steady state growth phase

At the end of Year 4 it is assumed that the steady state growth rate slows considerably. The steady state is unchanged in Year 4. Thereafter it is assumed that the growth rate falls to 2 per cent. This is in line with the growth rate of the economy (which for the sake of argument grows at a long-term rate of 2.5 per cent). This could be a little optimistic given the characteristics of the business.

To generate the terminal value we will use the formula:

Terminal value = steady state cash flow/ (WACC – growth rate)

We then need to establish the weighted average cost of capital.

Weighted average cost of capital

Cost of debt: we already know that Tin Can is highly geared and there are question marks over its cash generation. However, it has locked in long-term loan rates at an attractive 7.5 per cent.

The cost of debt is then 7.5×70 per cent = 5.3 per cent.

Cost of equity: we know that Tin Can is very sensitive to changes in volumes and pricing (which is highly competitive and subject to import competition) and so operational gearing is high. With 50 per cent gearing the company is also highly financially geared. As a result the beta of the shares is going to be high. We will use 1.3 (which is reasonably consistent with engineering shares in the market).

If we take the risk-free rate on a long-term government bond as being 5.5 per cent and a relatively high equity risk premium of 5 per cent given the uncertainty of the current environment then the cost of equity is:

Risk-free rate + (equity risk premium 2 beta) =
5.5 per cent + (5 2 1.3) = 12 per cent

The market capitalization is £138m, while there is debt of £60m. This gives a business funded 70 per cent by equity and 30 per cent by debt.

Therefore the weighted average cost of capital is:

$$0.7 \times 12 + 0.3 \times 5.3 = 10.2 \text{ per cent}$$

The calculation

We are now in a position to calculate the DCF of Tin Can. The series for the initial growth period runs:

$$5.5/1.102 + 11.1/ (1.102)^2 + 5.5/ (1.102)^3 + 12.4/ (1.102)^4$$

The terminal value is 12.4/ (10.2 per cent – 2 per cent) = £151.2m. As this is the value at the end of Year 4 we then have to discount this back to obtain a net present value. Discounting this back from the end of Year 4, i.e. £151.2m/ $(1.102)^4$, gives us £102.9m.

The total sum is then £129.6m.

This value is the value of the whole business, the enterprise value. To arrive at the value of the shares we have to take the debt off this amount to generate the equity value. Therefore on this basis the equity value is £129.6m – £60m = £69.6m.

From the market capitalization information we know that the stock market values the shares at £138m. Therefore we can say that the DCF is producing a value almost 50 per cent below that of the company's stock market value. On this basis, if we believe all our numbers and projections we would conclude that the shares are considerably overvalued. The stock market may be taking into account a more dramatic recovery in its earnings or a much higher growth at the terminal value phase. The characteristics of the business make this an unlikely expectation. However, there is often an overoptimistic view of the scale of earnings recovery. Furthermore, it may be that the price is assuming that the company may be subject to a bid approach – the characteristics of the industry certainly suggest this is needed. Whether it actually happens or not is another issue.

To illustrate the sensitivities involved, if we flex the terminal growth assumption to 4 per cent, the terminal value becomes £200m, which discounted back is £136m. This is a £33.1m uplift on the original valuation to give an equity value of £102.8m. Flexing the steady state growth assumption by 2 per cent equates to the shares going from being 48 per cent dear to a more modest 25 per cent expensive.

DCF advantages

- *Cash – key driver of value.* In theory the value of any asset is the discounted value of the cash it will generate. Therefore cash is the key driver of value. We have identified the manipulation that can occur in the profit and loss account to produce an earnings number that gives the impression of good performance. We have also seen that one of the weaknesses of earnings is that it may not bear any relation to the amount of cash being generated. However, it is much more difficult to distort the cash coming into (or going out of) the business.

- *Absolute measure.* One of the advantages of using a DCF is that it measures the absolute measure of a business – it does not rely on getting a value through comparisons with other 'similar' companies.

- *No accounting issues?* DCF valuation avoids all the accounting issues that have recently plagued markets. The methodology also means that different accounting policies for depreciation or amortization can be ignored.

- *Takes capital expenditure into account.* Unlike the use of Ebitda, the requirement of either growth or maintenance capital expenditure is explicitly taken into account. This spending is crucial to generate the growth on which the forecast cash generation is based or to maintain the competitive position of the business which also directly affects the company's cash flow profile.

- *Long term.* Another virtue (and possibly a vice) is that a DCF valuation relies on long-term forecasts of cash flows to determine value. It should not, therefore, be affected by one unsustainable good year or one exceptional bad year. It is the long-term value that matters. As we have seen, around 60 per cent of the value is determined by the 'terminal value'. This arguably overcomes the short-termist criticism often levelled at other valuation measures.

- *Takes early year losses into account.* An advantage of DCF is that it can be used for long-term growth companies that may be incurring heavy start-up losses. This method allows an equity value to be arrived at where other valuation techniques are clearly inappropriate.

● *Explicitly brings cost of capital into account.* The cost of capital is a crucial cost to the company that is often overlooked. Discounting the cash flows by the company's cost of capital explicitly recognizes its importance in generating value. In turn this reflects the risks attaching to the company and its funding structure. In particular the operational and financial gearing and the company's stage of development are brought into the equation. The higher the risks, the lower the value created by the cash flow when it is discounted back.

● *Sensitivity analysis ... playing with assumptions.* One of the key advantages with using a DCF approach is the way you can play around with various assumptions to see what impact these have on the valuation. Playing around with growth numbers enables you to work out what might happen to the share price if the market's view on growth changes. Similarly, if you feel the risks are higher than the market (or you have a lower tolerance for risk than the market), you can apply a higher discount rate and see whether the shares are still attractive.

An important way in which many analysts use this approach is to look at the EV (the company's market capitalization plus debt and other liabilities) and then see what assumptions the stock market is implicitly making about the growth rate of the company. If, for example, the EV is assuming a 2 per cent growth rate and you feel this is the very least the company can achieve, the shares are potentially cheap. You might then want to both explore the prospects for the company further and consider other valuation methods. You need to be aware of the cost of capital and growth assumptions being used.

DCF disadvantages

There have been a number of spectacular disasters for investors where DCF has been the major valuation methodology used to support the share price or bring a company onto the stock market. Eurotunnel, the cable companies, internet and many technology stocks have to some extent relied on DCF valuations to support their investment case. The example of an initial public offering (IPO) on page 187 highlights the range of values that can be generated by flexing the assumptions in favour of the company.

In many instances this poor record reflects the risks involved in forecasting for companies or projects that are start-ups or at an early stage of development where there are no sales, profits or earnings to value. Another issue has been the fact that the growth potential has attracted a lot of competitors hoping to profit from that growth. Unfortunately that high level of competition depresses returns – there is overinvestment in the sector or industry which leads to a price war to try to win market share. This inevitably depresses returns.

Overoptimism about the growth potential is also a major factor that leads to disappointment. The hoped-for demand often fails to materialize. In addition, the costs of many projects escalate, especially if they involve long-term construction expenditure.

Therefore great care should be taken when using this technique for valuing a share. Some of the key concerns are as follows.

- *Validity of short- and long-term assumptions?* As discussed under 'The risks in forecasting' section (page 131), significant risks attach to all the key variables that drive cash flow. This can affect both the short term and the long term with equal force, though longer-term forecasting is notoriously difficult. The problem with changes to the short-term forecast is that these tend to drive down forecasts over the entire forecast period. In addition short-term numbers are far more valuable in that they are discounted less heavily. Therefore getting the early periods wrong can see a very severe revision to the DCF valuation.

  Similarly, with the terminal value driving around 60 per cent of the result, assumptions made here are crucial. But this is the key problem: they are just assumptions – they are being applied to a point in the future beyond which forecasting is impossible. Given the volatility and difficulty in getting the near-term forecast right, why should assumptions of a company's growth rate in ten years' time have any validity?

- *Subjectivity and sensitivity – assumptions changed to get the 'right' result?* Assumptions made both for the initial growth phase and for the growth at the terminal value phase are highly subjective. This can lead to assumptions being changed to generate the 'right' result. This may be done to make an IPO attractive or an out-of-favour stock look more interesting on valuation grounds.

  The sensitivity of the value to assumptions made can be easily demonstrated. Let's take a company being prepared for a float on the stock market. The sponsoring broker has provided the forecasts and a DCF model as detailed in Table 3.4. The steady state growth is assumed to be 5 per cent occurring after Year 3.

Table 3.4   Discounted cash flow for IPO Plc

	Year 1	Year 2	Year 3	Steady state
Depreciation	20	25	28	30
Amortization	7	7	7	7
Ebit	100	110	122	135
Tax	−30	−33	−36.6	−40.5
Capex	−30	−35	−40	−40
Working capital	−5	−5	−5	−5
Free cash flow	62	69	75.4	86.5
DCF with WACC at 11%	55.9	56.1	55.2	1054.6
NPV	1221.7			
Steady state OPFCF/	86.5/6%			
WACC – growth rate	1441.7			
Discounted from Y3 to Y0	1054.6			

The DCF approach yields a net present value of £1221.7m. The company will have debt of £300m. This implies an equity value of:

$$£1221.7m - £300m = £921.7m$$

However, if we feel that the broker is being too optimistic about:

- the steady state growth assumption of 5 per cent
- the level of risks involved

we can input our own assumptions. Let's see what happens if the cost of capital rises to 13 per cent and the steady state growth rate falls to 3 per cent (Table 3.5).

Table 3.5	A rise in the cost of capital				
DCF at 13 per cent	54.9	54.0	52.3	599.4
NPV	760.6			
Steady state OPFCF/	86.5/10%			
WACC – growth rate	865			
Discounted from Y3 to Y0	599.4			

The 2 percentage point increase in the cost of capital and the 2 percentage point reduction in the steady state growth rate leads to an almost 40 per cent fall in the DCF to £760.6m.

With debt fixed at £300m the equity value would be:

$$£760.6m - £300m = £460.6m$$

This represents a fall in the equity value of 50 per cent. So a 'tweaking' of assumptions leads to a 50 per cent reduction in the value of the shares. The big impact is on the terminal value calculation, with the reduction in the growth rate and the higher cost of capital reducing the terminal value from £1054.6m to £599.4m. Instead of dividing the operating free cash flow by 6 per cent (11 per cent – 5 per cent) we are dividing by 10 per cent (13 per cent – 3 per cent). Therefore it can be seen how incredibly sensitive the company's value is to relatively minor adjustments to changes in the assumptions. (It should be noted that this example is illustrative only, as in most DCF projections the initial growth phase would stretch out to Years 7–10.)

With this approach we can examine what has happened to the valuation of the high-tech growth stocks. Having disappointed expectations, growth forecasts have been reduced dramatically as it has become clear that they were susceptible to trends in the broader economy and in particular falling capital expenditure. Whether these areas of the market offer real growth is now increasingly questioned.

Effectively both the period and the extent of super-normal growth have been reduced, with devastating consequences for the DCF. Similarly, the extent of the growth at the terminal value stage has been revised down substantially. The development of operating profits and hence cash flow has therefore been downgraded dramatically.

The rising cost of capital as well as the downgrading of cash flow forecasts has also exerted pressure on valuations. The greater risks and higher volatility that have become increasingly apparent translate into a much higher cost of capital. The whole market has seen the equity risk premium rise, increasing that component of the cost of capital.

The substantial downgrades, as the impact of operational gearing became apparent, highlighted the volatility and risks at the individual stock level. In addition, the companies' financial position deteriorated dramatically, with higher debt levels resulting from:

- debt taken on to fund deals that did not deliver hoped-for returns
- debt taken on for massive investment programmes
- the reduced profit forecasts and lower margins producing weaker cash flow and higher debt.

This combination of higher operational volatility and higher debt has led to the company's beta increasing significantly.

A combination of these can see the discount rate required rise rapidly. An increase of 2 percentage points in the equity risk premium (ERP) and the move of, say, 1.5 to 2 in the beta can see the cost of capital rise considerably. With the risk-free rate at 5.5 per cent, if the ERP was 4 per cent and rose to 6 per cent, the cost of equity would rise from 11.5 per cent to 16.5 per cent. This would seriously damage the DCF valuation, as the examples illustrate.

- *Forecast period of super-normal growth and returns?* As discussed earlier, one of the key components in the DCF calculation is forecasting out to the terminal growth phase. This early period tends to be the period of 'super-normal' or higher growth. Again, the difficulty is forecasting both the level of this growth and how long this phase will last. With a growth industry a lot of capital may be attracted which depresses pricing below forecast levels. In addition, maturity can happen very quickly and the industry settles down into a more mature phase much earlier than anticipated. Mobile telephony is an industry which has seen explosive growth but has arguably become mature sooner than anticipated. With massive investment in new technology (3G), the low growth level damages the DCF model considerably. Much debate is taking place over what will be the key driver that will enable superior growth rates to be re-established.

- *Complexity of calculation.* For private investors in particular, the complexity of doing both the forecasts of operating cash flow and arriving at the cost of capital makes this approach to valuation rather esoteric.

Finding the beta and the cost of debt can be awkward. Even if you do not intend to use this rather complex method, it is nonetheless important to be aware of its strengths and weaknesses to enable you to spot flaws in research that might be championing a share because of its attractiveness on DCF grounds and to help you approach it with a healthy dose of scepticism.

ENTERPRISE VALUE

Enterprise value features heavily in investment valuation procedures. Essentially it is the sum of all the liabilities required to purchase 100 per cent of a company's cash flow. In particular it takes debt into account with respect to valuations.

Many users of EV and definitions of EV simply add on debt. This is easy to compute and certainly has its advantages. It must be borne in mind, though, that there are other liabilities a company may have (pension fund liabilities in particular are topical and extremely important). These liabilities are potentially very significant. A takeover of a company with such liabilities could increase the acquisition cost considerably. Alternatively, of course, if the liabilities are expensed through the P&L, earnings may fall sharply. Critically, these liabilities will have an impact on earnings, cash or both. This obviously reduces the earnings and cash available to the company and its shareholders, damaging the value of the shares. Therefore if you invest in a company without being aware of these liabilities it could prove costly.

EV is especially useful when comparing companies that may have different accounting or tax regimes and is important in an increasingly cross-border/global investment environment. It has been useful also in valuations in European countries with a history of cross shareholdings and significant minority holdings. The implication here, of course, is that the company will not enjoy 100 per cent of the cash flows of its associate or majority-owned holdings. Enterprise value will take this into account and make comparisons easier.

The other important aspect of EV is a focus on trying to value the core business. Stripping away the effect of cross shareholdings and the presence of associates and minorities enables the key core business to be valued on a clean basis.

Reflecting these considerations, the formula that tends to be used is:

**EV = Market cap + average debt + buy out of minorities +
provisions – peripheral assets**

Because it takes into account debt and other liabilities it can be an effective check on looking at the share price/market capitalization in isolation. This overcomes one of the weaknesses of the P/E – which does not take into account the funding structure of the company.

In recovery-type situations, for example, many investors assume that as the share price has fallen from 100p to 25p it is potentially very attractive. If, however, there has been a significant cash outflow or the emergence of previously unknown liabilities (off balance sheet debt, pension fund shortfalls), the valuation on an EV basis might be identical to that before the share price decline. So a market capitalization fall of £1bn may be off-set by debt and other liabilities rising by a similar amount. The recent plight of Marconi is perhaps a good example of this.

Average debt

The average is used to give a much fairer view of the company's indebt-edness. Debt may swing markedly during the course of the year for seasonal trading reasons. In addition, a company will often make sure it manages assets, especially working capital, quite aggressively towards its year end to minimize year-end debt. Indeed, year ends may be selected to fit in with a seasonal low in debt levels.

Another important thing to bear in mind is any outstanding preference or convertible bonds; make sure these are reflected in the debt number. Companies may not include these in their definition of debt and gearing, so care is needed. These can be converted into equity if preferred. Similarly, off balance sheet debt and finance leases also need to be taken into account to get a comprehensive view of the company's indebtedness.

Buy out of minorities

Where a company has, say, 80 per cent of another company, while it consolidates 100 per cent of the profit, the owners of the other 20 per cent have a right to the income on their share of the investment. Therefore you would need to buy out the minority shareholders if you were to enjoy the benefit of controlling 100 per cent of the cash flows. They might or might not wish this to happen and again it can be difficult saying what this might cost. The value of the parent company can be used as an approximate guide.

Provisions

These may relate to the liability that would be assumed by a new owner in connection with, say, a pension fund or making good any environmental damage the company may have caused in the course of its operations. These can be very substantial amounts and need to be considered carefully. In a takeover situation, another form of liability may be the costs of closing operations and the associated costs of redundancy payments. As an investor these provisions will see a cash expense even if there is no impact on earnings.

Peripheral assets

With the EV you are trying to value the 'core' business. Accordingly, the value of non-core assets is subtracted. These may be property assets or investments in other companies or assets. Investments in other companies are called 'associates'. Normally a company will book its 'share' of the profits of that investment (for example it may 'book' 20 per cent of the profit of a company where it has a 20 per cent holding). If associates are treated as a non-core asset, care must be taken to strip out their contribution to profits and earnings. That is why ratios using EV tend to refer to 'operating' income or assets precisely to exclude the non-operating income from associates or investments. In addition, it is worth pointing out that while 20 per cent of profit may be 'booked', the income/cash flow effect is determined by the amount of dividends distributed by the company invested in.

Summary

The computing of all the liabilities of a company may appear daunting. It is a good discipline to try to establish potential drains on the company's earnings and cash flow. You may well find it much easier to use market capitalization plus debt as your proxy for EV. This is going to be useful as it takes into account a company's funding structure. However, being aware of other potential liabilities may help you walk away from investing in companies which are high risk because of those potential liabilities.

EV/Ebitda

The Ebitda can be worked out by taking the operating profit (from the profit and loss account) and adding back the non-cash costs of the business, depreciation and amortization (see advantages and disadvantages of Ebitda, page 100).

Ebitda on its own is of limited use because it tells you only what the cash stream is, not what you are paying for it. Therefore analysts compare the Ebitda to the enterprise value, which is the total cost of the company (market capitalization plus all its liabilities). As the Ebitda is generated by all the assets at the company's disposal, you need to take the whole funding structure into account to value it.

Example

In the case of Tin Can we are assuming it has debt of £30m and environmental liability to clean up some contaminated land which is expected to cost £10m.

Tin Can	
	Year 1
Pre-tax profit	£20m
Interest	£2.5m
Forecast operating profit	£22.5m
Depreciation	£20m
Amortization	£2m
Ebitda calculation (in millions)	22.5 + 20 + 2
Ebitda	£44.5m
Market capitalization	£138m
138m shares × 100p	
Liabilities	
Debt	£30m
Environmental liabilities	£10m
EV calculation (in millions)	138 + 30 + 10
EV	£178m

The next step is to divide the EV by the Ebitda (similar to a P/E, this gives a measure of how many years it would take to generate the cash to pay the full value of the company). This is normally expressed, again like a P/E, as a multiple. The average EV/Ebitda for companies in the stock market is normally between 8× and 10×. The lower it is, the cheaper the share is looking, although bear in mind earlier warnings about the quality of the company. In addition, all the issues surrounding the quality of earnings apply with equal force to Ebitda. Of course, again one must remember that it may be worth paying for an 'expensive' share if the company has both steady income and good growth prospects.

So for Tin Can the EV/Ebitda calculation is:

$$178/44.5, \text{ which gives a multiple of } 4\times.$$

As we would expect, this makes the share look very cheap. However, we have noted all the risks attaching to the forecasts and the quality of earnings. Therefore, as with P/Es, EV/Ebitda depends on the growth and quality of the number. In addition, it also depends on the capital intensity of the business – the more capital you need in the business, the lower the multiple. Obviously, it is more attractive to have growth that does not require a lot of capital investment.

The other danger with using this valuation, as we discussed when looking at it as a performance number, is the fact that it does not take into account the need for capital expenditure. Depreciation is a real cost of doing business and maintaining the fabric of the business is crucial. This is why the operating free cash flow measure is preferred as it explicitly takes into account the need for capital to generate the company's sales performance and growth. (It also takes into account the taxation impact on returns.)

As with P/Es, the issue of growth and the impact on returns needs to be considered. Many of the companies that promoted the use of Ebitda and focused on its growth have been consistent destroyers of shareholder value. The deals or investment undertaken, while having delivered growth in Ebitda, have failed to cover their cost of capital.

The advantages of Ebitda are that:

- it takes the whole funding into account (unlike P/Es)
- it allows comparisons between companies with different accounting policies towards depreciation and amortization
- it ignores exceptional charges, again allowing comparison
- it is a cash flow-based measure
- it can be used for growth companies incurring start-up losses.

The disadvantages of Ebitda as a valuation number are as follows.

- Is Ebitda being used when all other measures are disappointing?
- Depreciation is a very real cost of doing business.
- The need for maintenance capex within a business and the need to fund working capital suggest that Ebitda is not a true measure of cash flow.
- Ratio will vary with differing capital intensity.
- What does it measure, neither cash nor profitability?
- Earnings can still be manipulated.
- Earnings before interesting things . . . missing the crucial story of what is happening further down the P&L?
- Investment can grow Ebitda (ebit, depreciation and amortization), but what is the rate of return on that investment compared with the cost of capital?
- What is happening to interest costs?
- What is the impact on gearing and risk?
- It is used in capital-intensive, high-growth industries where no profits/ EPS are generated . . . but over-investment and low returns?
- Variations in tax charges may mean a different outcome for shareholders.

SALES

Another way to measure the value of shares is to consider the sales of a company compared with its enterprise value. This measures how cheap or expensive it is to buy the company's sales. One advantage of this method is that it is difficult to distort sales figures, so it is a useful way of comparing similar companies with quite different accounting methods.

The sales figure can be found in the P&L. The enterprise value is calculated by adding the market capitalization of the company to the debts and liabilities as outlined above. Some commentators use market capitalization to sales ratios as a valuation technique. EV/sales is more comprehensive and takes into account the fact that sales are generated by the whole capital structure, not just equity (which drives the market capitalization).

So assuming sales are £60m and the EV is £120m, the calculation is 120/60 which gives EV/sales equalling 2× or 200 per cent. This effectively means that you are paying £2 for each £1 of the company's sales.

EV/sales should not be used when comparing companies with very different profit margins. The EV/sales ratio will be much higher for companies that have a high profit margin. In theory, higher capital intensity should lead to higher margins (see returns, page 101–115).

These higher margins are often found in companies that employ a lot of capital, for example a cement works or complex manufacturing process where the plant is expensive. Of course, these higher operating margins are required to ensure that an appropriate return on capital is generated (see page 108). Conversely, where relatively little capital is needed, e.g. a distribution business, margins will tend to be lower and the EV/sales will therefore also be lower. Comparing the EV/sales of two diverse activities, with differing capital intensity, would tell you little of value.

The valuation of sales is critically dependent on the profitability of those sales. As we discussed when looking at sales as a performance number (page 76), a company that goes for market share might drive down the profitability (operating margins) of those sales dramatically. These low-margin sales are clearly worth less than very profitable sales.

The EV/sales ratio therefore is related to:

- the operating margins the company generates
- the confidence in those margins being sustained
- the growth rate of the company's sales
- the quality or visibility of those sales.

As a rule of thumb, a company with operating margins of around 10 per cent, generating sales growth of around 5 per cent would trade on around 100 per cent or 1 x sales.

With respect to our engineering company, Tin Can, there are a number of threats to prices and therefore the confidence in margins is correspondingly low. Accordingly one might expect to see a lower EV/sales ratio, perhaps in the range of 70–80 per cent of sales.

We have seen that a 5 per cent reduction in prices, an all-too-feasible possibility, would halve operating margins and see margins fall to 5 per cent. This would suggest that the EV/sales ratio would fall to 40–50 per cent or 0.4–0.5×. Interestingly, looking at the EV/sales ratio for Corus (previously

British Steel), by getting its market capitalization data, debt and sales figure from its R+A, reveals a value of around $0.3\times$. This suggests the market has a cautious assessment of its sales growth and likely margins.

Conversely, the high margin, predictable sales and potential from the research pipeline at Pink Tablet suggest that it should command a very high EV/sales ratio. The margins at 25 per cent would immediately imply a ratio of 250 per cent. The high sales growth would expand the premium significantly while the potential of the research pipeline would also need to be taken into account. (This pipeline will generate sales in the future.) In our example the ratio emerges at $4.5\times$ sales. This compares with an EV/sales ratio for the sector of around $3.5\times$ at the time of writing.

The risk in this case is if a major drug comes off patent and is subject to generic competition. This would see margins for this product fall dramatically. Clearly, while average margins for a drug company are high this will inevitably conceal a wide variation, with ex-patent parts of the portfolio generating low margins and best-selling, well-protected products very high margins. So the drug going off patent is likely to be achieving margins much higher than the average.

The sharp contrast between Pink Tablet and Tin Can's margins and corresponding sales valuations is important. You can also get a sense of an industry's margins by looking at the EV/sales ratio. If it is low you will have a reasonable expectation of margins and sales growth being low or uncertain to predict.

The food retailing sector has a ratio of around $0.5\times$ and margins for the individual companies do indeed tend to be in the region of 4–6 per cent. These companies have relatively little capital employed as the working capital tends to be financed by suppliers. As a result this low ratio is not a problem as the companies generate very good returns on invested capital. Automobiles and parts are trading around $0.4\times$. Margins due to competitive pressures and the purchasing power of the big car makers also tend to be very low. Unfortunately, unlike the food retailers, these companies tend to employ significant amounts of capital. As a result returns on invested capital tend to be low and not cover their cost of capital. This is why care is needed when comparing EV/sales ratios across sectors – capital intensity and the type of capital needed may vary enormously.

Historically it has been felt that sales were one of the few numbers not subject to widespread accounting manipulation. As a number tends to become popular as a valuation measure, however, there is an incentive to manipulate that number. This tends to boost profits as there is a 'mismatch' – the costs related to those sales are invariably not recognized until they are incurred at a much later date.

Therefore, when looking at the EV/sales ratio, things to bear in mind include:

- do not compare ratios of industries with different capital intensity
- be careful of sales manipulation, especially in long-term contract-type businesses
- ratio will be driven by margins and sales growth
- Falling prices will dramatically reduce margins.

EV/sales

Returning to Tin Can and Pink Tablet we can see how the interplay of a company's prospects, operating returns and financial position impact on the valuation of its sales. We also consider some of the risks to those prospects and returns and the dangers to the valuation of the shares.

Table 3.6   Tin Can – financial position and returns

Debt	£60m
Shareholders' funds	£100m
Gearing calculation	
Debt/shareholder's funds	60/100
Gearing	60%
Total sales	£250m
Operating profit	£25m
Depreciation and amortization	£20m
Ebitda	£45m
Operating profit margin	10%
Invested capital	£200m
Return on invested capital calculation	25/200
Return on invested capital	12.5%
Interest cover (operating profit/interest)	25/5
	5×
Share price	100p
Market capitalization	£138m (100p × 138m)
Enterprise value	£198m
Enterprise value/sales ratio	0.8× or 80%
Enterprise value/Ebitda	4.4×

Financial position

Gearing at 60 per cent (Table 3.6) is moderate to high, but not necessarily a major problem if the performance remains at current levels (a big if). The cash generation and the need for capital within the business do need to be watched closely however.

Similarly a 5× interest cover is reasonable, though subject to the same caveats (see below).

Returns

Operating margins at 10 per cent are reasonable. However, bear in mind that if a contract is lost, raw material costs rise or prices fall (all distinctly possible given the nature of the industry/business), these operating margins are very vulnerable.

Return on invested capital at 12.5 per cent before tax translates to 8.75 per cent after tax and is unlikely to be covering the cost of the capital (which in this instance would be around 10 per cent). Even before bearing in mind the risks shareholders are running, the return is not attractive.

How would you value these sales? Remember that both the sales and the return on those sales are difficult to predict, and that the sales are static (no growth in the medium or long term).

The stock market is giving a low valuation of the sales of Tin Can – each £ of sales is being valued at 80p. The (relatively) low margins, static/declining sales outlook and the vulnerability of those margins all suggest that the market is right to do this.

Risks to returns – key sensitivities

- Any fall in margins would of course reduce operating profit and the return on invested capital. In the example of the lost contract (see previous case study), this falls to 10 per cent.
- Falling prices would be even more devastating. A 5 per cent drop in prices would take 50 per cent off profits (5 per cent of the company's turnover of £250m is £12.5m). This is called operational gearing – price reductions come straight off the bottom line.
- The pre-tax return on invested capital also halves to 6.25 per cent.

Why is this important?

- Covering cost of capital – is it worth the risk? A 5 per cent reduction in prices (very feasible given the nature of the industry and competitive structure) automatically means that the company is destroying more value. The fact that it is failing to cover the cost of capital means that investors would be better off with their money in the bank (which would be risk free).

- The interest cover would also fall to $4\times$ in the lost contract scenario. This is not too problematic, but getting scary.

- However, on a 5 per cent price reduction, interest cover falls to $2.5\times$. This is potentially a very serious state, with banking covenants possibly being breached.

Conclusion

This example neatly demonstrates the interplay between performance and prospects on the one hand and the financial position of a company on the other. Deterioration in the trading environment, weaker volumes and/or prices could cause a serious decline in performance. This in turn would lead to question marks being raised over the company's financial position.

Pink Tablet's financial position

With gearing of 12.5 per cent the Pink Tablet balance sheet is very strong (Table 3.7). The excellent interest cover of $21\times$ reinforces this. Therefore there is little financial risk in Pink Tablet.

Returns

The operating margins at 25 per cent are at a very attractive level. The success of new drugs should help sustain or possibly increase these margins.

The pre-tax return on invested capital of 23.3 per cent translates to a post-tax return of just over 16 per cent, which is well above the cost of capital and rewards shareholders amply for the risks involved.

How would you value these sales?

- Remember not only the high returns but also the fact that these sales are growing rapidly driven by the new drugs coming through the pipeline.

Table 3.7	Pink Tablet – financial position and returns

Debt	£50m
Shareholders' funds	£400m
Gearing calculation	
Debt/shareholders' funds	50/ 400
Gearing	12.5%
Total sales	£420m
Operating profit	£105m
Depreciation and amortization	£21m
Ebitda	£126m
Operating profit margin	25%
Invested capital	£450m
Return on invested capital calculation – Operating profit/IC	105/450
Return on invested capital	23.3%
Interest cover (operating profit/interest)	105/5
	21×
Share price	875p
Market capitalization	£2415m (875p × 276m)
Enterprise value	£2465m
Sales	£425m
Enterprise value/sales ratio	5.8× or 580%
Enterprise value/Ebitda	19.6×

- The stock market is putting a high value on these sales – each £ of sales is being valued at £5.80. The high margins *and* the rapid growth in sales are being factored into this valuation.

- The EV/sales is also, in effect, putting a value on the pipeline of sales. If you assume that a certain portion of the drug pipeline converts into future sales and the value of these is discounted back, the ratio would be lower.

- These high margins translate into a very high post-tax return on capital employed of 16 per cent. This is well above the cost of capital.

- The risks would revolve around a) patent expiry, b) a withdrawal of a drug due to adverse side effects, c) government pricing pressure and d) a rival developing a more effective drug. While important, these are less likely to affect the company in the short-term than the issues affecting Tin Can.

Risks to returns are as follows.

- If a drug with £200m of sales goes off patent (or is affected by a new, more effective competitor drug), operating margins on that product may fall from, say, 30 per cent to 10 per cent. This would take £40m off profits – or 40 per cent off Year 1 forecasts. The share price would fall 40 per cent if the P/E was to remain constant.

- However, the stock market may also question the basis for that high P/E, i.e. that the previous earnings growth is no longer attainable and therefore the P/E falls from, say, 35× to 25×. In this latter scenario the share price falls to 380p from 875p – a fall of 57 per cent (25× (25.4p × 60 per cent) = 25× 15.2p).

- Clearly this is an unrealistic example, as these issues are unlikely to happen so suddenly. Nonetheless, they highlight the potential down-side and valuation risks for high multiple/high return growth stocks that lose that tag.

Conclusion

The returns and growth potential of Pink Tablet are clearly very attractive. In addition the financial position is robust. The difficulty is trying to work out when these strengths are fully discounted in the share price.

PRICE TO ASSETS

Finally, another way to measure the value of a company is to see how the share price relates to the book value of the company's assets. As a result it is often known as the price/book ratio.

Measuring value on an asset basis is particularly useful for property companies and financial organizations such as insurance companies and banks. Investment trusts are also valued this way. These companies are measured according to their net asset value, also sometimes known as shareholders' funds. This is simply the value of the company's assets. So in the case of a property company it would consist largely of the collection of properties in which it has invested (minus any debt). For an insurance company the assets are largely the group's investment portfolio, those things in which the company is putting its income and from which, in the future, it expects to pay any claims. Of course this is after liabilities have been deducted.

Increasingly, with many companies having few assets (e.g. service-related companies) or intangible assets or goodwill that has been written off, price to book-type considerations are irrelevant for many sectors or companies.

Net asset value (NAV) can be expressed either as an overall figure or, if it is divided by the number of shares in issue, referred to as NAV per share.

One key thing to remember with NAV is that companies often trade below their asset value. For example, a property company with net assets of £100m may trade at a market capitalization (price of shares multiplied by the number of shares in issue) of £80m. This would be expressed as trading at a 20 per cent discount to assets. There may be good reasons for this.

Shares may be on a discount due to the following factors:

- the assets may not easily be sold (illiquid)
- the assets may be difficult to value
- the assets may be overvalued
- there may be concerns that the assets are falling in value
- they are generating a very poor rate of return, with little prospect of that changing
- selling the asset would create a tax liability.

In other circumstances shares on a discount to asset value may be attractive. The question to ask is what will trigger the shares moving back towards their asset value. This may be a realization that the assets are correctly valued, are generating good returns and are likely to grow in value.

Of course it is possible for companies to trade above their asset value, known as at a premium to assets. This could be because investors are expecting an improved valuation of the assets shortly or the assets are generating excellent returns.

Another factor, which can cause a reassessment of asset values, is take-over speculation. The assets may be valued low by the stock market but might be worth a lot more to a competitor or another industrial company. Buying a share because you believe the company may be taken over is a high-risk strategy. For one thing it may not happen; more commonly you may have to wait a lot longer than you think and you would have been better off invested elsewhere.

Sum of the parts

A variation of looking at NAV is to do a 'sum of the parts' calculation. For a company with very different businesses it may be more appropriate to try to value each of the businesses separately, commonly by reference to similar companies quoted on the stock market. This is often done if one of the businesses is a 'jewel in the crown' and the overall valuation fails to take into account the quality of this division. It may be that there is pressure for the value to be unlocked by demerging the quality business, which would create value for shareholders.

SUMMARY

As the valuation section has demonstrated there are strengths and weaknesses with all commonly used valuation measures. Alas there is no holy grail, no one ratio that compellingly provides all you need to know. Focusing on one variable can be dangerous, especially if it is the variable preferred by management. This inevitably creates an incentive to manipulate that number, which distorts the performance of the company and may well lead to decisions that undermine the business in the longer term. Using a combination of valuations when assessing a share is crucial.

An appropriate, wealth-creating triangle would consist of:

- sales and earnings growth
- strong finances and cash generation
- economic value added.

These factors need to be scrutinized closely and in relation to each other when trying to arrive at a valuation. This will help avoid looking at earnings growth in isolation and therefore seeing value happily destroyed by management as everyone applauds the 'ability' to grow earnings. Again it is important to consider earnings quality as well as quantity. Taking sales growth into account will help establish the underlying performance of the business.

Similarly, large restructuring or exceptional charges earnings may produce earnings growth. However, cash will be affected by the restructuring charges and the write-downs will see net assets per share reduced. These concerns are particularly relevant in deal-driven companies, since as shown very few mergers and acquisitions actually add value. Considering organic sales growth will help focus on the underlying performance of the business and whether the company is delivering 'real' growth as opposed to earnings driven by one-off benefits.

You can see whether cash is being generated by looking at the trends in net debt. While clearly if the company is investing aggressively (a high capex to depreciation ratio) debt may rise, you can then focus on the next issue of whether those investment projects are critical to the performance of the core business and whether they are likely to generate value.

The inability to add value, especially over a long period, immediately highlights the dangers of investing in such a company or sector. The risks are clear from the outset – returns will not compensate for the risks involved. If the extent of value destruction is too great, why on earth will things change sufficiently for value to be added? Here it is always worth remembering Buffett's dictum on the reputations of management and industries/companies. If the business has a poor record in generating value, it is likely to reflect an industry with poor economics, a company with a weak competitive position, or both. It is highly unlikely that management will reverse it.

Therefore, looking at value creation can help eliminate potential disasters or investments that are unsuitable because they do not meet your appetite for risk. This suggests that there is an opposite of the wealth-creating triangle: a Bermuda triangle of wealth destruction, poor earnings growth (combined with poor earnings quality) and a weak financial position and weak cash generation.

It may help when considering all the various valuation techniques to think about which part of the P&L account is being valued. Then compare this to the market's rating of these measures. These are detailed in Table 3.8 for the UK market as at the end of 2002.

To ensure a blended approach to valuation you may want to use screening devices offered by some websites. This would enable you to combine, say, a P/E relative, sales and earnings growth, a given yield requirement with a certain level of dividend cover, a minimum ROIC number and a maximum debt/equity or minimum interest cover ratios. This would combine a valuation and income measure while the financial position and ROIC help protect the downside risk. Focusing on the potential risks is a crucial element of the investment process. The value destruction of the boom years – companies investing aggressively in growth or engaging in deals or investments that fail to cover the cost of capital – has hit share prices and valuations extremely hard. This has led to an increased focus on company's generating positive returns for shareholders and compensating them for the risks they as owners of the company are undertaking.

Table 3.8	Valuing different parts of the P&L
Valuation	
Sales	1.2×
Depreciation	
Amortization	
Ebitda	10×
Operating profit (ebit)	
Interest	
PTP	
Tax	30%
Earnings	13×
Dividends	3.5%

4

Decision – buy or sell?

Prospects + valuation = recommendation

Investment style guide

Key issues in the current market

Risk/reward profile

Timescale – investment v trading

Buy or sell?

When you have assessed the prospects for your target company and its sector and valued your company in two or three different ways you must decide whether to buy, sell or hold the shares. All the information gleaned must be pulled together. Having decided whether the share is good or poor value you need to reassess the risks and rewards. Then, in the case of buying a share, it is necessary to think about how long you plan to hold it. Finally there is the problem of deciding at which exact point to buy or sell the shares.

Reflecting these issues there are four key steps:

- pulling together prospects and valuation
- investment style
- the risk/reward equation
- timescale – trading versus investment.

This framework helps you reach your conclusion – whether you should buy or sell.

PROSPECTS + VALUATION = RECOMMENDATION

Deciding whether to buy or sell a share rests on the interplay of the company's prospects and how those prospects are valued (or rated). The prospects for the company may be excellent, but you may not make any money if the shares are very expensive (whether that be on a multiple of sales, earnings or other valuation basis). This is sometimes referred to as good prospects being 'in the price', 'fully valued' or 'discounted'. Similarly, a company that faces a difficult future may be priced very cheaply and all the difficulties correctly incorporated in the share price.

When a company's prospects deteriorate the share price will fall in line with the less rosy prospects – the valuation may remain the same as the share price falls in line with the lower earnings. However, the valuation (rating) may also fall as the market becomes concerned about the risks involved and less confident about the outlook. This is referred to as the stock being 'de-rated'.

Conversely, if the prospects improve and the market becomes more confident about the outlook, the shares may be re-rated (the valuation improves).

Do your homework and have respect for the market

Given the importance of the investment decision, it is well worth getting to grips with the issues highlighted, especially the prospects for the company and the sector in which it operates, the valuation of the company, and the risk/reward ratio. This will help produce a much better-informed decision.

When looking at the valuation it is important to remember that it contains the collective wisdom of the entire market – the balance of views of all the buyers and sellers. This is not to say that the market has valued the share correctly. There is an academic theory called the Efficient Market Hypothesis which suggests that shares are, on the whole, valued correctly. However, the stock market bubble of the late 1990s which burst so dramatically has cast strong doubt on the notion of market rationality. More attention now focuses on behavioural factors that determine share prices. This is summed up by the twin emotional factors of fear and greed that are always invoked to explain market movements.

Nevertheless, it is always worth asking what the market's valuation is and why it is attributing such a low (or high) valuation to a share. If, following your assessment, you believe the shares are cheap (expensive), ask yourself why you are right and the market is wrong. In effect, why do you know more than the market? This again underlines the need to do your homework and to be clear on why you have arrived at your conclusion.

What's in the price? What is the valuation saying?

As discussed earlier (in why P/Es may be low/high, see page 147) the market's valuation of a company may be telling you that a downgrade may be imminent, that the financial position is poor and deteriorating, that returns are low and will remain low or that management will continue to fail to add value (either due to its inability to do so or the economic constraints of the sector).

The share price is, in effect, conveying the market's view of the key valuation drivers:

- management and strategy
- financial position
- performance and returns
- outlook and prospects.

Therefore the share price is conveying important information on each of these aspects of the company's situation. A low valuation may be telling us that one or all of these factors is problematic. It is worth exploring therefore what you think of the market's view of these issues before you arrive at your conclusion. You can then take a view as to where you think the market is being too negative (or positive). It also helps you identify what might need to change and how likely that change is before the market reconsiders its valuation.

You can of course weight these components to suit your own risk/reward preferences. In the current market environment you may want to give greater weighting to a company's financial position and the returns it is generating. Given the difficulty in reading the outlook and the related uncertainty over profits and earning forecasts, you may wish to downplay this element (though it will always remain an important part of the equation).

There can of course be a wide variety of recommendations on the same company. The matrix of valuation drivers can be useful here. It is always worth road testing your conclusion by seeing what those with a contrary view are saying. If available, it can be worthwhile exploring where the disagreement lies – is it on the prospects for the company or the valuation? Is it the assessment of the management and strategy?

INVESTMENT STYLE GUIDE

As well as considering the prospects and valuation, it is worth knowing what 'type' of share it is. This will help you form a view of what drives the shares and how the stock market perceives the shares. The pros and cons of each investment style will be considered, which will provide a sense of the potential risks and pitfalls.

- Value investing
- Value investing – income stocks
- Value investing – investing in cyclicals
- Investing in growth
- Momentum investing

Value investing

This investment style has returned to favour as the demise of the growth-oriented sectors has caused such damage to the market. The fall from grace of many growth stocks has highlighted the risks inherent in this type of investment style. The share price of growth stocks that do not hit their projected growth rate suffer the double whammy of a) the earnings downgrade, and b) the collapse in the multiple as the P/E or sales multiple adjusts to lower projected growth rates. This has led to some spectacular share price collapses.

By contrast, standing on lower multiples, value stocks may well offer a more stable/lower-risk investment.

Value stocks tend to have a combination of the following characteristics:

- a significant P/E discount to the market
- a big discount to net asset value
- a higher yield than the market
- a very low EV (market cap plus debt) to sales ratio (i.e. it is very cheap to acquire the company's sales).

It may well be that the prospects for these companies are far from inspiring. A value investor might retort that the share price already tells us that and so we should not be put off.

Some investors adjust the P/E by looking at the earnings growth rate. This gives the peg ratio and is used by many investors as a means of valuing growth. Therefore, standing on lower multiples and having the protection of higher yield and asset backing, 'value' shares have tended to be relatively attractive in the current market. Those expected to benefit from the economic recovery/lower interest rates may be especially interesting.

One of the great difficulties with value stocks is that the P/E may be low for a good reason, the stock is not cheap. This often reflects the market's concern over the uncertainty/lack of predictability in earnings. It will normally reflect a combination of the following.

- The earnings forecast may be highly speculative and awaiting a major downgrade.
- The quality of earnings is very low.
- The company may be ex growth.
- The company may be in terminal/structural decline.
- Company/industry returns may be very low.
- Management is deemed to be poor.
- Financial position is very poor.
- The real economic value of the assets is considerably less than their stated value (a low ROCE may tell you that the assets are overstated in value).

Many cyclical stocks may emerge as value plays (see 'Value investing – investing in cyclicals', page 215).

What is the catalyst?

Another issue with respect to value investing is what will be the catalyst for a change in the shares valuation? If the shares have been standing on a low P/E relative for some time, what circumstances will lead to a change in this valuation? Will it be a good set of earnings numbers which highlight that the quality and quantity of earnings is (much) better than the rating gives credit for? Is a change in management required? Is a disposal or acquisition which improves the focus and growth prospects of the company and perhaps its financial position required?

Value investing – income stocks

With interest rates falling, many investors may be looking both to participate in any recovery in the equity markets this might lead to and to find an alternative source of income. This suggests that stocks yielding significantly more than the market may remain in favour. This is a subset of the value style of investing.

If looking for income, investors should consider whether the level of income is sustainable and how likely it is to grow. Assessing the following aspects of a company's financials may help in deciding both the attractiveness and the outlook for income.

- A high yield relative to the market.
- Dividend cover: a low level of cover suggests that any deterioration in trading will inevitably lead to the dividend being cut.
- If there is little or no cover, are dividends being distributed from reserves? Does this make sense? It may be appropriate if the poor year is a 'one off', but not if there is likely to be a prolonged period of poor volumes and prices. Otherwise declining net assets are paying for your income – as a shareholder you may not be any better off.
- If there is little or no cover, are the dividends being paid out of asset sales?
- Financial position (gearing and interest cover): this provides information on whether the balance sheet or cash flow can support the dividend.
- Earnings and cash flow: is the earnings figure coming from wholly owned business and effectively coming through in cash? Any accounting manipulation that improves earnings but does not alter the underlying cash flow undermines the dividend cover ratio. Cash pays dividends not earnings (see quality of earnings, pages 86–92).
- How much capital does the company need to invest? A need to replace a large amount of depreciated assets, for example, will restrict what the company can distribute to shareholders. Receiving a dividend while the competitive position is undermined through lack of investment is likely to prove at best a very short-term gain.
- Earnings forecasts: dividends are very much linked with earnings trends. So how confident you are in the forecast is an important factor in the sustainability and growth of the dividend.
- Dividend forecasts: will the dividend grow?

Dividend forecasts can be important as a high and growing yield is often a better predictor of good performance than just a very high initial yield.

As with the potential pitfalls expressed on value stocks, investing for income has the same list of reservations. It can be argued that if the company is paying out a lot of shareholders' money, precious little is left for growing the business; not necessarily an encouraging sign for the long term or for the company's competitive position. Importantly, it may be the case that the management does not have either the opportunities or the skills to generate higher returns.

In this sort of situation, shareholders may insist on the funds being distributed to them, as they believe that they can do a better job of reinvesting the funds. This questions shareholders' 'trust' in the management – if one is sceptical about its ability to invest shareholders' money effectively, why should one trust it to manage the existing assets well? And if it cannot manage the existing assets well, maybe investing in the company is not going to make you money.

Value investing – investing in cyclicals

The performance of cyclical stocks depends on the trend in the cycle and the trend in interest rates. While cuts in interest rates should benefit a cyclical stock it may be that demand does not revive or industry overcapacity threatens pricing.

However, there is a 'Catch 22' situation for cyclicals with respect to falling interest rates. Interest rates being cut is good for cyclicals as:

1. profits are very sensitive to GDP and falling rates should stimulate economic growth in time
2. often these companies are highly geared financially, so their interest burden is likely to be reduced.

This accounts for them having a high beta. However, the reason interest rates are coming down may also be important. If interest rates are cut because the economy is slowing rapidly and inflation is well under control, this may well see volumes and pricing come under pressure. The current concerns over the impact of deflation are important here. Deflation, to date, has been a particular concern to the manufactured sector for some time. Globalization and the transparency created by the internet have been deflationary forces for internationally traded goods.

This concern is particularly acute in the current environment given the very different nature of this cycle – a downturn not triggered by rising interest rates intended to choke off excessive demand and rising inflation but one of excess supply, with inflation well under control and prices for many products on a downward trend.

Any fall in volumes or prices has a massive impact on earnings forecasts, so there is a significant degree of risk attaching to earnings. Normally these stocks have high fixed costs and so small reductions in volumes have a big impact on profits (called 'operational gearing'). The effect of falling prices can be even more devastating. Any reduction in prices tends to come straight off profits, and with a vengeance. To illustrate this simply, take a company making £10m on £100m of turnover (a margin of 10 per cent). If prices fall 5 per cent, turnover falls to £95m . . . and profits are £5m (other things remaining equal). As can be seen, a 5 per cent reduction in prices leads to profits halving in this instance.

Pricing will be affected if there is overcapacity in an industry; this overcapacity is exacerbated by a volume downturn. Companies may look to maintain their volumes or defend their market share, which will inevitably lead to lower prices as their competitors follow suit. The extent of any price reductions will depend on the degree of market concentration that exists.

As well as market structure, pricing will be much more sensitive if the industry is subject to international competition. Structurally, pricing levels for manufactured goods have been subject to the twin forces of globalization and the deflationary impact of the internet for some time.

The effect of these two forces is to drive prices lower and lower. This depresses earnings. It also reduces returns on capital to levels that do not cover the cost of that capital, let alone compensate for the risks involved in such competitive markets. This has seen these internationally traded goods sectors underperform for some time. As a result a process of national and international rationalization has been initiated to try to reduce capacity levels and improve pricing and returns on investment.

Therefore, while an expected reduction in interest rates may provide a background that favours investing in cyclical stocks, the situation is far more complex. Some of these sectors rarely cover their cost of capital and struggle perennially in the face of swings in volumes and weak pricing power. Accordingly, earnings disappointments are virtually inevitable if there is a long economic slowdown, especially a global one. Critically there is a direct link between high rates of returns and outperforming the major indices.

So, while there may be value in cyclical stocks, great care is needed to establish that they have:

- good control of costs/start with a low cost base
- a degree of pricing power conferred by market share and/or product superiority
- financial robustness
- cash generation and are well managed with a proven track record of dealing with difficult trading environments
- relatively high returns.

It is important that these issues are considered thoroughly before making a long-term investment in this area of the market – though there may well be short-term trading opportunities to consider.

Investing in growth

In assessing a growth stock you may wish to check that it can deliver a combination of the following:

- sales growth well ahead of the market
- earnings growth well ahead of the market
- high rates of return on capital – growth adds value
- high capex to depreciation ratio
- strong financial position/cash flow to fund growth.

Falling interest rates are positive for growth stocks as they reduce the rate at which future earnings are discounted. Historically growth stocks (and especially cyclical growth stocks such as software) have performed well coming out of a bear market. This suggests that good-quality, lower-risk growth stocks with some GDP sensitivity might be an interesting way of playing market recovery. This is, of course, subject to the caveat that this economic cycle is very different and overcapacity exists in many cyclical growth areas that may weaken the earnings recovery this time round.

Looked at generally, growth can be delivered in a number of ways or from a number of sources:

- being in a growth market
- developing a new product or technology
- taking market share
- taking products/services into new regional markets
- investing in new facilities
- acquiring competitors.

It is important to fully understand what kind of growth a company is delivering. This is because the market will tend to favour, and therefore value more highly:

- organic growth over acquisition-led growth
- growth that is driven by sales rather than cost reductions.

The market takes different approaches to these growth generators largely because there may be more risks involved in, say, a new acquisition compared with an existing product that is taking market share in a growing market. Accordingly the market will value more sustainable and lower-risk growth more highly than 'one-off' growth. Frequently acquisitions may enlarge a business but not improve its longer-term growth potential (see M&A section, page 58, for a full analysis). The problem with cost reductions is that they again tend to be a one-off. They will boost earnings in the following year but not necessarily thereafter.

While growth is obviously an attractive feature for making money in the long run, it needs to be borne in mind that:

- growth attracts a lot of capital, which depresses returns
- growth may need a lot of capital in the early phases and not generate cash
- growth may not add value
- you do not know how long the growth will last (e.g. mobile telephony)
- valuing growth can be difficult
- the share price will tumble dramatically if growth falls short of expectations.

Momentum investing

Momentum investing is based on the 'trend is your friend' philosophy. Run with your winners and cut (or sell) your losses is another way of putting it. This is important because momentum investing places as much emphasis on selling as it does on buying. Given that selling well often poses a real problem, this can be a useful and disciplined aid to the decision-making process.

The two key trends that are monitored by momentum investors are earnings surprises (positive and negative) and relative share price performance.

Earnings momentum

Momentum investors will favour shares which have started to beat – or are anticipated to beat – consensus expectations (as defined by analysts' forecasts). These expectations are displayed on a variety of websites.

Results coming in above or below these figures are referred to as 'earnings surprises'.

If the earnings have beaten, or are thought likely to beat, consensus expectations this is taken as a sign that a process of improvement has started. Money can be made, the argument goes, as the improvement is expected to continue and will attract extra investor interest, fuelling share buying and hence share price rises. The improvement may reflect a pick-up in the trading conditions the company is facing (better volumes and pricing) or internally generated improvements such as a cost reduction or investment programme yielding positive results.

As a proxy for earnings momentum we can look at the relative change in consensus estimates over various periods (any changes over one month or three months are obvious ones to monitor). At any one time this can give us a fairly clear picture as to how optimistic or pessimistic analysts are becoming.

A momentum investor will not be too concerned about what is causing the surprises, what the recent trading record has been, what sector the company is in, what the long-term growth outlook is or how good the management team is thought to be (all of which a growth investor would focus on).

If a company disappoints – or is anticipated to disappoint – consensus expectations, a momentum investor will sell straight away. This is likely to herald a profits downgrade or other bad news and trigger an extended period of poor performance – so sell on the first downgrade, as invariably more will follow. Falling volumes and prices tend to damage earnings numbers far more than is initially appreciated and the difficult conditions last a lot longer. (See 'The risks in forecasting', page 131). The continual downgrading of technology and telecoms stocks since 2000 bears witness to this. The extent of the difficulties and the damage caused to share prices have been far greater than many anticipated, and most companies have endured far more than one downgrade.

Share price momentum – relative strength

Relative strength basically means that a share price is rising more rapidly than the market overall. This suggests continued demand for the stock. A share price hitting new highs may well be deemed a buy signal for the momentum investor. (Paradoxically, a more traditional fundamental investor would more likely take this as a sell signal!)

Most momentum investors will watch the volumes being bought as well as the price trend as an expression of the degree of support/interest. A rising share price with little volume may indicate that the period of out-performance is coming to an end. The volume provides an indication of the sustainability of the trend. However, it must always be borne in mind that supply/demand imbalances – the lifeblood of share price momentum investors – can be brought into balance by extra supply (rights issues, placings, etc.), not just higher share prices.

Importance of trends in the current market

Given the great volatility that has been an increasing feature of the market recently, and the lack of confidence in the numbers following an array of accounting crimes and misdemeanours, the use of charts and trends has become more popular and arguably more useful.

In addition, the advantage of selling on negative earnings momentum has been very effective – downgrades remain a dominant feature and share prices react sharply to earnings disappointments. On a news flow basis, credit rating changes also appear to be a clear sell signal.

Having the discipline to sell well can be difficult. There is often a high degree of attachment to the original decision and emotional factors take over. There is a tendency to hope that things will get better or that the price fall is temporary. However, using a momentum-type approach can provide good discipline when it comes to the effective selling of shares.

Conclusion

It can be seen that all the various approaches to investing have potential strengths and weaknesses, especially in an environment that remains very difficult to read. The 1990s were characterized by a preference in a low-inflation environment to seek out real growth opportunities. Interestingly one of the issues in the celebrated case of *Unilever* v *Merrill Lynch Asset Management* revolved around the underperformance of an investment portfolio that was dominated by value stocks when growth stocks were performing more strongly. Conversely, with the onset of the bear market, value stocks have been the better place to be.

The preference for growth in the 1990s ultimately led to the stock market bubble and the (over) allocation of capital to the perceived high growth TMT sector. Investors buying on momentum, and index funds which have to buy shares that become a larger and larger portion of the index, exaggerated the upside for these shares. With hindsight what is crucial to appreciate is how increasingly arcane valuation methodology was becoming to justify valuations. The more complex or more arcane things become, the higher the risks involved. As many of the features traditionally used in valuation, sales, earnings and cash, were not being generated, valuations would rest, for example, on the number of people visiting a website. Obviously this has no clear correlation with revenues being generated or money being made. It is worth pointing out that the further the basis of valuation moves away from core valuation numbers such as cash, earnings or sales, the greater the risk and the more money you are likely to lose.

Ebitda was promoted by many of these companies as a valuation measure as all the other performance criteria were irrelevant. Sometimes this may have been perfectly legitimate as the company was in an early stage of development. Often, however, it reflects the weaknesses and issues associated with the use of this figure discussed on page 100. If the company was at an early stage of development with no track record or a very short one, then in effect investors were being venture capitalists – which is fine if one realizes the much greater degree of risk involved with companies at a very early stage of development. And as stressed, if the risks are that much greater, the cost of capital is much higher, so you need much higher returns to compensate.

The other element is, of course, that the timescale for growth stocks (and stocks at an early stage of development) was being pushed further and further into the future. Even if they delivered this growth (which they did not), the valuation was, at the very least, fully reflecting the prospects. This long-term perspective was reflected in a stock such as Cisco. At its peak, the shares were on a P/E of around 150. Using the definition of a P/E that it is the number of years it takes to pay for the shares, you would be taking a very unhealthy view of your life expectancy. In effect it is a 'hereafter' valuation.

On a value-added basis, as discussed in the growth section, high growth attracts capital which drives down returns. A lot of the investment in the boom period will never cover its cost of capital and will in all likelihood be written off.

KEY ISSUES IN THE CURRENT MARKET

Macro factors

At an economic level the combination of low growth, weak corporate spending and the corporate sector's weak financial position and concerns over the indebtedness of the consumer on both sides of the Atlantic create a difficult backdrop. Concerns over deflation are also a major issue. To the extent that price pressures continue to be exerted, earnings downgrades will remain a feature of the market landscape. Companies with clear and sustainable pricing power are clearly very attractive in this environment.

Focus on risk

The increase in volatility and the preference for defensive and low-beta shares clearly suggests that the appetite for risk among investors has fallen considerably. As well as there being a great difficulty in reading current trends and the future direction of earnings, the financial position of the corporate sector is a key concern. The frequency and extent of earnings downgrades dramatically illustrates the difficulties the corporate sector faces. With this degree of uncertainty, risk minimization is likely to remain a feature. This may lead to a very circumspect approach towards growth, especially if there is no value being added.

Defensive v growth – defensive attractions in the price?

Value stocks, especially high-yield value, and defensive stocks have been the relative winners in 2002. Tobacco, food manufacturing and household products have shown absolute gains. Sectors that did well in 2001 continued to do well in 2002, suggesting that the momentum of following earnings and share price momentum has also been winning strategy. The recent outperformance of value stocks has also reflected disillusionment with growth stocks; valuations put on growth were excessive and the growth failed to materialize. The fact that so much value was destroyed by growth companies has also seen attention return to value creation, not growth. The issue now is whether the attractions of these defensive shares are fully valued. This clearly depends on your view of the economic outlook – if you feel that a strong recovery is likely, you will want a more growth-oriented portfolio. Alternatively, if you are cautious about the economy you will still want the stability and security of defensives, especially if they offer a secure yield.

High or low beta?

This choice between defensive or growth stocks is sometimes referred to as the preference for high-beta or low-beta stocks. Buying high-beta stocks will maximize the upside from any market rally – they will outperform a rising market. However, you may be taking on risks if the recovery fails to materialize.

Expected market returns

The central expectation for the total returns (share price appreciation plus dividends) from equities has fallen to around 8 per cent. With the volatility of markets and relatively low level of total returns, the security of income is a compelling attraction. A yield of, say, 4.5 per cent will deliver more than half of any expected total return. The dangers of chasing very high-yield stocks (where the yield flags a company in trouble, not an attractive source of income) should, however, be borne in mind.

A serious examination of the pros and cons of all styles and stock types is of paramount importance to improve the chances of outperformance. A blend of approaches may well be appropriate to give a balanced basket of stocks for long-term holders.

RISK/REWARD PROFILE

When investing in shares it is crucial that you consider one of the key fundamentals of investment: the balance between risk and reward. For accepting a higher degree of risk you must be compensated by a much better return on your investment. However, you need to be comfortable with the degree of risk you are taking on.

It is a good discipline to think about what the potential risks are to your target company and what the potential downside is. This will help determine whether it fits in with your overall risk tolerance. Avoiding disasters is an extremely important element in good investing!

There are two main types of risk for share buyers.

- *Market risk* – the market as a whole may fall for reasons outside the control of the company. Inflation fears, an economic slowdown, poor trade figures and rising interest rates will affect share prices across the board.

- *Company risk* – this includes external factors such as a recession or a rise in interest rates when the company is highly indebted. Falling demand, rising raw material costs and new competitors would affect the whole sector in which the company operate. The company may do badly due to internal factors such as weak management, high borrowings or a poor acquisition. This is why you need a portfolio of shares to diversify away what is called 'stock-specific risk'.

Warren Buffett identified the company-specific and general risks.

- Evaluating long-term economic characteristics of the business – how certain are they?

- Management – is it running existing assets properly? Will it use cash flows properly? Is it working for shareholders or for itself?

- Inflation and taxes – long-term impact on purchasing power.

- Purchase price.

Beta

We have discussed and debated beta as a measure of risk or volatility. If you can find that data, it is worth establishing what the beta is irrespective of any theoretical debates. It will give you a sense of how the share is likely to perform in a rising or falling market. It provides an effective shorthand for the operational gearing and financial risks involved in the stock.

Table 4.1 highlights just some of the risks that may affect the value of shares.

Benchmarks

When considering whether your investments have been successful you need to consider a couple of benchmarks.

- *Risk-free returns* – your first benchmark should be the interest you would get per year in a savings account. This is a risk-free rate (though

Table 4.1	Risks that may affect share value
Sector	Cyclical industry, low barriers to entry, overcapacity, low margins and the risks associated with a new or emerging industry
Company	Financial risk (high debt/weak cash flow), poor management, poor market or product positioning, and strategic errors (for example poor acquisitions)
Valuation	Share becomes valued too highly by the market and suffers a setback
Stock market	Possibility of a sharp fall in the stock market

also a limited-reward rate) and represents the 'opportunity cost' of putting your money into shares. Therefore you need to earn progressively more than the risk-free rate the higher up the risk curve you go.

- *Index returns* – the other key benchmark is the return you earn when compared with the stock market overall. Without running the company-specific risk of buying an individual share, you can benefit from equities with no company-specific risk by buying the whole market. This can be done cost effectively through an index fund. The point of buying individual shares and constructing your own portfolio is to try to achieve a higher return than the index. This is known as 'relative performance' and something that professional money managers often focus on. This can lead to the claim that in their attempts not to under-perform the index, they become closet tracking funds.

Absolute v relative

You may be more concerned with the absolute amount of money you make rather than performance against an index. This is very much how hedge funds operate. This can make sense for a private investor. However, remember that the opportunity cost is either a risk-free rate of return or what you might get from investing in a low-charge index fund. Again, your absolute targets should also bear in mind the risks you are undertaking.

TIMESCALE – INVESTMENT V TRADING

Long-term. If you are planning to hold the shares for several years, you should be looking in a fundamental way at both the prospects for the company and its valuation. You need to feel comfortable with both. The earlier section on key performance and financial ratios will help you to quickly establish the company's recent track record and financial position.

For long-term wealth creation the triangle identified earlier of a company that generates sales and earnings growth, has a strong financial position and cash generation, and adds value (i.e. the return on capital exceeds the cost of capital) is crucial. The key is to not overpay for these characteristics.

Short–term trading. If you are thinking of trading on a shorter timescale, you will be taking a view that the share looks 'cheap' (or expensive). You may be indifferent to the company's prospects in this situation and more concerned about 'sentiment' in the stock market, share price or earnings momentum and anticipated news flow. It is worth stressing that this 'timing' decision is extremely difficult to get right, even for the professionals. Academic evidence suggests that making trades at the right moment is almost impossible statistically.

BUY OR SELL?

Having got to this stage it is worth having fairly clear criteria for your desired outcome. This will depend on the risk/reward ratio, which will be different in each instance.

Buy

To reach a 'buy' conclusion you will obviously need to be convinced that you will make more money in the share than simply putting the money on deposit. How much in excess of the risk-free rate you are looking for will depend on your individual approach to risk. You will also need to take into account dealing charges and any dividends likely to be received.

The greater the risks, the more demanding the total return target you need to set. An anticipated 20 per cent return from a well-managed, well-financed, company with a good spread of activities, say, may suit your risk tolerance a lot more than a hoped-for 30 per cent from a company that is operating in a difficult market with a poor financial position. The downside in the latter case could be considerable if something goes wrong.

Sell

A 'sell' decision may be expected to underperform the market by 20 per cent or to have an absolute downside of that amount. Being prepared to sell, and having the discipline to do so, is one of the most difficult aspects of good investment management, even for the professional. Facing up to your mistakes and drawing a line under losses is much easier said than done for most people, but it is a critical part of protecting your portfolio. This reinforces the need to continually monitor your portfolio and make sure that your investments continue to have the risk/reward profile you are comfortable with.

If a share you buy goes down, analyze why, as far as you can, and react accordingly. A natural – albeit somewhat illogical – tendency when seeing shares fall is simply to hold on and hope things will improve. Much better to try to ascertain why this has happened. Have prospects deteriorated since you bought? Has the general outlook changed materially? Has new information come to light? Looking at the shares today, would you still buy them? If so perhaps you should buy some more; if you think the valuation is now expensive, you should have the discipline to sell even if the price is lower than you paid.

Sector case studies

Media sector
Pharmaceutical sector

INTRODUCTION

To provide practical illustrations of analyzing a sector as shown in Chapter 1, we have chosen two very different sectors as case studies – the media sector and pharmaceuticals. I had no prior knowledge of these sectors and mine is certainly not an 'expert' view. However, the analysis shows how applying the structure used in Chapter 1 can provide a very useful framework for understanding what drives companies' ability to make money in these areas.

The media sector is a highly cyclical one, as it is affected by discretionary corporate expenditure. It is also very diverse, which presents a challenge in constructing a sector framework. The pharmaceutical sector tends to have growing demand, independent of the economic cycle, but can face politically led price pressure, given the power of government both as a consumer and regulator. Success very much depends on company-specific characteristics, most notably the portfolio of products (the degree of product maturity and patent expiries) and the quality of the research pipeline.

The various approaches to, and influences on, valuation discussed in Chapter 4 are then applied in the context of these sector characteristics.

We first look at the media sector before turning our attention to pharmaceuticals.

MEDIA SECTOR

- High correlation with GDP growth
- Strong link with corporate profits
- Doubts over timing and extent of advertising expenditure recovery
- Growth and risks from new media channels
- Growth in new digital channels (and the web?) creates extra demand for content
- Control/ownership of content is becoming increasingly valuable
- Consolidation and acquisitions likely to remain a feature?
- Sector performance historically mirrored Nasdaq, reflecting its role as a 'new economy' proxy and being the M in 'TMT'

The media sector includes a number of diverse activities. The common thread is that the companies are involved somewhere in the process of creating 'content' (entertainment, knowledge or news) which is then distributed (by an increasingly wide variety of means) to an audience.

Such companies make money either by charging the audience for the content and/or from charging companies which wish to reach that audience with advertising. Content may be free for consumers (the ITV companies), with revenues/profit being derived from advertising revenues. Alternatively, a significant proportion of profit may be generated from charging for content through subscription charges (cover price for print media) and a much lower proportion from advertising.

The sector therefore includes:

- companies that create and sell pure content (whether it be a TV/radio programme, music, magazine or a book)
- those that distribute that content (e.g. TV, satellite, radio or indeed internet companies)
- companies that make adverts that feature alongside this content.

As a result the sector can be broken down into the following sub-sectors:

- TV companies (network), including pay TV and satellite
- TV production (programmes)
- newspapers (local and national)
- magazines
- radio
- book publishing
- music
- internet
- advertising agencies
- PR and market research agencies.

These categories may not be mutually exclusive – some of the TV companies may create their own content which they then distribute to their audience.

Demand outlook

Advertising accounts for approximately 75 per cent of TV companies' revenues, 60–80 per cent of newspapers' and virtually all of the advertising agencies revenues. The outlook for advertising expenditure, therefore, is the common denominator in this diverse sector.

Advertising expenditure has been weak since 2000 as companies in the face of a weak economy and severe pressure on corporate profits have sharply cut their discretionary expenditure. With uncertainty over the economic outlook there is inevitably a debate as to when advertising will pick up and by how much.

In 2000 the national market for advertising in the UK was around £9.8bn, equivalent to 1.1 per cent of GDP.

Demand drivers

The main long-term drivers of advertising growth are as follows.

- GDP growth – there is a very high correlation with trends in the overall economy.
- Profits – the trend in profits (in turn dependent upon GDP) is crucial to

advertising expenditure as it is often a discretionary item of expenditure. Accordingly, as profits fall companies may quickly cut their advertising spend to cut costs and save money.

- Many European markets are relatively immature as far as advertising as a proportion of GDP is concerned. The European average is around 0.7/0.8 per cent compared with the USA at 1.4 per cent of GDP. Many of these countries are still highly regulated, which may explain a significant element of the difference.

- Privatization and liberalization in areas such as telecoms and finance were until 2001 a big influence on demand in Europe, being the highest growth areas for advertising expenditure. Following deregulation and privatization, advertising benefits from new entrants who advertize to build market share combined with advertising undertaken by the newly privatized company.

- Longer term there may be increasing emphasis on brands, especially as a barrier to entry (as other barriers to entry are being dismantled).

- Companies are becoming increasingly cost and brand focused, e.g. Unilever in 2001 embarked on a cost-savings programme (expected to yield around £2bn) that involved promoting fewer core products. Of the cost savings, Unilever was expecting to allocate an additional £250m a year to its marketing budget of £1.65bn.

- It is also likely that any divested brands will receive greater attention from the new owners.

- New technical products and services including broadband, new generations of mobile telephony and digital technology will all need promoting. This will inevitably increase advertising expenditure as companies seek to persuade consumers of the advantages of these products.

However, while the above factors are important in driving advertising expenditure, these trends are susceptible to:

- recession – a downturn in the economy tends to hits circulation, which in turn affects advertising rates

- pressure on corporate profits/funding – the discretionary nature of much advertising expenditure means that it is often an area to be cut when profits are under pressure. For many established products it may be that a short period of no spending does not materially affect consumer loyalty for the product. With high levels of indebtedness and weak cash flow, pressure is likely to remain on discretionary spending

● recruitment – falling demand and profits lead to employers cutting back on recruitment advertising which can have a big impact on revenues for newspapers and magazines.

Within the overall advertising market there is a wide range of growth in different types of advertising. This is obviously very important to monitor, as it will affect the growth rates and valuations of companies that are exposed to these differing trends. Historically radio and outdoor advertising has tended to outpace the overall market.

Price outlook

The price of any advertising slot will depend on the size and profile of the audience, i.e. how effective it is for the advertiser to hit the target audience. In the future there are likely to be two conflicting forces at work as a proliferation in channels/media leads to a reduction in audience size, but where the specific characteristics of that audience mean that the effectiveness of the advertising is enhanced. ITV has seen a serious erosion of its share of audience under competition from other channels. This will affect its pricing power, although it retains, of course, a significant reach in terms of addressing a mass audience.

The price of content looks set to rise, reflecting its scarcity and the growing demand from the increasing variety of channels. However, the pricing of sports content is seriously under pressure.

Cost structure

It is naturally difficult to generalize across all the sub-sectors. Staff costs are perhaps the most significant feature. For example, at an advertising agency around 60 per cent of all costs are wages. For newspapers around 25 per cent of costs are staff related while 27 per cent is the cost of the newsprint.

Television companies have to pay towards the costs of the entire network (this is a third of total costs at Anglian/Meridian/HTV). Programming is then the other key element of costs at around 25 per cent.

An important point to note is that most of the companies in the sector employ relatively little capital to generate their turnover. Nonetheless a lot of costs are fixed and profits are highly geared to revenues. The fall-off in advertising revenues has hit sector profitability very hard. This, as well as other strategic issues, has seen consolidation occur. The proposed Carlton/Granada merger is partly about cost reductions in the face of revenue pressure, as well as a response to competition from new channels.

Cost outlook

Given that one of the key areas of costs is wages, the availability and price of skilled employees is a key driver of the cost base. Service sector wage inflation is an important area to monitor, especially for those companies based in London and the South East. With pressure on revenues, cost cutting has risen up the agenda at all sector constituents.

Profitability

Given the disparate nature of the sector's activities there is a wide distribution of margins. There may even be a wide range within the same sub-sectors. With high operational gearing, margins have been under significant pressure.

Factors influencing margins

Profitability is strongly influenced by advertising revenue, which means that the factors that allow you to charge more for that advertising space are a key determinant of profitability. This in turn depends on:

- audience size – advertisers will pay more to reach a bigger audience
- growth of that audience – this again allows a company to charge more
- audience profile – if the audience belongs to a specific demographic group with certain interests (and preferably a high level of spending power), advertisers can closely target their marketing effort, which again allows the company to charge more for that space.

Creating this audience in the first place depends on the media in question developing and carrying appropriate content. Profitability may then depend on what price that content can command – if any. So, for example, a specialist newspaper or magazine may well be able to have a high cover price. Similarly, having a clearly defined target audience helps achieve higher advertising rates. A combination of a higher cover price and hence higher advertising rates will enable higher margins to be generated.

While there is no charge for terrestrial TV, satellite and cable channels charge the consumer directly for content. Accordingly, at BSkyB, for example, only 14 per cent of revenues derive from advertising, with around 80 per cent relating to direct charges to the customer. Alternatively, a terrestrial TV company that is free to its audience may be able to generate significant profits by selling the programmes it makes to other networks or overseas. Again programme sales could benefit margins quite significantly. The other form of content that is sold in the sector is data. Reuters generates a considerable proportion of its revenues from selling financial data – an extremely difficult and competitive market.

Non-trading influences on profitability

It is worth noting that some companies in the sector generate profit from the sale of investments. This is normally disclosed separately but care should be taken not to boost the assessment of profitability by including one-off benefits. Reuters and Pearson have, historically, benefited significantly from the disposal of investments in related media and internet companies in which they have taken a stake. Given the pressure on stock markets and corporate valuations these are likely to be less important in the future. It is important to strip them out of profits and certainly not assume peak profits can be regained if they included these disposal benefits.

Profitability – ROIC, little invested capital

The fact that these businesses often use relatively little capital (being very much more labour intensive) means that using return on capital employed as a measure of profitability is less relevant. Where acquisitions have been made, considerable amounts of goodwill are likely to have been written off. These sums need to be reinstated to calculate ROIC. As well as using operating margins, profit per employee is another way of assessing profitability/efficiency given the high proportion of staff costs.

Financial profile

Given that there are relatively few assets involved, the conventional debt/equity measure of gearing is not particularly useful (this is especially the case if acquisitions have been made and significant write-offs of goodwill incurred). Accordingly it may be more appropriate to look at interest cover as a more useful guide to the company's financial position and ability to service its debt.

Industry structure

Again, given the diverse nature of the sector's activities, the structure is best assessed by looking at the sub-sectors.

TV companies – percentage of TV audience/percentage of total TV advertising

The structure of the quoted television sector is determined by which franchises the companies have. This determines the total population available to the company. The three largest are London (5.5m or 20 per cent of TV households), covered by Carlton and LWT, Midlands (4.5m or 16 per cent of TV households), where the franchise is held by Central (part of Carlton), and North West (3m or 11 per cent of TV households), which is held by Granada.

Naturally the proportion of national TV advertising is closely correlated with these population patterns.

For competitive and regulatory reasons (The Broadcasting Act) any commercial company is limited to a 15 per cent share of the total television audience. This has been an important consideration in the recent amalgamations of the TV companies. The holding of franchises obviously acts as an automatic barrier to entry during the length of the franchise.

Advertising agencies

While there are some large advertising companies in the UK, the market is less concentrated than many others. WPP, the largest player in the UK in terms of market capitalization, has around 13 per cent of the pan-European market. The US companies Omnicom and Interpublic have 20 per cent and 16 per cent of the European market. This highlights the importance of US companies in an increasingly global market (many advertisers are consolidating all their worldwide expenditures with one player). Inevitably this regional representation has been built up by acquisition.

Many advertising companies are increasingly looking to offer a broad range of marketing-related services to clients, such as market research, direct marketing and PR. These markets are growing more rapidly than the core advertising business, reflecting the increasing complexity of markets and consumer behaviour (which is likely to accelerate as the web impacts on consumer behaviour).

Another area of integration is media buying (the buying of the space/ slots for the advertising). This has often been subcontracted out, although some agencies appear to be looking to take this function back in house.

Sector integration and expansion

Given developments in technology (especially broadband) and the (related) convergence of functions of PCs and TVs, there is an increasing desire for companies such as internet service providers to have content (AOL/Time Warner). Indeed, many telecoms companies have also indicated a long-term desire to have ownership of content. Similarly, many traditional media companies are looking to develop their online offering. Increasingly there will be a number of platforms disseminating content. These developments will inevitably affect the valuation of content-rich companies.

Barriers to entry

There are many barriers to entry in many of the sub-sectors. Invariably these involve a combination of:

- the need for high-quality content
- brand
- franchise
- distribution economies
- the size and diversity of established players (which makes them difficult to take on as they can engage in a price war in one product area without too much harm being done to the overall group).

A good example of these factors combining to deter new entrants is the newspaper industry. *The Independent* is the only new national daily to be successful in the past 15 years. There have been many failures – *Today*, *Sunday Correspondent, Evening News*. Meanwhile, the restricted number of licences in TV networks automatically limits the number of players and restricts entry.

The availability of content may in certain circumstances also prevent new entrants from entering a media-related market.

Against these barriers, it is worth noting that the internet has in many instances lowered barriers. In the advertising world, the barriers to entry are arguably lower (though note the globalization trend). With few capital assets needed, a handful of people with a lot of creative skills could set themselves up relatively easily.

Industry risks

- *Advertising revenues.* As advertising revenues depend on economic growth and levels of corporate profitability, a key risk is over the outlook for these two variables. With the corporate sector heavily indebted it may take a considerable recovery in profitability before advertising expenditure improves. Having been under considerable pressure, the timing and extent of recovery is difficult to assess.

  Looking into the future, the proliferation of options for delivering content to an audience (given the possibilities of the net, broadband and digital) may lead to more competition for, and fragmentation of, audiences. This in turn may lead to a fall in the price achieved for advertising space. (It should be borne in mind, however, that with more narrowly defined audiences, rates may actually increase.)

- *Costs/investment risk.* The competitive need to invest in these new platforms, whether it is the net, broadband or digital, will involve extra layers of costs. This will be the extra investment cost associated with the new technology, and new delivery platforms as well as the operating costs of the new ventures.

  There has to be a risk that the investment in these new areas, will fail to generate an appropriate return. For example, a newspaper or magazine publisher may invest aggressively in a website which costs a lot more to run and/or fails to generate as high a level of traffic as anticipated. Alternatively, the target audience uses the web (not paying for content) but stops buying the magazine/newspaper. It is early days, but there are signs that consumers may start paying for web content. The *Financial Times*, for instance, has recently followed the *Wall Street Journal*'s lead in charging a subscription.

It should also be highlighted that there is a risk of *not* investing in new methods of delivery – that the magazine's circulation/advertising revenue turns down as web-based competitors steal a march on an 'old economy'-based supplier, eroding its market share. A good example of this might be the pressure on local classified advertising if people start to use the web rather than local newspapers to advertise goods or services.

- *Content risk.* Given the importance of content, there has to be a risk (as well as potential reward for the owners of content) that the price (and/or the availability) of content will increase sharply. Similarly, there has been a suggestion that some of the Hollywood studios might combine forces to set up their own cable/satellite brand and subsequently restrict availability (and/or raise the price) of their films. This would raise serious competitive/cost pressures for established cable/satellite companies specializing in films. Again this raises the issue of just how important control over content can be.

- *Consolidation/acquisition risks.* Given the pace of consolidation and acquisitions occurring in virtually all of the media sub-sectors, there have to be risks associated with such deals. These include overpaying and failing to integrate the businesses effectively, as well as being left behind if others make the most effective strategic moves first. In view of the people-oriented nature of many of these businesses, there is always the danger of key personnel leaving if they don't wish to be part of the new, larger entity.

Industry opportunities

- *Broadband/convergence.* Changes in technology, especially the arrival of broadband and new delivery methods such as WAP, digital TV and radio, interactive TV and of course the web, create a lot of exciting developments for the sector. As ever there are risks attaching to these changes, especially if the older media companies are comfortable with the old technologies and have become complacent due to the previously high barriers to entry.

- *Audience segmentation/targeting.* As multi-media platforms develop and the media becomes more targeted (i.e. more and more is known about the specific customer), the audience becomes more valuable to an advertiser. This represents an important opportunity.

● *Content/data providers.* Clearly, with the proliferation of new technologies and applications, there is likely to be strong demand for providers of data and content.

Valuations

It is difficult to generalize about levels of valuations in a sector with ten defined sub-sectors. Bearing this in mind, the key drivers of valuation are as follows.

● *Recovery.* Having fallen so sharply since 2000, there are signs of stabilization in advertising expenditures. However, the timing, pace and extent of any recovery is debatable. Many recovery hopes are based on the combination of the presidential election in the USA and the Olympics in 2004. Longer term, with advertising in Europe at much lower levels than in the UK or the USA, a higher level of longer-term growth might be expected, thus improving the prospect for those companies with European exposure. There is a danger that valuations will start to 'price in' a recovery, which may cause disappointment if it fails to materialize.

● *Growth in demand for content.* Given the importance of new technologies and convergence, content is an increasingly important component of any company's valuation. Leveraging that content and data (information is an increasingly important feature in many new economy areas) is likely to be highly profitable. Conversely, lack of content (or ownership of that content) can put companies at a significant disadvantage. Reuters has suffered considerably from falling demand for financial content and market share concerns.

● *Growths in certain types of advertising.* Certain categories of advertising are expected to grow more rapidly than the average. Radio and web-based advertising are good examples.

● *Growth of net/new media channels.* There is a danger that the growth in the use of web-based information/content sites will eat into existing 'old media' titles. This may force many companies to have a multi-media approach, leading to higher levels of investment and costs. This will inevitably reduce returns on investment and hence valuations.

Bringing these factors together it can be seen that key elements are:

- circulation/audience
- advertising revenue and its rate of growth
- content.

Given the issues influencing the valuation, it is also worth highlighting the trends and developments that influence the behaviour of the sector in stock market terms.

- *GDP growth*. The high correlation with GDP means that any change to growth expectations (domestically and globally) affects the performance of the sector. In particular weak demand from consumers will affect companies thinking of advertising campaigns.
- *Profit growth and financial position*. The weak financial position of the corporate sector and pressure on cash flow has led to significant cutbacks in advertising expenditure.
- *GDP and profits recovery?*. At the end of 2002 sector performance was affected by the stock market trying to anticipate when a recovery in GDP and corporate profits would benefit the sector. The market will tend to look 18–24 months ahead in this situation. However, disappointment can still set in if the recovery is delayed.
- *Advertising revenues*. Share prices tend to be influenced by how well advertising revenues are performing (in turn this depends on audience/circulation figures).
- *Correlation with Nasdaq*. During the stock market boom the sector was highly correlated with the performance of the US technology index, the Nasdaq. This connection is perhaps not surprising given that the sector was widely deemed to be part of the new economy (the middle component of TMT) and the fact that, relative to the Nasdaq, there were fewer tech/internet plays in the UK.

Having been overinflated by these factors, valuations had a long way to fall as more modest growth and more difficult trading conditions set in. High levels of operational gearing saw profits and earnings fall significantly.

PHARMACEUTICAL SECTOR

- Good growth outlook underwritten by ageing population
- Demand not affected by economic downturn
- Highly profitable sector with operating margins of around 25 per cent and ROCE of 30 per cent
- Company profitability (and valuations) reflect product maturity and patent expiry issues
- Governments and health care purchasers flexing their purchasing power
- Quality of research pipeline key to future success
- Question marks as to the value added by mergers and acquisitions
- Valuations reflecting pressure on returns and pipeline concerns

Demand outlook

Pharmaceuticals is an unusual sector as there is almost always demand if the product is effective at curing an ailment. Therefore the emphasis tends to focus more on supply-side issues, i.e. the quality of drugs being researched and developed, what types of illness they treat and how effective they are.

Demand drivers

Below are some of the most important factors influencing levels of demand for medicines. Some may be straightforward demand influences; others may raise the efficiency and reduce health services' costs by reducing the need for (expensive) surgery or hospitalization. This is a critical issue when health services are financially stretched.

- *Demographics.* An ageing population inevitably leads to demand as people live longer and become more prone to illnesses. This leads to attention being focused on the diseases of the elderly.
- *Affluence.* As people become more affluent, they are in a much better position to address their health care needs. This also applies to countries as they benefit from economic development.

- *Scientific advance/new products.* These allow diseases that were previously untreatable to be dealt with – creating new demand. New products may meet demand needs that are not currently satisfied or dealt with only inadequately.

- *Health care efficiency.* There will be strong demand for any products that reduce the need for surgery or hospitalization. These products will command a premium given their overall impact on health services' costs.

Prices

The pricing of a drug depends on where it is in its lifecycle and how much competition exists in that area of illness. The more mature a drug, the more likely it is that there will be price pressure. When ultimately the drug goes off patent, the competition from generic products is likely to see prices fall significantly.

With new drugs the pricing power will depend on how successful the product is in curing the complaint, how many drugs are already targeted at that type of complaint and how much it saves the health authorities.

Concerns over policy changes in the USA to cut the costs of the Medicare budget (health insurance for the over 65s) have highlighted the political issues influencing the pricing of pharmaceuticals. The pressure on health budgets worldwide is likely to see attempts to control drug prices. It is worth noting in this context that pharmaceuticals account for only around 12 per cent of total health care budgets.

Nonetheless, the importance of the purchasing power of health authorities and the political sensitivities involved mean that this will remain an important influence on pricing in the longer term.

Cost structure

Table 5.1 provides an estimate from looking at the report and accounts of a 'typical' pharmaceutical company. It demonstrates the percentage of revenues that each cost category accounts for.

This cost structure is interesting as the actual cost of producing the good at 27 per cent is a relatively small proportion of revenues. Marketing and research are the key cost areas for a pharmaceutical company.

The table is for a 'typical' drug company with a wide portfolio of products; the spread of margins between new products and older off-patent drugs

Table 5.1   Cost and margin structure for a 'typical' pharmaceutical stock

Revenues	=	100%	
Costs of goods sold	=	27%	
Selling and admin	=	34%	(how much is marketing?)
R&D	=	14.5%	
Ebitda (Depreciation = c4.5%)	=	29%	
EBIT	=	24.5%	

subject to greater competition is likely to be very wide. This becomes clear when a product comes off patent – profits can fall sharply. Generic competition can cause sales to fall up to 80 per cent once the patent is lost. For a very successful drug, margins pre-patent expiry could be in excess of 50 per cent. Operating margins for new products, which are especially effective in treating diseases and with a long-running patent, can be significantly higher than the 24.5 per cent detailed above. This is why so much attention focuses on the research pipeline and the timing of new product launches.

Operating margins of around 24.5 per cent are at very attractive levels, though this is needed to compensate for the risks and costs associated with the research and development process. (Significant sums may be spent on drug compounds that never make it to the market.) The R&D spend and the effectiveness of that expenditure is the key to the future growth and prosperity of a drugs company. The level of R&D can vary widely from company to company – anywhere between 11 per cent and 16 per cent. It is difficult to assess how much is research and how much is development. It may be that the development spend increases as products get nearer to the market. The management of the R&D process and the targeting of key areas of illness are clearly critical.

An element of R&D may be discretionary and trimming this expenditure would in the short term benefit margins. However, this could jeopardize the longer-term growth and profitability of the company.

Outlook for costs

The outlook for costs will be broadly affected by:

- *research* – heavier spending on late-stage clinical trials and more rigorous regulatory environment, while the disappointing pipelines at some companies may see greater investment in research

- *impact of mergers* – recent consolidation has seen rationalization savings and further consolidation is possible, though reservations exist as to how much value is added by deals in this sector.

Profitability – margins

The sector is distinguished by very high margins. Operating margins tend to be in a range of 25–35 per cent. The range is obviously influenced by a number of factors. A key issue is whether the company is a 'pure' drug company or whether it has divisions that sell over-the-counter 'consumer' products or drugs/chemicals aimed at the agricultural sector. These latter two areas are characterized by much lower margins.

Even for pure drug companies, margins may vary significantly, essentially reflecting the quality and age profile (i.e. patent life/expiry) of the product portfolio. Below are some of the key factors influencing margins for companies in this sector.

- *Product/sales mix.* Where in the product lifecycle the group's products are will be a main driver of margins. The more mature the portfolio, the lower the margin is likely to be.

- *Patent expiry.* When patent protection drops away, margins may come under significant pressure due to lower sales as competitor generic products take market share and lower prices.

- *Therapeutic category.* It may be that certain segments of the market have less competition as very few efficacious drugs have yet been developed. Therefore a new drug in an underprovided area (e.g. Aids-related illnesses) may well command very high margins.

- *Cost saving to health care provider.* A drug that enables a patient to avoid surgery or to be treated at home rather than in hospital will save the health authorities a considerable amount of money. A product that helps in this way will therefore enable the drug company to charge a premium price and achieve premium margins.

- *Research pipeline.* The future margin of any company will very much depend on the products in the pipeline (i.e. under development and awaiting regulatory approval). A healthy pipeline, i.e. with a high number of products with good sales potential, will be the key driver of the company's future margins.

Patent expiry

The following issues will affect the company's profitability in the case of a drug that is about to lose its patent protection.

- How far do sales fall when a product comes off patent?
- How far is the drop in sales due to lower prices and generic substitution?
- Will there be a significant rise in marketing expenditure to compete with generic products?
- How far will the margin drop when these factors occur?

Profitability – ROIC

Returns on invested capital at around 30 per cent are clearly very attractive. These returns are required given the risk/reward profile and costs involved (up to $500m) in developing a drug and bringing it to market.

Given the role of patent protection and high barriers to entry, the sector is unusual in that such returns make it difficult for competitors to compete away these high rates of return. Again this rate of return is an average. The reward for a 'blockbuster' type product could considerably exceed this figure. Another factor influencing the level of returns is the fact that the pharmaceutical sector is knowledge/research driven. Accordingly, relatively few fixed assets are used in the business.

Financial profile

In financial terms the sector is very attractive. The high returns on sales and capital employed lead to strong cash flow. This in turn enables the companies to finance R&D expenditure and the marketing of new drugs. The strong cash flow also means that the companies have little debt. This low level of gearing means there is little financial risk.

Industry structure – merger activity

Despite the fact that half of the top ten drug companies (by sales) have merged since the beginning of 1998, the sector is still highly fragmented when considered on a global basis. However, the mergers have created enormous companies in stock market terms. The newly created companies are significant in the context of their local stock markets, accounting for a large percentage of the total market.

Why size is increasingly important

The incredible pace of merger activity in the late 1990s has highlighted the desire for size in the industry. While it is too early to assess the success of these mergers, it should be borne in mind that the evidence of the financial success of mergers in the economy generally suggests that few add value for shareholders.

The rationale for the combinations that have occurred has tended to focus on the economies of scale that can be generated in the areas of research and development (as it becomes increasingly expensive to bring drugs to market) and marketing.

Research economies

The importance and benefits of economies of scale in research and development reflect the following factors.

- The increasing cost of bringing drugs to market – greater research costs and drug trials. It is estimated that it costs around $500m to bring a drug to the market.
- The portfolio effect – i.e. one can take more risk as research is spread across therapeutic categories. In addition, this reduces reliance on off-patent products.
- The funding of a wider range of research and the avoidance of duplication.

Marketing economies

The benefits of size with respect to marketing include:

- a larger and more effective market presence, which enables earlier and more rapid take-up of a product (this has significant advantages in terms of maximizing returns and cash flow) and helps maximize patent time (normally around 20 years)
- companies can offer a broader range of products to customers

- marketing presence can be used in partnership to sell new biotech products.

A more cynical interpretation of the trend towards mergers could be the defensive one of a company looking to save face as a major product(s) goes off patent. A deal/merger diverts attention from its drugs pipeline not providing any meaningful medium-term earnings dynamic to compensate for the patent expiry. Cost cutting from the merger then drives the earnings momentum.

It is perhaps a little too early to assess whether these deals will add value for shareholders. The questions they will have to answer are:

- whether the enlarged companies can grow more quickly than they would independently
- whether businesses of this size can be managed effectively, especially the R&D facilities.

A company that has consistently maintained its desire to remain independent is US pharmaceutical company Eli Lilly. Following the decline in sales of Prozac, Lilly has developed an excellent pipeline with eight products in phase iii clinical trials.

Given the spate of mergers in the late 1990s and the perceived attractions of scale, the sector is polarizing in operational and stock market terms between the very big and the very small. Glaxo/SB and Astra Zeneca account for around 95 per cent of the market capitalization of the UK pharmaceuticals sector.

The smaller companies are often involved in the rapidly growing biotech areas. Small-scale biotech companies can be volatile investments, but obviously high risk. The risks can be mitigated by diversifying through funds that invest in a wide range of biotech companies.

Given the funds and resources needed to bring a drug to market, many smaller companies may seek out larger partners to help:

- fund/organize clinical trials
- with access to research
- with marketing/distribution.

This may lead to a series of alliances between biotech companies and larger mainstream pharmaceutical companies.

Barriers to entry

Given the role of patents, there are clear barriers to entry for a given product. If the patent is for a product that is incredibly effective in treating an illness, there may be no competition over the life of the patent.

With up to $500m required to develop a product from inception through to approval, this establishes a capital barrier to entry to begin with. In addition there are likely to be 'knowledge' barriers – the know-how and expertise required in increasingly specialized areas to identify and develop ideas for the effective treatment of illness.

Industry risks

The inevitable risk for any drug company is that a considerable sum of money is spent on developing a new drug, processing it to the final stage, only for it to fail to get regulatory approval. This could cost several hundred million dollars. Regulators are keen to prevent potential problems and to get value for money.

Another potential risk is that the product gets regulatory approval – only for there to be unforeseen side effects that seriously damage the health of the patient. The other risks are perhaps less dramatic than these but nonetheless worth bearing in mind. A competitor product with better healing properties being launched at the same time is another product development risk. As mentioned earlier, there is the political/regulatory issue that is likely to put pressure on pricing levels.

Industry opportunities

These include:

- developing a blockbuster
- mergers
- biotech
- new technology.

Valuation

The sector is valued very highly relative to the stock market averages. This is driven by a number of factors, including:

- growth – sales and earnings
- high quality/predictability of earnings
- independent economic cycle – defensive demand
- patent protection and barriers to entry
- high returns – returns on invested capital of around 30 per cent
- high returns – margins 25-35 per cent
- cash flow profile – function of high returns, companies generate strong cash flow and strong balance sheets
- where the company stands in the product cycle – early, mid, patent expiry
- new product launch
- drug pipeline – future earnings potential (also influences EV/ sales ratio)
- merger activity – will they add value?

The influence of these factors can be seen in the valuations.

Sales valuation

The EV/sales ratio for the UK majors demonstrates the high valuation. Glaxo, for instance, trades on 3.5 × sales. These valuations reflect:

- high operating margins
- growth in sales
- estimated future sales from the company's research pipeline.

Variations between companies will therefore reflect the differing product mixes (especially the maturity of the product portfolio), achieved operating margins, and the quality and potential of the group's research pipeline.

Earnings valuation

The characteristics noted in the sales valuation, combined with the growth and quality of the sector's earnings, lead to sector constituents having a premium to the stock market. However, the premium has narrowed considerably due to concerns over patent expiry and research pipelines.

Stock market performance is influenced by various factors, including:

- being independent of the economic cycle – earnings visibility implies 'defensive growth'
- new product news/research developments which lead to volatility
- currency exposure – US dollar exposure
- political pressure on prices – Medicare, postcode rationing, etc.
- weightings/merger activity – mergers in the US and the UK
- biotech – high-risk high-growth area, but volatile.

Glossary

adding value When a company's post-tax return on invested capital (*Nopat*/invested capital) exceeds its cost of capital. See *economic value added* and *weighted average cost of capital*.

AGM (annual general meeting) A meeting held each year by a company to which every shareholder is invited. At the meeting, some members of the board of directors submit themselves for re-election by the shareholders. The *annual report and accounts* are presented and any business requiring the approval of the shareholders is discussed, including the level of dividend to be paid.

amortization Following changes in accounting standards, any goodwill paid on acquisition of a company must be written off, or amortized, over the useful economic life of the assets acquired (this time period can vary quite significantly, depending upon the type of assets acquired) and charged to the *profit and loss account* (see *depreciation*).

annual report and accounts A report made by the board of directors of a company, summarizing its performance over the preceding year. Normally it will give some indication of the expectations for the year ahead and will carry detailed comments about the company's trading position. Accompanying this will be the financial statements, notably the *balance sheet, the profit and loss account* and the *cash flow statement*.

associate company A company in which a substantial stake (more than 20 per cent but less than 50 per cent, a level above which the company would move from being an associate to a subsidiary) is held by another company and where the owner of that stake is in a position to influence its operations. When looking at the accounts of companies that have associates there are rules for how money earned from the investment is recorded. If 20 per cent is owned, 20 per cent of the *operating profit* will be shown together with 20 per cent of any interest paid on borrowings. This does not mean, however, that the associate company hands over 20 per cent of its profits – the only cash that changes hands is in the form of *dividends*. In the vast majority of cases, the actual dividend paid would be much less than the percentage of profit credited.

attributable profit Profits, after tax and other charges (e.g. *minorities* and preference dividends), which 'belong' to the ordinary shareholders (see *preference shares*). Used in the calculation of *EPS (earnings per share)* and *return on equity*.

balance sheet A statement showing the *assets* and *liabilities* that a company has at its year end. It is essentially a 'snapshot' of a company's position and can and does change, reflecting seasonal factors within the business. The balance sheet is normally prepared at the company's *year end* and should always be read together with the *profit and loss account* and the *cash flow statement*.

beta A measure of the volatility of a share relative to the stock market overall. A share that moves in line with the market would have a beta of 1. A beta of 1.2 would imply that a share should rise 12 per cent for each 10 per cent rise in the market and conversely falls 12 per cent for each 10 per cent drop. A beta of less than 1 normally offers a degree of safety in a falling market as it should fall less rapidly than the stock market overall. Likewise, low beta stocks tend to underperform rising markets. Betas are not set in stone, but can – and do – change over time. Generally the beta is influenced by the degree of *operational and financial gearing* a company has as these affect the sensitivity and volatility of profits. Defensive stocks tend to have a low beta and cyclical, highly indebted stocks a high beta.

bonus issue An issue of new shares where the intention is not to raise new money for investment but to a) increase the number of shares and correspondingly b) reduce the share price. Normally the intention is to improve the *liquidity* and appeal of the shares to investors – if the share price is high (for example over £10), it may be a deterrent to small investors.

The value of the company does not change – if a company has 100 shares trading at £10 each and makes a 1 for 1 issue, the number of shares will double (to 200) but the price will halve (to £5). No new money is being raised so the overall value of the company should be unaltered. Also known as a scrip issue or capitalization issue as an element of the group's reserves are transferred to the shareholders' premium account. See *share split*.

book value Normally shown on a company's *balance sheet*, the book value is calculated by subtracting a company's liabilities from its assets. Book value will frequently differ from the share price as the latter is more open to short-term influences such as market sentiment and economic outlook.

capex/depreciation ratio The relationship between how much a company spends on *capital expenditure* and the level of *depreciation*. In theory, the higher the ratio, the more the company is investing in future growth. A mature company will be investing at or below its depreciation charge. The returns generated from capex need to be monitored – there may well be different returns from replacement and growth capex and differing risk profiles attaching to them.

capital employed The total amount of funds used by a business in its day-to-day activities. The figure includes *shareholders' funds* and net debt.

capital expenditure (capex) The amount the company invests in physical assets such as plant, machinery and equipment to generate revenue. In effect it is all assets that have an economic life of greater than one year. See *capex/depreciation ratio*.

capitalization (or market capitalization) The total value of a company, defined by the value of its ordinary *shares* (based on the mid-market price) multiplied by the number of ordinary shares in issue.

cash flow statement A statement showing the source and destination of all monies received and spent by a company in the course of the financial year. The annual cash flow statement in the *annual report and accounts* reconciles how a company's cash balances have changed during the financial year. It contains important information on whether the company is actually generating cash.

closed period The period between a company's year end (and half year end) and the date of reporting its results. During this period, the management cannot, without a stock exchange announcement, disclose new information that would affect the share price.

convertible loan stocks In the same manner as bonds, convertible loan stocks pay a fixed rate of return and may be redeemable at a given date in the future. In addition, however, they offer the opportunity to convert the stock into *shares* at specified times in the future on set terms.

convertible shares See *convertible loan stocks*.

corporate governance Following earlier work done by committees chaired by Cadbury, Hampel and Greenbury, a Combined Code on Corporate Governance was issued in 1998. The essence of corporate governance is to ensure that management is acting in the best interests of shareholders. Examples of issues involved include the role and composition of the board, the number of non-executive directors, a clearly defined separation between the chairman (who should be non-executive) and the chief executive, and levels of executive pay, length of contract, share options and so on. A statement made by the board of directors of a company confirming that it has complied with agreed and accepted standards of best practice in their day-to-day management activities should be contained in the group's *annual report and accounts*.

cost of capital A company will normally fund its business activities using a combination of debt and money from shareholders. The cost of capital then simply becomes the 'weighted' average of the *cost of debt* and the *cost of equity* (i.e. in proportion to the equity/debt funding of the business). See *weighted average cost of capital (WACC)*.

cost of debt Straightforward to appreciate and to calculate. If the company can borrow from the bank or in the debt markets for, say, 8 per cent, this tells you the cost of servicing the company's debt. Importantly, the interest payments are tax deductible, which makes the debt even cheaper relative to equity. So in this case the cost of debt would be 8 per cent × 0.7 or 5.6 per cent (i.e. deducting the 30 per cent tax charge).

cost of equity The equity component is somewhat more difficult but nonetheless crucial to assess. Essentially, the cost of equity must reflect what rate of return an investor requires to compensate for the risks attaching to shares in general and to a particular company (which may be more risky than the stock market overall).

Reflecting these considerations, it is calculated by reference to 1) the risk-free rate of borrowing, which is normally based on the interest on a government bond, 2) an *equity risk premium* to allow for the risks associated with investing in shares, and 3) the volatility of the individual share which is measured by its *beta*. The cost then becomes $1 + (2 \times 3)$. If the risk-free rate is 6 per cent and the equity risk premium is 4 per cent, a stock with a beta of 1.2 would have a cost of equity of 10.8 per cent (i.e. $6 + (4 \times 1.2)$). As this example shows, the cost of equity is significantly higher than the cost of debt – essentially reflecting the higher risks associated with shares.

credit rating An indicator of the financial strength of a company. A number of factors are taken into account when establishing a credit rating, such as overall assets and liabilities, the debt/equity ratio known as *gearing*, *interest cover* and *cash flow* profile. The rating is set by credit rating agencies such as Moody's and Standard & Poor's.

cum-dividend If a stock or share price is quoted as being cum-dividend, the purchaser will receive the most recently declared *dividend*. See *ex-dividend*.

current assets Short-term assets such as stock, short-term debtors and cash. Used to establish short-term solvency. How quickly stock can be converted into cash varies enormously from sector to sector. A food retailer will be able to 'turn' its stock into cash rapidly. For a manufacturer the process is likely to be much longer subject to the production cycle.

cyclical stocks Companies whose shares are directly linked to the business cycle. These stocks are influenced by outside factors such as the overall business climate, interest rates, commodity prices and trends in the globa! economy. Cyclical stocks tend to be the heavier, more traditional industries such as construction, chemicals, engineering, motor manufacturers, paper and pulp, and steel, though clearly some service-sector activities can also be cyclical, e.g. media and advertising, pubs, hotels and restaurants. Profits in these industries are very sensitive to changes in volume and price as *operational gearing* is high.

defensive A stock with a low *beta* believed to offer a safe haven in difficult economic circumstances. Food manufacturers and retailers, and utilities would tend have these characteristics.

depreciation Reduction in the value of an asset. Most commonly applied in company accounts where the initial value of an asset is reduced each year to reflect the wear and tear and/or obsolescence of the asset. The reduction is called the 'depreciation charge' – a cost incurred in running the business deducted before arriving at operating profit. However, it is not a cost that involves spending additional money – the book value of the asset is merely written down. Therefore this charge to the *profit and loss account (P&L)* is referred to as a 'non-cash cost'.

The life of an asset will vary – it may be very short and so annual depreciation charges are commensurately high where technological change is rapid (such as computers), or much longer for assets such as a cement kiln or land and buildings. The shorter the period the assets are written down, the more financially conservative the company (and the greater the short-term negative impact on profits).

derivatives Essentially, financial instruments that derive their value from the price of an underlying security (such as a *share* or a bond) or commodity. Derivatives are used by investment professionals to manage risk, as they offer a way to limit losses on other investments and also to get greater exposure to a company than that available by going solely down the ordinary share route. The most commonly encountered types of derivative are options and futures.

dilution Refers to the impact of a transaction on ordinary shareholders. It is normally calculated as the impact on *EPS (earnings per share)* of a transaction. So if a company announces a takeover, the new earnings per share number will be calculated to see how the new earnings number compares with the situation before the deal. The deal is dilutive if earnings are below the pre-deal number. It is normally expressed as a percentage and will depend on how the deal has been financed (i.e. *shares* or debt) as well as the price paid for the deal.

It may sometimes be used to refer to the dilution of the shareholders' holding in a company. This may occur, for example, in a refinancing involving equity for bond swap. Ordinary shareholders may find they have been 'diluted' from owning all the company to holding a very small percentage.

discount rate The rate at which future cash flows are 'discounted' to a present value. This rate is normally the company's *weighted average cost of capital (WACC)*, which is a composite of the cost of debt and cost of equity.

discounted When the prospects for a company are fully known by the market and therefore reflected in the share price. Phrases such as 'in the price' or 'fair value' are also sometimes used. A company may be well run, highly regarded with excellent prospects, but the share price is on such a premium to its sector/market that it is fully 'discounting' its qualities. Therefore the shares will not make money unless the prospects turn out to be even better than first thought. Conversely, a very poor company, in a weak financial position and with a difficult outlook, may be valued very low. Again it is 'in the price'.

discounted cash flow (DCF) One of the key fundamental valuation techniques (though not the easiest for private investors to use). The *operating free cash flow* (cash generated by the business, operating profit after tax plus *depreciation* and *amortization* less cash invested in the company and working capital needed as it expands) of the business is projected out into the future. It is then 'discounted' back using the company's *cost of capital* to generate a present value of the income stream. Lots of 'assumptions' are made which are both subjective and highly susceptible to change and significant error.

dividend A payment made by a company to its shareholders. Usually dictated by overall level of profitability. Many companies do not pay a dividend at all if trading conditions have been particularly poor or if the company is in a start-up situation and can use the cash more effectively in the development of the business. See *interim dividend* and *final dividend*.

dividend cover EPS divided by DPS. The number of times a company's *dividend* is covered by the *earnings* it generates. It is normally expressed as a multiple. The higher the level of cover, the more sustainable the payout and the better the scope for future dividend growth. Low level of cover raises the possibility that the dividend is not sustainable and may be cut (depending on other aspects of the company's financial profile and need for capital within the business).

earnings Profits attributable to ordinary shareholders. Earnings are post tax and after minority or preference dividend charges. Care needs to be taken to ensure consistency of use, i.e. prospective or historic, pre- or post-*exceptional* and *amortization* charges.

earnings momentum The trend in both the reported and projected earnings of a company. Where a company's reported earnings beat market expectations and profit forecasts are upgraded, the earnings momentum is described as positive. This can be a critical factor in the shares outperforming the market as the improving earnings momentum reflects a better performance of, and outlook for, the company in question. Clearly, where a company reports earnings that are below expectations and profit forecasts are downgraded, the shares are likely to underperform the market. See *momentum investing*.

ebit Earnings before interest and tax. Also commonly known as *operating profit*.

ebitda Earnings before interest, tax and *depreciation*. A measure of performance used in valuation. The advantages of this measure are that it takes into account the whole funding structure of a business (equity and debt), unlike the *price/earnings (P/E) ratio*, and allows comparisons of companies with different accounting policies towards depreciation and *amortization*. It also ignores *exceptional* charges. It has become increasingly controversial as a method of valuation because many companies have promoted it as all other performance measures have been disappointing and they have run into serious financial trouble. Similarly, there has been a focus on the growth of Ebitda at the expense of returns. Another problem is that depreciation is a real cost of doing business and needs to be taken into account.

economic value added (EVA) *Nopat – WACC* × capital invested. A critical way of assessing the performance of management in its use of assets. Value is added when the post-tax *ROCE (return on capital employed)* (normally done as net operating profit after tax divided by the amount of capital invested in the business) exceeds the *weighted average cost of* *capital (WACC)*. The cost of capital reflects the risks shareholders undertake – risks that need to generate an appropriate reward. A useful way of assessing the success of capital investment and mergers and acquisitions.

enterprise value (EV) The sum required to secure 100 per cent of the company's cash flows/acquire all its liabilities. It takes into account its funding structure and any cross shareholdings that might exist. Importantly it takes into account all provisions. In effect it is the sum of all the company's liabilities. Normally calculated by adding market capitalization, average debt, provisions and subtracting peripheral or non-core assets.

EPS (earnings per share) *Attributable profit* / number of *shares*. The amount of profit attributable to each ordinary share in issue. For example, if the company's attributable profit is £1m and there are 1m shares in issue, the EPS would be £1. The attributable profit is post tax and is struck after any *preference* dividends or *minorities* have been deducted. See also *price/earnings (P/E) ratio*.

equity risk premium The return required by investors over and above the return on risk-free investments such as government bonds to compensate for the additional risks involved in equity investment. This is normally calculated by looking at the historic return on equities compared with government bonds, with the difference being deemed the premium required for investing in shares. However, investing in shares is forward looking, which creates a problem. Generally the equity risk premium is thought to be between 3 per cent and 6 per cent. See also *cost of capital*.

exceptional items Items in a company's *profit and loss account (P&L)* that are deemed to be 'one off'. Examples may include a profit or loss on the disposal of fixed assets or business operations, large redundancy charges as a result of restructuring, costs associated with the integration of acquired companies or bid defence costs. Some definitions of exceptionals treat as exceptional only those items of a financial or capital nature (e.g. disposals) while excluding those items that relate to the core business.

EPS numbers in the UK are normally quoted before the impact of these one-off exceptional charges, as this gives a truer measure of the underlying performance of the business. However, exceptional costs that appear frequently (e.g. redundancy costs) or relate to the company's core operations should be scrutinized to ensure that they are not in fact a normal cost of doing business and therefore should not be treated as exceptional.

ex-dividend When a stock or share price is quoted as being ex-dividend, the purchaser will not receive the most recently declared *dividend*. See also *cum-dividend*.

final dividend The dividend payable by a company after its year end. Normally this dividend is higher than the *interim* and typically represents anywhere between 60 per cent and 75 per cent of the year's total. This is because the interim dividend (declared at the half-year stage and on unaudited numbers) carries more question marks.

fixed assets Tangible and intangible assets the business requires to generate turnover. The tangible assets may include land, plant and machinery. The intangible assets might consist of *goodwill* relating to brands or patents. Intangible assets are *amortized* while tangible assets are *depreciated*.

fundamentals The most basic aspects of a company that need to be examined before making an investment decision – essentially what a company does, how well it does it and how much money it makes doing it. Key factors in this assessment include type of company, market position, efficiency, financial position, cash-generation ability, management record, past profitability and future outlook. An examination of these issues is referred to as 'fundamental analysis'.

gearing
1. Net debt/equity. A measure of the level of debt carried by a company related to its *shareholders' funds*, normally expressed as a percentage. See also *interest cover*.
2. The performance of an investment, especially warrants or options, which move in a sharp manner relative to the underlying security. See also *operational gearing*.

goodwill The premium over *net asset value* a company pays when acquiring another company. Obviously, in service- or brand-based businesses, where there are few tangible (or physical) assets, the goodwill element of the amount paid can be significant.

gross domestic product *(GDP)* The total value of goods and services produced by a country over a specified time period. This is normally quarterly or annually. See also *gross national product*.

gross national product (GNP) *Gross domestic product* plus the income from overseas investments less the income due to overseas investors in the domestic economy.

growth investment An investment strategy where the main objective is to identify companies with the potential for high, long-term growth in sales, earnings and *dividends*. Ideally, these companies should be growing at a rate well in excess of the stock market average and should also be able to demonstrate good growth rates even when the economy slows down.

hedge fund A collective investment that tries to make money for its investors in absolute, not relative, terms. So it will try to make money when share prices go down as well as up. It does this by *shorting* stocks and by buying put options as well as simply buying (or 'going long') stocks (the traditional investment management route sometimes referred to as 'long-only funds'). Allied to this, hedge funds usually 'gear up' (sometimes alarmingly so) to fully exploit market opportunities. For a traditionally run investment fund, it is hard to make money in bear markets; for hedge funds, bear markets are a key opportunity. With opportunity comes risk and hedge funds are not for the financially conservative. In addition, charging structures are high.

illiquidity

1. The inability to deal quickly in a reasonable size in certain classes of security, especially in volatile markets.
2. Where there is little or no cash available for investment, either at hand or within a portfolio.

interest cover operating profit divided by interest paid. This is an important measure of a company's financial strength as it reflects the company's ability to service its debt. This measure may be a more relevant indicator of financial strength than the debt/equity ratio *(gearing)* for companies such as those involved in service industries that have few assets on the *balance sheet*.

interim dividend When companies pay *dividends* twice a year, the interim dividend is declared for the first half of the company's year at the time the interim results are announced. See also *payment date*.

interim report Companies that are listed on the stock exchange are required to submit trading figures twice a year. The interim figures give the company's trading position at the end of the first half of the financial year; the final report (or preliminary report) shows the position at the close of the year as a whole.

investment bank As distinct from a clearing (or high street) bank, an investment bank is generally involved in larger, corporate-style banking, providing finance for takeovers, overseas expansion and so on.

They also frequently act as advisers for companies seeking a listing on the stock exchange. Sometimes referred to as merchant banks, investment banks tend to be integrated in the sense that they carry out a full range of activities, including corporate finance, stockbroking, market-making and fund management. This has recently led to concerns over conflicts of interests and this integrated structure is being questioned.

liquidity

1. The level of cash either held in a portfolio or available for investment.
2. The ability to deal easily in a class of asset or *share*.
3. The amount of cash and funds that are easily accessible in the economy generally.

minorities (or minority interests) The deduction of the share of profits that outside interests have in a partially owned subsidiary. For example, if an 80 per cent-owned subsidiary is consolidated, 20 per cent of its after-tax income would be due to the owners of the remaining 20 per cent of the company. Minority charges are deducted before calculating the profit attributable to ordinary shareholders – and hence determining EPS (*earnings per share)* and *retained profit*.

momentum investing The practice of buying shares that are showing an upward trend relative to the stock market overall. This may reflect positive *earnings momentum* or may simply reflect a trend/fashion towards a particular sector or share. Naturally, if a sector or share is doing well, this will generate interest from investors. See also *technical analysis*.

multiple A term used in describing the valuation of a *share*. The shares may be said to be on a multiple of $15 \times$ earnings. The term is used with any valuation measure used, e.g. sales multiple, *Ebit* multiple or *ebitda* multiple.

net asset value (NAV) The value of a business as defined by the difference between the value of its assets and liabilities. Sometimes this is expressed on a 'per *share*' basis, that is, where the NAV is divided by the number of shares in issue. This is a useful way of assessing the relationship between a company's share price and its NAV. For example, investment trust and property shares are valued in this way by referring to the *discount*/premium to NAV the shares are trading at. In addition, *value stocks* can be assessed in this way.

nopat Net operating profit after tax. A key component of *discounted cash flow (DCF)* and also used to assess the post-tax returns on capital (Nopat/invested capital).

operating free cash flow Net operating profit after tax (*Nopat*) + *depreciation* + *amortization* – maintenance *capital expenditure (capex)*. A useful definition of cash flow used in *discounted cash flow (DCF)* valuations.

operating loss Losses incurred by the core operations of a company before taking into account any interest charges/credits or the contribution from *associate companies*.

operating margin *Operating profit*/sales. This is a useful measure of a company's profitability and management efficiency. It is perhaps most useful when comparing operating performance with companies in the same sector. Operating margins should vary directly with the capital intensity of the business (i.e. the greater the amount of capital, the higher the margin). A key driver of sales valuations.

operating profit Profits made by the core trading operations of a company before taking into account any interest charges/credits, asset disposals or the contribution from *associate companies*.

operational gearing The impact of a percentage change in revenues on the operating profit of a business. It is determined by the relationship between fixed and variable costs – the higher the fixed costs, the greater the operational gearing. It will also be affected by whether the revenue reduction is driven by a fall in price or volumes with the greater impact coming from price movements.

overweight A position where a fund has more invested in a stock or sector than the proportion in the relevant index/benchmark. For example, if a share represents 5 per cent of the All Share index and the fund has 8 per cent of its investments in that share, the fund is said to be overweight. (In this case, 60 per cent overweight).

payment date The date that *dividends* are sent to shareholders.

P/E ratio See *price/earnings (P/E) ratio*.

P/E relative A measure of how the company's *price/earnings (P/E) ratio* relates to that of the market overall. This is normally expressed as a percentage. For example, if a company is on a P/E of 20 × and the market is trading on 25 ×, the P/E relative is 80 per cent.

pre-exceptional pre-amortization profit Profits before both any *exceptional items* or any *goodwill amortization* are taken into account.

pre-exceptional profit Profits before any *exceptional items* (credits) have been deducted (credited).

preference shares In return for receiving a fixed rate of return (even if the company prospers dramatically in the future), preference shareholders have a certain level of protection in that, if the company goes bankrupt, they will receive their money back (if there is any left to give) before the ordinary shareholders. There are a variety of preference shares which can include those that are redeemable (where the initial investment is repaid) and/or convertible into ordinary shares. For example, a 'cumulative convertible redeemable preference share' offers the following characteristics.

1. It is cumulative in the sense that, if the preference *dividend* is not paid in any one year, it 'rolls up' in subsequent years (during this time, ordinary dividends cannot be paid).
2. It is convertible into ordinary shares on an agreed basis.
3. It may be redeemed at par at the end of the agreed period if not converted.

price/earnings (P/E) ratio The share price divided by the *EPS (earnings per share)* of the company. It provides a simple and often effective way of valuing a *share* price. In effect, this tells you the number of years that the investment takes to pay for itself. It is normally expressed as a *multiple*, e.g. the shares are on 12 × earnings. This 12 × ratio is also referred to as the *rating* on the shares.

The P/E may be for the company's last financial year (this is referred to as 'historic') or for future financial years (referred to as 'prospective'). Prospective P/Es are generally used by analysts. Normally, a high P/E reflects a high degree of confidence in the company's growth profile and/or the sustainability of those earnings (often referred to as the 'quality of earnings'). A low P/E will normally reflect a combination of much lower-than-average growth, high cyclicality of earnings and 'low-quality' earnings. Sometimes a high P/E can be the result of very low earnings, e.g. a *cyclical stock* which suffers from the impact of falling demand and prices at the bottom of the cycle (in these circumstances the shares may be attractive despite the high *multiple* as the shares are at the bottom of the cycle).

profit and loss account An integral part of a company's *annual report and accounts*, this is a statement that outlines the company's income, costs and profitability (or lack of it) in the period to which it relates.

rating Describes the valuation put on a *share*. The shares may be said to be on a rating of, say, 15 × earnings, but the term can be used to describe any of the valuation measures used, e.g. sales, *Ebit* or *Ebitda*. In investment terms the key is to determine whether the rating is fair given the quality and outlook for the business. If the shares are cheap, investors may buy them on the basis that they will be re-rated (i.e. the *multiple* increases). Conversely, a high-growth company that does not meet the expectations placed on the shares will see its rating fall, i.e. de-rated.

retained profit When a company makes a profit, some of this is normally distributed to shareholders in the form of a *dividend*. The remainder, the retained profit, is transferred to the company's reserves and may be applied to the expansion of the business.

return on equity *Attributable profit/shareholders' funds.* This is a key measure of how hard the share capital is being made to work and how efficient the management is being.

return on invested capital (ROIC) *Operating profit/shareholders' funds +* debt + *goodwill* (and other asset) write-offs. Goodwill on acquisition is often deducted from shareholders' funds and therefore reduces the amount of capital employed. The invested capital focuses on how much the company actually spent (invested), not the book value of assets employed. Accordingly, a more comprehensive and preferred way of gauging how efficiently the company allocates resources.

rights issue Where a company seeks to raise additional money from its shareholders. The shareholders will be offered the opportunity to buy new shares at a given price and in proportion to their existing holdings (e.g. one new share for every four shares held); the rights to buy them at this price then become tradable in their own right.

ROCE (return on capital employed) *Operating profit/shareholders' funds +* net debt. This is a very important measure of the company's profitability and ability to use efficiently all the funds available to the management. It is important to be clear whether the number is pre or post tax. The post-tax number is used when calculating whether the company is *adding value*, i.e. whether the returns are exceeding the *cost of capital*.

scrip issue See *bonus issue* and *share split*.

sector *Shares* that have common characteristics and are grouped together. The FT All Share Classification consists of a number of clearly defined sector groupings, for example Resources, General Industrials, Cyclical Consumer Goods and Information Technology. These broad sector groupings break down further into individual sectors such as Chemicals, Health, Pharmaceuticals and Telecommunication Services.

share buy-back When a listed company buys back shares on the open market for cancellation. When the *balance sheet* is very strong (the company may have cash in hand or have very low levels of debt) and the management believes that the stock market is failing to value the company properly, the company may seek to remedy the situation by using the surplus money to purchase what it believes to be its undervalued shares. This has the effect of reducing the number of shares in issue and the cost of servicing the *dividend* and may improve the *EPS (earnings per share)* figure. Companies often do this in order to reduce the *cost of capital*.

shareholders' funds The net assets of a company belonging to ordinary shareholders, i.e. the balance of assets and liabilities.

shares Shares, also known as ordinary shares (as opposed to preference or convertible shares), represent ownership of a company. Shareholders are entitled to receive *dividends* (if the board of directors decides to pay them) and to vote at the company's *AGM*. See also *preference shares*.

share split Done for the same reasons as a *bonus/scrip issue*, i.e. to improve *liquidity* and reduce a heavy share price. It differs from a bonus issue as it involves reducing the nominal value of the company's shares. For example, a five-for-one split would see the shareholder holding five new shares for every one held but the nominal value would fall from, say, 25p to 5p. No adjustment takes place to the company's *balance sheet*.

shorting The act of selling a share you do not own in the expectation that it will fall in price. As you do not own the shares concerned it is referred to as going short of the shares.

technical analysis As opposed to *fundamental* analysis, technical analysis attempts to predict the future direction of *share* prices (or markets and other assets) by examining the trend in the share price represented in chart form (hence sometimes called chartism). Certain key patterns are held to be predictive because of historical repetition.

trading statement A review of how a company has performed over the half or full-year trading period. These statements are normally issued either immediately before or after the trading period in question. The review is normally phrased with respect to the market's expectations for the company. They are useful as they provide investors with an assessment of the company's performance before it enters its *closed period*.

value investing A fund management style that focuses on the selection of *value stocks*. Normally, a screening process will be adopted to identify those *shares* which meet the preferred criteria. For example, the shares may have to be on a certain *price/earnings (P/E)* discount to the market, *yield* premium to the market or *discount* to *net asset value (NAV)* to be considered worth adding to the portfolio. Historically a very important and successful method of investing which has returned to favour over recent years following the fall from grace of growth stocks post the TMT bubble. By contrast, *growth investments* have performed poorly.

value stock A *share* that appears cheap on a combination of the following criteria (among others):

1. a significant *price/earnings (P/E) discount* to the market and/or its sector
2. a high *yield* relative to the market
3. a *discount* to its *net asset value (NAV)*
4. undervalued cash flow stream.

While a share may be cheap on one or indeed all of these criteria, there can be good reasons why this low valuation is appropriate, normally reflecting a combination of poor outlook, poor financial position, poor management.

weighted average cost of capital (WACC) The *cost of equity* multiplied by the proportion of funding that is made up by equity (the *capitalization (or market capitalization)*/market cap + debt) added to the *cost of debt* multiplied by the proportion of funding made up by debt (debt/market cap + debt). See *cost of capital*.

yield *Dividend/share* price expressed as a percentage. Sometimes the yield will be expressed in prospective terms, that is, the yield for the current financial year, taking into account any dividend growth that may be projected. In the case of a bond, the yield is determined by the coupon payable divided by the price paid for the stock.

Index